Innovation, Technology, and Knowledge Management

Series Editor
Elias G. Carayannis, George Washington University, Washington D.C., USA

For further volumes:
http//www.springer.com/series/8124

Nagy K. Hanna • Peter T. Knight
Editors

Seeking Transformation Through Information Technology

Strategies for Brazil, China, Canada and Sri Lanka

Springer

Editors
Nagy K. Hanna
5852 Marbury Rd.
Bethesda, MD 20817, USA
nagyhanna@comcast.net

Peter T. Knight
3830 9th Street N, Apt. PH1W
Arlington, VA 22203, USA
ptknight@gmail.com

ISBN 978-1-4614-0352-4 e-ISBN 978-1-4614-0353-1
DOI 10.1007/978-1-4614-0353-1
Springer New York Dordrecht Heidelberg London

Library of Congress Control Number: 2011932677

Printed on acid-free paper

Springer is part of Springer Science+Business Media (www.springer.com)

Preface

We have been motivated to write this book to capture some of the richness of country experiences in their journey toward e-transformation. From our own practice and observation of the aspirations and challenges of developing countries, we believe there are a lot of lessons to learn from sharing these experiences. They transcend the formal descriptions of national ICT strategies, which typically describe objectives and list of actions and investments based on static assessment of e-readiness. We attempt to capture the dynamics of formulating and implementing a strategy, for some countries how the journey started, and for others who have been pursuing e-transformation for two or more decades, the evolution of a series of strategies.

Country cases attempt to cover all components of e-transformation, polices, institutions, human resources, communications infrastructure, ICT industry, the vast array of possible ICT applications in public and private sectors, and the synergies and interdependencies among these components. These case studies also reflect the hard choices and tradeoffs that must be made in designing and implementing e-development within real-life human, financial, and institutional constraints. They attempt to capture the gap between blueprint design and implementation, the lessons to be learned from implementation, and the instruments used to meet implementation challenges.

We drew on the in-depth observation of the authors who have been actors or participant-observers of the country they are reporting on. That gives these authors a position or perspective that can capture the *process* of formulating and implementing e-strategies and appreciate the roles of various stakeholders and the underlying forces and dynamics that shape both design and implementation. All cases follow a common conceptual framework, to facilitate cross-country comparisons of e-strategy design and implementation. Yet, the story is told in ways to emphasize the unique features of each county's conditions and journey.

Initially, we thought of having many country case studies, briefly told. But as the drafts emerged, it became clear that the limits on the length of each case would deprive the readers of some interesting innovations and concrete examples of the initiatives taken, or the long-term perspective taken by some countries over a series of strategies, or the interdependencies among various elements of e-transformation.

Hence, we decided to have two companion books, each focusing on four countries and a comparative analysis, done in more depth than would have been possible in one volume. This is the first of the two books. It covers Brazil, China, Canada, and Sri Lanka, and compares their characteristics along key design and implementation parameters. A companion book covers Singapore, Finland, The Philippines, and South Africa. We hope more cases will be developed and more comparative studies will be done and published as the list of such country cases becomes longer, and country experiences get better documented and analyzed.

We owe many colleagues special thanks for helping us on our own journey in coauthoring and coediting this book, and first and foremost, the coauthors with Nagy Hanna of two country cases: Christine Zen-Wei Qiang for China and Garth Graham for Canada. Ciro Campos Christo Fernandes and Maria Alexandra Cunha were coeditors and authors of a book on e-development in Brazil with Peter Knight. The experience of working with them and the many other contributors to that book helped greatly in developing the Brazil case study. The case of e-Sri Lanka, which inspired and validated much of the e-development framework used to guide all cases in this book also owes much to Sri Lanka's National ICT Agency and its leaders, as they first developed the e-Sri Lanka strategy, in collaboration with Nagy Hanna, and then pursued implementation and integration of their continued learning into an evolving e-strategy. We also acknowledge the valuable comments we received from: Sandor Boyson, Research Professor, Robert H. Smith Business School, University of Maryland; Irfan Haque, Special Advisor Financing for Development, South Centre, Geneva; J.P. Auffret, Managing Director, Center for Advanced Technology Strategy. Finally, we must acknowledge the many policy makers and innovators, in part cited in the publications in the four selected country cases, as they led the way toward e-transformation.

Bethesda, MD Nagy K. Hanna
Arlington, VA Peter T. Knight

Contents

About the Editors

Nagy K. Hanna is an author, academic, and consultant with extensive experience in advising policy makers and business leaders in designing policies and programs in support of e-transformation, innovation, competitiveness, private sector development, and public sector reform. He was the World Bank's first Senior Advisor on e-strategies. He has more than 35 years of experience at the highest levels of development policy, strategy, finance, and operations, and covering all geographic regions. He advises the World Bank, UN, and other international organizations, global ICT companies and consulting firms on designing strategies and institutions for ICT-enabled innovation and transformation. He founded and first chaired the World Bank's global community of practice on e-development. He pioneered the first World Bank lending operation in support of comprehensive ICT-enabled development, now being replicated in several countries.

Dr. Hanna holds a PhD from the University of Pennsylvania, Wharton; and executive development, Harvard Business School. He is also currently Senior Scholar at University of Maryland, Advisor to national CIOs and several boards of national ICT agencies, and member of the Board of Springer International Journal of the Knowledge Economy and Springer book series on Innovation, Technology and Knowledge Management. He is a Commissioner of World IT Forum (WITFOR); and cochair of its e-Government committee. He has published over 100 books, reports and articles on e-transformation, innovation, ICT industry, knowledge economy, national innovation systems, and state modernization.

He can be contacted at nagyhanna@comcast.net.

Peter T. Knight is an economist and consultant specializing in e-transformation and working with international organizations, governments, and private sector enterprises. He is President of Telemática e Desenvolvimento in Rio de Janeiro, and partner of Telematics for Education and Development. From 2005 to 2009, he coordinated the *e-Brasil* Project. Before joining the private sector, he led the World Bank's pioneering Pilot Electronic Media Center (1994–1997), and before that was

Chief of the National Economic Management Division in the Bank's Economic Development Institute (EDI) and Lead Economist for Brazil. His World Bank career spanned over 20 years, with more than eight devoted exclusively to work on Brazil. Earlier, he held positions at Cornell University, the Ford Foundation, the Brookings Institution and the *Centro de Treinamento para o Desenvolvimento Econômico* (CENDEC).

Dr. Knight received his PhD and MA degrees in Economics from Stanford University and holds degrees in Government from Dartmouth College (US) and Politics, Philosophy and Economics from Oxford University (UK). He has published over a hundred books, monographs, chapters, and articles in various languages. His latest three books were published in Portuguese in Brazil and deal with e-development in Brazil and other countries. He is a member of the Board of the *Journal of E-Government* and speaks French, Portuguese, Russian, and Spanish in addition to his native English.

He can be contacted at ptknight@gmail.com.

Contributors

Garth Graham is a consultant and community networking activist with extensive Canadian and international experience in enabling communities and governments to apply ICT in community development and plan national strategies for ICT use. In a career that spans work in Yukon Territory, East Africa and Vietnam, he has been dedicated to ensuring that decision-making about the development choices which communities face occurs at the community level. Via his work with Telecommunities Canada, a national voice for the practices of community networking, and with a variety of other community networking associations and government agencies, he now has 17 years experience in the collaborative development of community Internet projects and networks. He has also been active in a variety of Canadian citizens' organizations concerned with digital inclusion and the public policy debate on Canada's transition to an Internet economy.

He can be contacted at garth.graham@telus.net.

Christine Zhen-Wei Qiang is lead Economist of the ICT Sector Unit at the World Bank, where she manages the Information and Communication for Development flagship reports. Her main responsibilities include overseeing the World Bank's analytical work on ICT policies, economics, and impact analysis, as well as leading ICT operations and policy dialogue in countries in Asia. She has published a large number of journal articles, book chapters, and reports on ICT for development, economic growth, and poverty reduction. She holds a PhD in economics and a Master's degree in computer science and engineering from Johns Hopkins University.

She can be contacted at cqiang@worldbank.org.

Chapter 1
E-Transformation as an Integrating Strategy

Nagy K. Hanna

There is a growing awareness that Information and Communication Technology (ICT) revolution is opening up new sources of growth and new opportunities to solve long-standing development problems and is transforming industries and services so fundamentally as to change the competitive advantages of countries. This revolution also poses major risks and uncertainties as it raises the bar for competing in the global marketplace, accelerates product and process change, demands experimentation and innovation, and calls for openness, flexibility, adaptation, and fast learning.

Developed and emerging markets alike are learning to cope with and in some cases to smartly leverage the ICT revolution to enhance their competitive position in various industries, improve governance and public services, and build an inclusive information society. Obviously, there is much to be learned, in view of the fast pace of technological change, the emergence of the digital economy, the uncertain payoff of ICT investments, the malleable nature of ICT as a general purpose technology, and the need for complementary policies and investments to realize the potential benefits. E-enabled transformation involves deep changes in institutions and practices, and consequently demands new types of leaders and change managers.

As during the early stages of all major technological revolutions, before large scale diffusion and transformation, experimentation and innovation are essential. There are no recipes or standard strategies that can be taken by early adopters or fast followers. Countries and enterprises alike have to discover for themselves what this technological revolution means for their constituencies, markets, institutions, practices, and future.

Some of the common challenges facing all countries are: How to diffuse the adoption of ICT as fast, and tap its benefits as broadly as possible? How to ensure an appropriate mix of investments (in hardware, software, skills, institutional change) at the local and national level? What is the optimal path or sequencing among such investments? How to ensure appropriation and adaptation of the technology to diverse local contexts? What degrees of decentralization are necessary for different elements of e-transformation? What kinds of policies and institutions will be needed to facilitate coordination among these elements? What synergies can be tapped and how to identify them? What balance may be struck among various stakeholders

N.K. Hanna and P.T. Knight (eds.), *Seeking Transformation Through Information Technology*, Innovation, Technology, and Knowledge Management,
DOI 10.1007/978-1-4614-0353-1_1, © Springer Science+Business Media, LLC 2011

(public agencies, private sector, civil society) and among various development objectives (growth, poverty reduction, sustainability) in designing e-transformation strategies? The list is long. In short, how to pursue e-transformation?[1]

What Is E-Transformation?[2]

E-transformation stands for e-development, ICT-enabled development, information society, and knowledge economy, collectively. It signifies deep changes in the economy and society brought about by the effective deployment and diffusion of ICT. These changes typically lead to increased production and use of information and communication; reduced cost and increased pace of transactions and interaction throughout the economy; empowerment of individuals, communities, and enterprises with connectivity and knowledge; and increasing the share of information-based production and services in the economy. E-transformation is a process of fundamental structural change, a shift to a new techno-economic paradigm. As a general purpose technology, ICT is a transformative tool for all kinds of economic activities: financial services, manufacturing, transportation and logistics, education and health care, media and entertainment, public services, science and innovation, and more. Within organizations, e-transformation goes beyond automation of existing processes to encompass fundamental redesign and innovation of processes and practices and of the organizations that carry them out.

The ICT revolution offers an avenue for shortening or leapfrogging some early stages of low-level adding industrialization for some countries and that route has been in part taken by some inspiring examples like Korea, Finland, and Singapore. This route is still open to other larger countries, such as India and China.

But e-transformation is not the domain of the few who moved fast ahead or of some privileged sectors. It is not just about knowledge-intensive development, "weightless" growth, or IT-based services. It is not be limited to ICT as a sector, or to high tech and knowledge-based sectors. Much of the gains in total factor productivity (TFP) come from technology-embodied imports, of which ICT is an integral part. They also come from institutional and business process innovations, increasingly enabled by ICT. E-transformation is about mobilizing and leveraging key sources of growth across all key sectors of the economy.

E-transformation is a broader concept than *high technology* or the *new economy*. It is more linked to knowledge-based, innovation-driven, competitive economy, and to inclusive, learning, information society. But unlike the knowledge economy, which deals with the intangible resource of knowledge, it focuses on ICT as a focal point and takes a holistic approach to harness this technological revolution to

---

[1] The use of "e-" (originally standing for electronic) before a word is used to refer to the use of ICT, especially the Internet, in connection with the word so modified.

[2] For those interested in full treatment of the concept of e-transformation and the broad implications of ICT for development and techno-economic paradigm shift, see Hanna (2009a).

transform the economy and society. This means acting on all elements of the e-transformation process, including policies, institutions and capabilities to leverage the new technologies, and not just promoting the ICT industry or ICT investments.

E-transformation should not be confused with e-readiness indicators. E-readiness indicators attempt to measure progress in the ICT sector and to some extent, its use in government and business. But e-readiness indicators do not tell the whole story, provide a static picture of inputs and outputs, and are not ends in themselves. E-transformation is really more about the effective diffusion and use of ICT (measured in part by e-readiness indicators) as well as the deep structural and capability changes in the economy and society that accompany ICT use and diffusion. E-transformation is a process of structural change, and e-readiness indicators provide measures of context and ICT-enabled conditions for that change. The ends of e-transformation depend on the overall development vision, goals, and strategy of the country itself – sustainable growth, elimination of poverty, effective and transparent governance, competitive economy, innovative economy, learning society, information society, etc.

Why Case Studies of E-Transformation?

In-depth country experiences are indispensible in learning new practices, capturing tacit knowledge and building frameworks and theories. Case studies of country experiences convey a more realistic picture of the messy, creative, and emergent processes involved – providing researchers with a rich source for theory building and hypothesis testing, and providing practitioners with examples that capture best or promising practices. Case studies can thus help engage scholars and thoughtful practitioners and enhance their dialogue on strategies for building the knowledge society. They also show the role of frameworks and conceptual models in guiding strategy design and implementation and the need for further elaboration or improvements on such models.

National e-transformation strategies and programs are typically communicated in planning documents in terms of their final design. Similarly, aid agencies present these national ICT programs and projects for financing in final blueprint terms, not process terms. That gives the impression of a highly controlled, deductive, linear planning exercise, starting from a comprehensive analysis and ending with a comprehensive blueprint, or starting from an isolated pilot that is fully designed and appraised upfront.[3] The reality is quite different. Like all strategies, those related to e-transformation seldom emerge full blown.

Examining e-transformation strategy formulation and implementation as a process through a case study can make important contributions to our understanding and practice. First, it offers a model for practitioners to reflect on their own practices, become participant-observers, and help contribute to multidisciplinary research on national ICT strategy. Second, it captures the political and institutional dynamics that

[3] For relevant discussion of the project cycle and its limits for nonengineering investment projects, see Hanna and Picciotto (2002).

shapes e-development[4] strategies. Early political backing and coalition formation, timely mobilization of resources, dynamic negotiation of priorities and sequencing of implementation are often neglected in the reductionist recasting of ICT application in development. Yet, these are critical aspects of strategy design, implementation, and sustainability. Finally, a case study of the strategy development process allows for contextual understanding of the linkages and interdependencies among the various elements of e-development.

Unlike common descriptions of national ICT strategies, these case studies go beyond static assessment of the knowledge economy and e-readiness to capture the dynamics of developing and implementing a strategy and of building partnerships within the country for e-transformation. They go beyond the typically long laundry list of recommendations for transforming a country into a knowledge economy. They reflect the hard choices and tradeoffs that must be made in designing and implementing e-development within real-life human, financial, and institutional constraints. They take account of initial conditions, stakeholder interests, institutional learning, and political dynamics.

The literature on country experience in developing and implementing e-transformation is scarce. With few exceptions, that literature is theoretical or descriptive. Descriptive literature typically depends on official statements of national ICT polices and strategies, with scant attention to implementation experience, evaluation, and lessons learned.[5] Even scarcer is the literature on cross-country or comparative experience in pursuing e-development or e-transformation. One such notable exception is a World Bank's review of national e-strategies (World Bank 2006).[6] However, this review was based on desk exercises of examining written e-strategy plans. Thus, it missed capturing the gap between blueprint design and implementation, the rich lessons to be learned from meeting implementation challenges, and the instruments used or created to meet these challenges.

One key contribution of this book (and a companion book on additional country case studies) is that it draws on the in-depth observation of the authors who have been actors or participant–observers of the country they are reporting on. That gives these authors a position or perspective that can capture the *process* of formulating and implementing e-strategies and appreciate the underlying forces and dynamics that shape both design and implementation. Moreover, all cases follow a common conceptual framework, to facilitate cross-country comparisons of e-strategy design and implementation, without reducing country experiences into some aggregate measures of readiness or indicators of outcomes. This has not been an easy task, since most practitioners do not have much time to reflect on and evaluate such experiences. This is perhaps one contributing factor to the scarcity of such literature.

---

[4] We use e-development and e-transformation interchangeably since development is fundamentally about economic and social transformation, and the terms overlap and complement each other, emphasizing both development and transformation as the goals of using ICT.

[5] Individual country case studies have been covered in successive issues of the annual Global Information Technology Report, published by INSEAD and the World Economic Forum.

[6] Trends in "National E-Strategies: A Review of 40 Countries" Chap. 5 in World Bank 2006.

Case studies are more accessible to a broad audience of development practitioners, policy makers, and national and international development consultants and researchers – not just ICT and technology policy specialists. This broad audience is the primary target of this book. For some readers, particularly general development practitioners, the case studies may be more concrete and contextual and thus more appealing than the first and last chapters. Comparative analysis of country experiences may be of special interest to the researchers and students of ICT for development.

Why a National E-Transformation Strategy?

Most of ICT for development literature has been also focused on single innovation, single application, single institution, single enterprise, or a microlevel intervention.[7] The business and development literature tends to portray ICT as an endless stream of technological innovations or the "next best thing" for consumers, businesses, or governments. At the national level, case studies are primarily focused on one element of e-transformation: telecommunications, ICT industry, e-government, etc. Much of current development policy and practice treats elements of e-transformation in isolation, yet most of the documented failures of ICT applications in e-government, e-business, e-education, or rural development are traced to fragmented approaches that miss key enablers, operated within separate bureaucratic domains, and ignored synergies for sustained transformation and ecosystems for sustained innovation.

Some observers of the ICT revolution argue that national ICT strategies do not add much value, since ICT is driven by the private sector, involves much serendipity,[8] and continues to advance at breathtaking speed. Just note the recent emergence and advance of wireless and broadband communications, mobile devices, search engines, Google maps, collaborative technologies and social networks, analytics and business intelligence tools, and cloud computing. There are many theoretical arguments for pursuing e-transformation at the national level, to capture substantial economies of scale, network effects, positive feedbacks, etc. (Hanna 2009a, b; 2010). However, can governments and aid agencies really play a role in such a dynamic and encompassing technological revolution? Can societies develop a national consensus on a strategy to advance e-transformation at a national level? Can these strategies remain relevant and robust in the face of such technological upheavals?

---

[7] This literature is best represented by the well-respected International Journal: *Information Technology and International Development.*

[8] Note how the demand for programming to address the Y2K problem, and the overinvestment in telecommunications during the dot com boom helped the early growth of India's export of software services.

This book contributes to this debate. The country case studies show the merits of pursuing e-transformation strategies at many levels, and particularly at the national level. They show specifically how governments are partnering with the private sector and other stakeholders to purse such strategies. These cases can shed light on new strategies that are adaptive and dynamic, in some cases pursued and adapted over decades, and in consultations with various stakeholders. These strategies may not come close to an idealized integrated e-transformation process. Most cases in this book (and its companion one) suggest that countries have a lot to learn to capture economy-wide benefits of ICT. But these cases suggest that many countries are working hard to design and implement such national strategies, and are learning this new development game – drawing on their own experience, and those of early leaders and late bloomers. While there is no one common recipe, the book sheds light on key characteristics of strategy formulation and implementation of e-transformation, the instruments and policies being used, the role of various stakeholders, and the lessons learned. Even the most advanced among these countries are not content to rest on their early achievements in such a fast but long race.

Why a Framework for Studying E-Transformation?

This book advances the framework of *e-transformation* as an integrated approach to leveraging ICT for development, or ICT4D – pursuing coherent policies and mutually reinforcing ICT-enabled development initiatives at the national and regional levels. E-transformation can also be accelerated by identifying and influencing key stakeholders to help create an "ecosystem" for the information society and knowledge economy – a holistic approach that generates a shared vision, mobilizes stakeholders, and both maps the connections and shapes the relationships among diverse players. This broader approach to ICT4D seeks to build national consensus, facilitate systematic thinking about ICT as enabler of development, strategically manage ICT4D programs, tap synergies among interdependent elements of ICT, and communicate to a broad community of practice.

A holistic approach to e-transformation also focuses on the organic links between information, communication, and knowledge and broader national development goals. It enables new and advanced strategies for development. It bridges the boundaries of the government agencies dealing with communications, IT, science and technology, innovation, education, training, research, trade and industry, small and medium enterprise development, etc., and goes beyond organizational "silos" reflected in ministries' isolated information and communication systems. And it goes beyond aid agencies' common approach of focusing on ad hoc ICT applications in development projects while neglecting shared information infrastructure, systemic constraints, and sustainability.

Creating an information society is facilitated by a national ICT-enabled development strategy. Such a strategy should provide a guide to policies, investments, and implementation mechanisms for developing ICT capability and using it to achieve a country's development objectives.[9] It focuses the actions and resources of different stakeholders – but especially the government – on national priorities for harnessing ICT for development. It taps the interdependencies among these actions and investments over the medium term to realize a shared vision of ICT-enabled development. And it explains how institutions collaborate and share responsibilities for this development.

Country experiences can be analyzed and assessed, and gaps and weaknesses can also be identified using the e-transformation framework. The value added of this framework has been validated, among others, by a case study of e-Sri Lanka, a comprehensive e-development program already underway for several years, with World Bank assistance (see Chap. 5). The experience of using an integrated e-development framework to guide the design and implementation of e-Sri Lanka and capture lessons of implementation is documented elsewhere (Hanna 2007a, b). The World Bank has since applied this framework to its assistance in a number of other countries.[10] Thus, all country case studies of this book examine national ICT strategies through the lens of this framework. They demonstrate how the e-development framework has guided – or might be enlisted to guide – the design and implementation of national ICT-enabled development strategies.

An E-Transformation Framework

E-transformation can be conceived as composed of key, interdependent elements: an enabling policy and institutional environment, an affordable and competitive information infrastructure, a dynamic ICT industry that can adapt the technology to local needs, broad ICT literacy and education to promote adoption and applications for development, a coherent investment program to apply ICT to modernize the public sector, and incentives to promote the effective use of ICT for developing the private sector and empowering civil society (Fig. 1.1). The figure is a highly simplified representation of the key enablers and application areas of ICT and the many possible interdependencies among them. The first four elements are the enablers to the effective use and wide diffusion of ICT in government, business, and society.

Collectively, these elements – or foundations – of e-transformation cover the package of policies, investments, and institutions that enable an economy to apply and leverage ICT for social and economic development. At the heart of e-development are e-leaders and e-leadership institutions – individuals, networks, and institutions that develop a vision of information society, set policies and priorities, seek to forge national consensus on reforms, and coordinate and create synergies among the elements of e-development. To succeed, leaders should rethink and act simultaneously

[9] For a review of many national e-strategies, see World Bank (2006, 87–124).

[10] Such as ongoing Bank-financed projects for e-Ghana, e-Rwanda, and proposed projects for e-Armenia and e-Moldova.

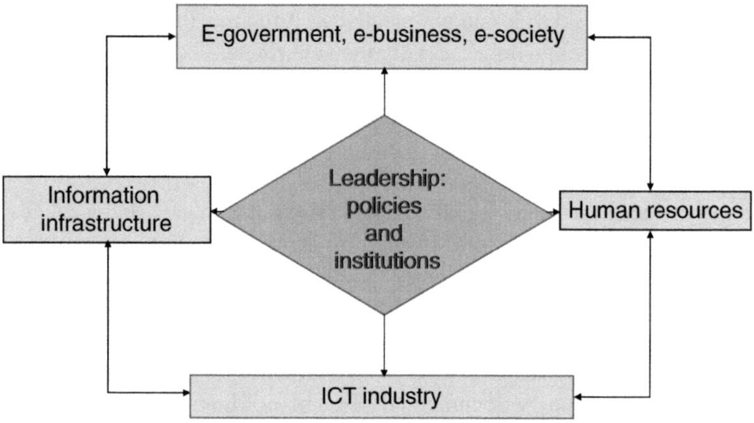

Fig. 1.1 Simplified links among key elements of e-transformation (e-development)

on the ICT infrastructure, human resources, ICT innovation system, policy and institutional regime, and ICT use and diffusion throughout the economy.

This framework can help explain e-transformation as a process enabled by ICT as a sector and as a general purpose technology. It can also be used to guide the design and implement integrated ICT4D programs at the national level, much in the same vein as Porter's system of competitive advantage (Porter 1990; Heeks 2006) is used to both explain sector development and guide the design of programs to enhance national competitive advantage. Porter's competitive advantage theory takes a holistic and systemic view of four elements or determinants: factor conditions; demand conditions; related and supporting industries; and firm strategy, structure, and rivalry. It views these elements together as a mutually reinforcing system. These elements and their interrelationships are continually evolving. The proposed e-development framework functions in the same fashion to explain the dynamics of ICT-enabled development and to guide the design and strategic management of ICT4D programs. Appropriately coordinated and sequenced, programs covering these key elements can exploit synergies, transforming the economy and accelerating development.

Integrating E-Transformation into Broader Strategies

Experience with national ICT strategies suggests that their links with overall development strategies tend to be weak, particularly in low-income countries (World Bank 2006, 87–124). When linked to national development strategy, they tend to focus ICT as an industry, but often neglect ICT as a cross-sector enabler and transformer. Even when such links are mentioned in planning documents, they are often forgotten in practice. The reasons are many: scarcity of e-leaders, poor understanding of the links, low awareness, and ownership of ICT among most public administrators, weak involvement of core ministries, such as finance and economic planning, and the pursuit of technology-driven agendas by ICT ministries or their equivalent. Meantime, all other ministries are confined to their sectoral mandates, defend their own turf, and do not naturally think about leveraging the new technologies, tapping synergies among e-development components or realizing returns to scale in shared applications and information infrastructure.

E-transformation is about promoting a new development strategy paradigm, one adapted to the opportunities and challenges arising from ICT – the general purpose technology of our times (Hanna 2009a, b). A national e-transformation strategy is shaped by the broader goals of national growth and development that are set in relation to the imperatives and opportunities of a technological and knowledge revolution. It may leverage ICT to improve governance and the delivery of public services, bridge economic divides, promote social inclusion, and/or drastically cut transaction costs across the economy. It may seek to exploit new sources of growth, employment, innovation, and competitiveness by promoting the ICT and ICT-enabled services industries and the use of ICT by small enterprises to network, create, and compete.

The e-transformation framework integrates ICT into development strategies by placing ICT interventions within a broader development context and making them meaningful to policy makers.[11] Thus, it facilitates the process of creating a shared and energizing vision of how a society will harness the ongoing ICT revolution – and its companion process of globalization – to access knowledge, address development priorities, and meet competitiveness challenges.

By tightly linking national ICT strategies to broader development visions and strategies, the holistic e-transformation strategy engages policy makers in driving the ICT agenda in response to national development priorities – rather than the other way around. It helps focus the attention of policy makers and program managers on ICT-enabled development results. ICT becomes an enabling force for pursuing policy reforms, transforming institutions, and improving governance and transparency. It can catalyze reforms in education and mobilize knowledge and other resources for social inclusion. Enlightened leaders become engaged in shaping this vision and in using it to build consensus on institutional change and economic transformation.

An e-transformation strategy is not a mere vision; it operates within institutional and financial constraints. Thus, it seeks to guide the allocation of resources, focusing scarce public resources on investments with the greatest development impact or those that can produce quick wins in line with political demands for tangible and timely results. Investments have to be sequenced and phased. Defining the national ICT strategy in terms of development outcomes (such as growth or rural development) rather than ICT sector indicators (such as teledensity and ICT investments) helps focus the attention of policy makers and program managers on ICT-enabled development results.

The e-transformation framework reframes what were typically seen as specialized technology debates, isolated ICT interventions, and separate

[11] Little theory or research has linked concepts of development studies to ICT-for-development research. See Heeks (2006).

infrastructure investments into a broader whole and an integral dimension of the country's development strategy.[12] Considered holistically, these interventions can be linked to a broad development vision that keeps the focus of debate on development outcomes and the focus of program design on linking means to ends. Rather than assuming causality between individual elements of e-development – such as connectivity, content, e-literacy, and e-government – and development outcomes, these elements are strategically combined to secure the intended development outcomes.

Integration of ICT with development strategy is not a one-way street or a one-time exercise (Hanna 2007a, 2009a). The e-development vision can evolve as political leaders, policy makers, and top administrators learn and change. As implementation proceeds and awareness grows, the links become clearer to leaders and implementers alike. The experience of leading corporations suggests that, through practice and institutional learning, business leaders begin to own the ICT function, and ICT becomes increasingly central to overall business competitiveness and transformation strategies – not just a facilitator, follower, or support function.

These links to the development agenda cannot be taken for granted. Unless systematically built and rebuilt within an e-development framework, the links may weaken over time and be displaced by narrower, technology-driven or purely ICT sector agendas.

Taking Account of Interdependencies; Exploiting Synergies

The interdependencies among e-transformation components are significant in advanced knowledge economies and even greater in developing and emerging economies. Studies in OECD countries indicate a strong link between ICT investment, productivity growth, and competitiveness (OECD 2004). Moreover, they show the significance of "interaction effects" – for example, interactions between ICT investment, infrastructure, skill levels, and the policy environment (Economist Intelligence Unit 2004). A critical mass or minimum threshold of ICT development can have a significant positive impact on a country's economy. Integration offers many opportunities for tapping synergies among the elements of e-development and reaping returns to scale when investing in information infrastructures.

For a developing country in particular, with circular and multiple causation for information poverty (Hanna 1991; Myrdal 1957), the impact of one element of e-development is heavily dependent on progress in others. Investments in ICT must be accompanied by investments in human resources, process innovations, institutional changes, and policy reforms to fully realize the potential benefits. This is consistent with a key lesson of development experience in general, that is, the need for a comprehensive approach to development (Hanna and Picciotto 2002).

---

[12] On the issue of reframing, see Wilson (2005).

Consider e-government and e-business. Making e-government and e-business services broadly available to citizens and enterprises requires accelerating Internet penetration and affordable connectivity. And the take-up of online services depends critically on the development of digital literacy and an information culture. Education and the policy environment are keys to making technology work. Moreover, when governments tap domestic firms to act as partners in providing e-government solutions, they support private sector development in ways that can broaden e-development and create competitive domestic markets and learning opportunities for developing the local ICT industry.

Potential synergies and key interdependencies are seldom identified and tapped in designing national ICT strategies. An integrated approach to ICT poses a challenge for aid agencies and developing country governments alike. Both face incentives that militate against collaboration and integration across sectors (see Hanna and Picciotto 2002). Aid funding and public budgets follow sectoral lines, and it can be hard to get new money for cross-sectoral initiatives. Whatever the source of funding, ICT efforts – e-government investments, telecommunications reforms, connectivity programs, ICT industry promotion, human resource development, content development, sectoral applications – are typically pursued in isolation. Even within an e-government program ICT investments are typically pursued agency by agency or system by system (see Fountain 2001).

Governments can play a critical role in shaping all these interdependencies. They may build e-leadership institutions to promote, govern, coordinate, monitor and evaluate the e-development process (Hanna 2007b, 2009a). Over time these e-leadership institutions should be able to identify more and more synergies among applications in e-government, e-business, and e-society. The benefits of tapping these synergies should outweigh the cost of coordination. Guided by the e-development framework, these institutions may search for strategic opportunities to tap potential synergies, realize returns to scale, build cross-sectoral links, and leverage entry points.

A comprehensive view of ICT for development does not imply addressing all constraints, opportunities, and investment possibilities at once. Instead, it challenges designers and implementers to prioritize, select, and sequence the most critical interdependencies in view of overarching objectives and the overall availability of resources and capabilities. It helps anticipate, recognize, and manage the key interdependencies over time. Also, without taking account of key synergies and interdependencies in a timely manner, true transformation is unlikely to occur, to be sustainable or to be diffused on a large scale.

The e-transformation approach may use various tools to prioritize, select, and sequence projects and programs. It calls for dynamic investment programming – pursuing selective activities for maximum impact and maintaining flexibility to reallocate resources among interdependent programs. Tough tradeoffs in managing and sequencing activities must be made all the time – between quick wins and long-gestating investments, between sectoral and cross-sectoral applications, between core and noncore activities.

Engaging All Relevant Stakeholders

National ICT strategies typically describe plans and initiatives in lifeless and bureaucratic terms, devoid of actors and stakeholders. They make little use of coalitions, partnerships, stakeholder participation, social interactions, governance mechanisms, conflicting interests and perspectives, power relations, pull platforms, and authorizing environments. Yet these factors drive the success or failure of efforts to diffuse ICT (Hanna 2009a, b).

The e-transformation framework should help policy makers and strategists in thinking holistically about all key stakeholders of an information society or all key players in a knowledge economy ecosystem. It is an approach to help map the connections, shape the relationships and coordinate the work among diverse players. It helps clarify the roles of the government, the private sector, civil society, academia, and aid agencies, with the aim of building partnerships among them. Over the medium term, this framework helps transformational leaders tap the interdependencies among the actions and resources of different stakeholders to realize a shared and compelling vision.

As a vision, e-transformation should appeal to broad and diverse groups of stakeholders, not just ICT champions and specialists, telecom operators, IT entrepreneurs and service providers, or owners of single issues or applications. The e-development framework helps articulate an inclusive vision, linking interdependent actions to coproduce sectoral as well as cross-sectoral outcomes. It seeks to identify the competitive advantages of the country that ICT could best leverage and the development programs that ICT could enable. Presenting e-development programs as an enabler of other sectors and programs, such as rural and entrepreneurial development, should help gain the support of key partners and ministries.

Leaders of e-transformation need to understand stakeholders and engage them as enablers, partners, and implementers. By shaping an integrated national program, an e-development strategy clarifies the comparative advantages of all potential actors: government, private sector, civil society, and academia, and determines what roles each can best play in designing and implementing e-transformation programs. In doing so, it helps build partnerships and coordinate agendas among these stakeholders. By building these partnerships, it provides an enabling policy environment for implementation and a healthy ecosystem for the information society.

Partnerships should be promoted across all components of e-transformation. For example, in a number of country cases, the need to retain key constituencies as partners has influenced the final scope of the e-development investment program and the balance of funding among its components. Contextual factors influence partnerships of all kinds, including public–private partnerships. Building partnerships in highly polarized and inequitable societies tends to be difficult because such partnerships inevitably demand trust and reconciliation of interests. Programs and incentives had to be developed to build trust, align interests, and pilot and nurture cross-sectoral partnerships.

Balancing Top-Down Direction with Bottom-Up Initiative

Most national ICT strategies have been driven by the desire of political leaders and central authorities to leapfrog to the knowledge economy and by their fear of being separated by the digital divide. Often designed by international consultants or the central staff of the ICT ministry, the strategies have centered on large investments and complex projects that can be centrally funded and managed to achieve economies of scale. At times, they have been intended to balance the many isolated pilots and fragmented investments suffering from duplication and lack of sustainability and scalability. But many of these centrally driven programs have lacked mechanisms to promote bottom-up initiatives, to build capacity at the grassroots, and to induce innovative partnerships – all critical to mobilizing local knowledge and capabilities and achieving scalability and sustainability.

The e-transformation approach promotes systems thinking or "ecosystem thinking," that is, the development of an environment that enhances innovation, scaling up and sustainability. Centrally driven programs need to be complemented by bottom-up initiatives, creative partnerships, and grassroots empowerment. National policies and institutions matter for creating healthy ecosystems and for enhancing developmental payoffs of local initiatives. And local initiatives accelerate learning, facilitate adaptation and coordination, and promote innovation and diverse experience on the ground.

The balance between centrally driven programs and locally driven initiatives varies depending on a country's size, the diversity of its regions, and its tradition of political and administrative centralization. But since ICT is a new dimension of development and a malleable general purpose technology, the balance should favor mechanisms to empower grassroots organizations, promote local ownership and innovation, ensure local fit and flexibility, and meet the special needs of communities. It is at the local level that many of the links between elements of e-development must be sought and built – such as those between telecenter development, content development, e-literacy, and the delivery of e-government services. Accordingly, an ecosystem can be created at the local level whereby telecenters[13] are used as platforms to deliver diverse services, connect local enterprises to extended supply chains, and engage local communities with the knowledge economy (Hanna 2010; Fillip and Foote 2007).

Several mechanisms may be used to institutionalize and support bottom-up initiatives, including innovation funds using matching grants. These mechanisms and the corresponding communities of practice can unleash a flood of ideas and energy. They encourage small enterprises, ICT associations, and nongovernmental

[13] There are many definitions for telecenters, but one good one is "a facility that offers community members the ability to use ICTs in a publicly shared manner. Telecenters often provide the only connectivity available to many community members, and their services may be offered with or without a fee." See http://cyber.law.harvard.edu/readinessguide/glossary.html.

and local community-based organizations to engage with the national ICT agencies in creating and integrating parts of the e-development program. When appropriately targeted, they help the central agencies understand their most vulnerable clients – rural communities and the poor – and the impact of regulation and policy at the grassroots level.

Using Pull Strategies

Top-down strategies have tended to rely on "push" programs, based on forecasting needs and then designing the most efficient investment programs to ensure that the right people and resources are available at the right time and place using scripted processes and standardized applications. Such push programs have their place in driving e-development, and they have dominated development planning and policy making. They remain amenable to elite control and central institutions. But fundamental shifts are changing our world and making it possible to use pull strategies (Hagel et al. 2010). The digital infrastructure is advancing and spreading rapidly and in turn intensifying competition, enabling outsourcing; lowering barriers to entry; and enabling the flow of capital, talent, and knowledge within and across organizations and countries. In turn, these fundamental changes allow for new institutional innovations and new "pull" techniques and practices: open innovation, pull or collaborative platforms, cross-sector and cross-institutional partnerships, and leveraging change agents.

Pull or shaping strategies pull participants into large ecosystems, energized by a passionate vision or "shaping view," encouraging them to invest in ways and platforms that amplify and scale up the investments of all participants (Hagel et al. 2010). By vividly and explicitly describing what the world would be like once it has been e-transformed, a pull strategy would set entrepreneurs and institutions in motion toward a common goal and direction. The digital infrastructure would be leveraged to give individuals, communities, and institutions new ways to make the most of their knowledge, learning, and other resources. It would strengthen the hands of leaders to reach out to, connect with and coordinate investments by large numbers of actors, increasing the potential for leverage and rapid and sustained innovation and distributed learning.

E-development involves a large number of participants, substantial opportunities and uncertainties, and potential for significant performance improvement or even transformation, and thus could be ripe for new forms of pull platforms and shaping strategies. Various ecosystems and platforms can emerge around a shaping strategy: Examples of pull platforms or ecosystems may include incubators, telecenters, grassroots innovation funds, innovation networks, ICT diffusion programs, open source software, open government data, etc. Connected cities and communities may act as pull platforms. A shaping strategy would mobilize such large ecosystems of players. It would promote shared infrastructures to enable innovators and application providers to leverage shared infrastructures and resources and minimize the investment required to build products and offer services. Shaping platforms may also include governance, interoperability, and policy frameworks that help coordinate complex investments and facilitate interactions.

Balancing Short- and Long-Term Objectives

Neither the design of national ICT strategies nor the reporting on them captures the dynamics of implementation and the tradeoffs between responding to short-term imperatives and staying the course on strategic and foundational investments. The country case studies in this book attempt to capture the dynamics of transformation and of formulating and implementing these strategies. Policy makers and e-leadership institutions face tremendous pressures to attend to quick pilots and visible interventions, to diffuse resources across many initiatives, and to limit attention to short-term political horizons.[14] And newly established ICT agencies are likely to face a diversity of legacy systems, backlogs of demands from powerful ministries and resistance to establish government-wide standards for ICT investments and architecture.

A holistic e-development strategy needs to strategically balance and orchestrate the ICT investment portfolio, to give a sense of quick payoffs while progressing toward sustainable transformation. It gives due attention to the less tangible investments that take a long time to yield results – such as the development of e-literacy, e-leadership, e-policies, e-institutions, core competencies, and ICT human resources – but that are fundamental to sustainable e-development. Short-term quick wins, deemed necessary for political sustainability, need to be balanced with long-gestating investments necessary for economic sustainability.

Building Flexibility and Learning into Strategy

National ICT strategies are often conceived of as detailed, long-term investment plans, to be centrally financed, monitored, and controlled. Their outcomes are monitored largely through ICT indicators, which focus mainly on inputs and outputs such as equipment, teledensity, and information traffic flows. But there are big gaps between access to ICT and its use. Moreover, establishing causality between interventions and changes in development impact indicators is difficult; as many other factors come into play, most of which can be understood only in the local context.

[14] At times quick wins are driven by an economic rationale and the need to learn, build user capacity, and sustain confidence in a program. Politicians may also prefer smaller, citizen-oriented initiatives that have lower risks and fewer implementation problems. Here, however, the discussion focuses on tensions and tradeoffs between high-impact but long-gestating investments and low-impact but short-term initiatives.

ICT is a new and fast-changing technology, and diffusing it across diverse social and economic settings requires contextual adaptation, experimentation, and learning. E-development programs need to be flexible. Innovation, learning, monitoring, and evaluation should be central functions and critical success factors. The need for flexibility and adaptability in e-development demands an emphasis on social learning, user-driven innovation, and participatory monitoring and evaluation.

Pursuing e-transformation as an inclusive shared vision and a holistic strategy – rather than a detailed blueprint – encourages learning from pilots and sharing experience from successes and failures. It also points to the need to discover complementarities and synergies over time, not just at the design stage. This cannot be done only from the center, top down, or as a one-time event. Deliberate strategy, emphasizing focus and control, has to be complemented by emergent strategy, emphasizing continuous learning and venturing (Mintzberg et al. 1998). An e-development strategy thus requires institutionalized learning, user-driven innovation, multiple feedback mechanisms, tools for managing and sharing knowledge, knowledge partnerships among stakeholders, and participatory monitoring and evaluation.

Overview and Organization of This Book

The e-transformation framework proposed above is inevitably a simplified view and stylized description of a complex process and rich experience. Most of the country experiences we analyze here were not guided by an explicit and complete version of the e-development framework we propose here. So we use e-development as an organizing framework to glean the strands of causal order and key synergies underlying what may seem a chaotic process and to structure the unwieldy mass of historical events into a meaningful sequence of change and transformation. The holistic e-development framework is mainly a heuristic device or conceptual model, not a straightjacket to be forced upon the infinite richness of real life and the real journey of each country toward an ICT-enabled and transformed economy.

The following chapters, each covering one country, do not follow each aspect of this model in a rigid manner, or present all the values and synergies that may be captured by using this framework. Rather, each country's story is organized along the e-development framework, but broadly interpreted to allow for bringing in selected aspects of the infinite enrichment of real life and to highlight some of the unique experiences of each country. Each chapter deals with a unique story for a unique country. We try to capture each country's initial conditions and individual paths to e-transformation. Yet, we adopt a basic and common framework of e-transformation to show how taking an integrated view of the process can provide a powerful synergistic dynamic in practice, and a clear explanatory framework of a country experience.

In this volume, we focus on two key countries from the BRICs (Brazil and China), mainly because they represent major and fast-growing emerging markets.

Moreover, these countries share a lot in common in terms the challenges of regional diversity and inequality (including digital divide) within each country, and the need to use federated approaches and other mechanisms to experiment, scale up successes, and meet the needs of transformation in different contexts and at different levels of government and the economy. Given the similarities and magnitude of the challenges, policy makers and business leaders of these countries (Brazil and China), together with other members of the BRICs (India and Russia) should be interested in mutual learning. Multinationals and investors are also interested in their huge emerging markets.

The other two cases represent countries with small- to medium-size populations, but at opposing levels of e-transformation: Canada and Sri Lanka. Canada is an example of a country that started early on the e-transformation journey. It is not only a country with high levels of e-readiness and excellence in online government services, but also a country with vast geographic coverage, yet high levels e-inclusion and Internet connectivity. The Canada case poses key issues about the role and locus of leadership for e-transformation for countries at advanced stages of connectivity and transformation.

By contrast, Sri Lanka is a relatively poor country that started on its e-transformation journey relatively recently and is deliberately trying to catch up. The Sri Lanka country case examines the process of designing a deliberate e-development strategy from a participant–observer point of view, as one of the authors engaged in collaborating with the country's leaders in shaping a national ICT-enabled development strategy, guided by a holistic view of e-development. It shows how a deliberate strategy would attempt to overcome initial conditions of weak institutions and unstable political environment to pursue long-term e-transformation and digital inclusion. This case also shows how strategies and initiatives emerge during implementation and can then be tapped and combined with an upfront, deliberate strategy to create an adaptive and learning planning process for continual e-transformation.

A companion volume covers Singapore, Finland, South Africa, and the Philippines. Neither volume includes a representative sample of countries. But both attempt to give a stratified sample, as we strived to include countries at different levels of development, different sizes of population, different political systems, from different continents. Perhaps the only common thing among them is their aspiration and conscious search for e-transformation, so they can have interesting lessons and stories to tell. But we did not include only frontrunners, such as Finland and Singapore, but also recent followers, such as Sri Lanka, so we can capture lessons from countries at different stages of e-transformation.

The final chapter conducts some cross-country analyses along key e-strategy design and implementation issues. The key issues include the degree of centrality, linkage or integration of e-transformation into the country's development strategy; search for comprehensiveness, synergy and coherence of the strategy; and attention to e-leadership, stakeholder engagement, and institutional mechanisms for implementation. They also cover the balance taken between top-down direction and bottom-up initiative, between pursuing long-term and short-term objectives, and between ICT as a cross-sector enabler and as an industry or sector on its own.

The final set of issues or criteria for comparing e-strategies includes degree of reliance on innovation and adaptation during implementation, emphasis on monitoring and evaluation or measuring outcomes, and attention to the digital divide and social inclusion. These issues correspond to those outlined above. Lessons are organized along these key design issues and options.

It is not possible for any book that shares and compares country experiences in a highly complex and intangible process as e-transformation to search for and come up with an ideal e-strategy, a best option or an optimal balance along the above criteria. In fact, this search would be counter-productive, in view of diverse contexts and sociopolitical conditions, and the need for innovation and learning along the way. This book simply aims to share the diverse experiences of diverse countries and to provide a framework for thinking about and informing policy options, investments, and actions. It aims to provide concrete examples of what has been done in different contexts and conditions, and thus enrich the set of tools and options available to policy makers and development practitioners. It shows that design and implementation of e-transformation strategies is contingent on many contextual factors and local stakeholders.

Countries are still at early stages of this journey, and have much to learn from their own experiences, from each other, and particularly from the pioneers. No framework or overarching theory can substitute for this process of experimentation and self-discovery, which is also an intrinsic part of e-transformation. We hope this book can help countries share the policy lessons and discoveries arising from their exciting journeys.

References

Economist Intelligence Unit. 2004. "Reaping the Benefits of ICT: Europe's Productivity Challenge." http://graphics.eiu.com/files/ad_pdfs/MICROSOFT_FINAL.pdf.

Fillip, Barbara, and Dennis Foote, 2007. *Making Connection: Scaling Telecenters for Development,* Washington, D.C.: Academy for Education Development.

Fountain, Jane E. 2001. *Building the Virtual State: Information Technology and Institutional Change*. Washington, DC: Brookings Institution Press.

Hagel, John, John Seely Brown, and Lang Davison. 2010. *The Power of Pull*. New York: Basic Books.

Hanna, Nagy K. 1991. *The Information Technology Revolution and Economic Development.* World Bank Discussion Paper 120. Washington, DC: World Bank.

——. 1994. *Exploiting Information Technology for Development: A Case Study of India.* World Bank Discussion Paper 246. Washington, DC: World Bank.

——. 2004. *Why National Strategies Are Needed for ICT-Enabled Development*. Information Solutions Group Paper. Washington, DC: World Bank.

——. 2007a. *From Envisioning to Designing e-Development: The Experience of Sri Lanka.* Directions in Development Series. Washington, DC: World Bank.

——. 2007b. *Leadership Institutions for the Knowledge Economy*. Washington, DC: World Bank.

——. 2008. *Transforming Government and Empowering Communities: The Sri Lankan Experience with e-Development*. Directions in Development Series. Washington, DC: World Bank.

——. 2009a. *e-Transformation: Enabling New Development Strategies*. New York: Springer.

—. 2009b. *Enabling Enterprise Transformation: Business and Grassroots Innovation for the Knowledge Economy*. New York: Springer.

—. 2010. *Transforming Government and Building the Information Society: Challenges and Opportunities for the Developing World*. New York: Springer.

Hanna, Nagy K.and Qiang, Christine. 2009. "Trends in National E-Government Institutions" in *Information and Communications for Development 2009: Extending Reach and Increasing Impact*. Washington, D.C.: World Bank.

Hanna, Nagy K., and Robert Picciotto, eds. 2002. *Making Development Work: Developmental Learning in a World of Poverty and Wealth*. New Brunswick, NJ: Transaction Publishers.

Heeks, Richard. 2006. "Theorizing ICT4D Research." *Information Technologies and International Development* 3 (3): 1–4.

Mintzberg, Henry, Bruce Ahlstrand, and Joseph Lampel. 1998. *Strategy Safari*. New York: Free Press.

Myrdal, Gunnar. 1957. *Economic Theory and Underdeveloped Regions*. New York: Harper Torchbooks.

Porter, Michael. 1990. *The Competitive Advantage of Nations*. London: Macmillan.

OECD. 2004. *The Economic Impact of ICT: Measurement, Evidence and Implications*. Paris: OECD. http://www1.oecd.org/publications/e-book/9204051E.PDF.

Raiti, Gerard C. 2006. "The Lost Sheep of ICT4D Research." *Information Technologies and International Development* 3 (4): 1–7.

Wilson, Ernest J., III. 2005. "Engaged Scholars and Thoughtful Practitioners: Enhancing Their Dialogue in the Knowledge Society." *Information Technologies and International Development* 2 (4): 89–92.

World Bank. 2006. *Information and Communications for Development 2006: Global Trends and Policies*. Washington, DC: World Bank.

Chapter 2
Toward E-Development in Brazil

Peter T. Knight

Brazil can more effectively harness ICT to increase competitiveness, reduce inequality, and perfect its democracy – goals that most Brazilians espouse. This chapter presents evidence of the importance of leadership and a broadly shared vision in order to drive coordination of e-development policies and programs, leverage local innovations and lessons of experience, and scale up successes for a large, diverse, and democratic country.

Over the last 30 years, Brazil's economic growth has been unsteady and averaged only about three-fifths of the 5.5% rate reached over the period 1920–1980. Brazil's growth has also been much less than that of India and China, to mention two large and complex countries. The Asian "Tigers," Chile and Costa Rica in Latin America also did better than Brazil by this measure (Table 2.1).

Despite its remarkable dynamism and significant social and economic progress following the end of high and unstable rates of inflation in 1994, Brazil has lacked a unifying vision of its development objectives. The country suffers from deep-seated social problems rooted in a highly unequal distribution of income, wealth, and access to education and health services. These inequalities, the current expression of Brazil's centuries-old "social question," threaten social cohesion and undermine public safety. But they also cut economic competitiveness. Brazil's deep social and economic inequalities have begun to be addressed in important social and economic programs during the governments of Fernando Henrique Cardoso (1995–2002) and Luis Inácio Lula da Silva (2003–2010). Income inequalities have been reduced following the economic stabilization and monetary reform (Real Plan) in 1994 and the introduction of conditional direct transfers to poorer citizens which were consolidated and greatly expanded during the Lula administrations under the family subsidy (*Bolsa Família*) program. Brazil weathered the great recession of 2009 better than most countries, and in 2010 GDP growth is expected to exceed 7%. Further progress is crucial to realize the country's economic potential and to secure political stability.

N.K. Hanna and P.T. Knight (eds.), *Seeking Transformation Through Information Technology*, Innovation, Technology, and Knowledge Management,
DOI 10.1007/978-1-4614-0353-1_2, © Springer Science+Business Media, LLC 2011

Table 2.1 Average annual percentage rates of growth of GDP, 1980–2008

Country	1980–1990	1990–2000	2000–2008
China	10.3	10.6	10.4
India	5.7	5.9	7.9
Korea	9.0	5.8	4.5
Hong Kong, China	6.8	3.6	5.2
Malaysia	5.3	7.0	5.5
Thailand	7.6	4.2	5.2
Singapore	8.7	7.6	5.8
Chile	4.2	6.6	4.4
Costa Rica	3.0	5.3	5.4
Brazil	2.7	2.7	3.6

Source: 1980–1990, World Bank (2005); 1990–2008, World Bank (2010)

Public frustration with crime, corruption, unresponsive political institutions, inefficient government services, tortoise-like judicial systems, and lack of economic opportunities is rampant. There is still no real consensus on development strategy among key elites or the public at large, though better education, health, public safety, and infrastructure seem to be broadly accepted goals. The federal and state elections of 2006 provided an opportunity to discuss these problems and promote a national debate on how to accelerate socioeconomic development, improve competitiveness, and induce massive investments – from domestic and international sources – that Brazil requires. To a certain extent this happened, but in general the necessary debate was derailed by political scandals that captured headlines and dominated national attention. Something similar occurred in the run-up to the national and state elections held in October of 2010.

Brazil needs a new development vision with a mobilizing power similar to that which inspired Brazilian President Juscelino Kubitschek's campaign slogan, "Fifty years of progress in five," and his Plan of Goals (*Plano de Metas*) for his government (1956–1961). Building the automobile industry, a national highway network, and a new capital, Brasília, in the nation's heartland together were central to Kubitschek's vision. JK, as he was known, remains one of Brazil's most respected presidents.

Innovative governments – good examples such as Canada, China, Finland, Ireland, South Korea, and Singapore – have shown that with focused strategies and leadership, ICT can help accelerate economic and social development. Developing countries around the world, with Sri Lanka and India in the lead, have been developing national e-development strategies and attracting financing for their implementation from both domestic and international sources of funding, including the World Bank. Brazil is well positioned to develop and implement an e-development strategy, and now appears to be moving in that direction. Given Brazil's size and diversity, e-development may have to proceed at different paces for different states, with leadership from all levels of government, and with progressive state governors at the forefront.

Vision, Leadership, Consensus, Policies, and Institutions

Developing a Brazilian Vision for E-Development

Developing the information society in Brazil was the subject of a pioneering effort by the Ministry of Science and Technology back in 1999–2000, during the second administration of President Cardoso. A team coordinated from that Ministry produced a report known as the Green Book (*Livro Verde*) in the year 2000.[1] This report was the closest Brazil's federal government has come to a comprehensive e-development strategy. It included a wide-ranging analysis and proposed goals and actions elaborated with the participation of over 300 specialists from different parts of government, the private sector, academia, and civil society organizations. Some 150 of these participated in 12 thematic groups. The Green Book covered all the key elements in the e-development framework. Legislative, programmatic and other actions were proposed though in rather general terms, without budgets. Unfortunately, this integrated and comprehensive strategy was never executed in a coordinated fashion with strong guidance from the President's office, though various elements of it were pursued by separate ministries. E-government got the most attention during the period 2000–2002. An institutional framework was created to develop e-government programs at the federal level in 2000 with coordination from the President's Chief of Staff as explained in greater detail later in this chapter. Then in 2004 the subject of e-government in Brazil was treated in a pioneering way in *e-gov.br – a próxima revolução brasileira* (*e.gov.br – the next Brazilian revolution*).[2] Contributions by 44 specialists documented and analyzed Brazil's achievements in building an information society and conducting a wide range of e-government activities in education, health, public safety, justice, elections, legislation, public administration, and digital inclusion (bridging the digital divide). Brazil's major regions and the federal, state, and local governments were covered. Shortly after this publication another book appeared, *e-government – o governo eletrônico no Brasil* (*e-government – electronic government in Brazil*)[3] with contributions by 30 specialists.

A major project on strategic scenario development was carried out by the Presidency of Brazil's Strategic Studies Nucleus (*Núcleo de Assuntos Estratégicos* – NAE) in 2005, and this included scenarios for ICT use (*Núcleo de Assuntos Estratégicos* 2005; Takahashi 2007). But through 2009 there was little evidence that they had much impact on national development strategy, perhaps in part because of staff changes at the NAE, now the Secretariat for Strategic Affairs (*Secretaria de Assuntos Estratégicos* – SAE).

[1] Takahashi (2000).

[2] Chahin et al. (2004).

[3] Ferrer and Santos (2004).

The *e-Brasil* Project (Box 2.1), initiated in October 2005, was a continuation of these pioneering efforts to mobilize the intellectual capital needed to raise the priority of a more focused e-development strategy at the national, state, and municipal levels.

Box 2.1 The *E-Brasil* Project

The *e-Brasil* Project sought to raise awareness first of politicians and their advisors and then of the population at large concerning the advantages of a coherent e-development strategy to help build a more equitable society and a more competitive economy – goals widely accepted in Brazil. The project team reviewed international and Brazilian experience and produced recommendations for public policies to achieve these twin goals (see the concluding section of this chapter).

The e-Brasil team members had diverse institutional and political affiliations: they occupied or had held key positions in the Brazilian federal and state governments, governments of other countries, international organizations, the private sector, and academia. What united them was the conviction that with the intensive use of ICT it is possible for Brazil to overcome the obstacles that prevent it from being a developed first world country – most notably its highly unequal distribution of income, wealth, and knowledge and factors reducing its competitiveness, such as corruption, excessive bureaucracy, and a tortoise-like judicial system.

During 2006 and 2007 the e-Brasil project published three books, two of them before the state and federal elections of October 2006, and the last and by far the most complete in September of 2007.[4] An interactive web portal promoting the e-Brasil vision and policy program and offering links to institutions of the Brazilian ICT sector was established in 2006. The Portal was intended to be part of a broader strategic communication campaign to raise awareness not only of political leaders, but also of the public in general, through the electronic and print media, concerning the opportunities that intensive use of ICT can offer Brazil to achieve economic, social, and political goals.

Progress was visible at the political level, especially in important states such as São Paulo, Rio de Janeiro, Paraná, Ceará, and Minas Gerais. The state of Acre (on the border with Bolivia and Peru in the Amazon) initiated programs to make broadband Internet available to its residents free of charge while enhancing its e-government offerings. A nationwide movement to

(continued)

[4] Knight (2006), Knight and Fernandes (2006), and Knight et al. (2007).

Box 2.1 (continued)

create more digital towns and cities was developing. In the municipal elections of 2008, candidates for mayor in many *municípios,*[5] including the largest in the country, São Paulo and Rio de Janeiro, called for adoption of some of the key e-Brasil policies, such as free or low-cost Internet connectivity for their populations. At the federal level there were important initiatives to bring broadband Internet and computers to all the nation's schools, develop a National Broadband Plan, and to support the rollout of interactive digital television with a huge development potential for education, health, e-government, and e-commerce applications as well as entertainment and information.

Weaknesses of the e-Brasil project included its lack of an institutional base and sufficient resources to develop a more effective strategic communication campaign.

During 2009, in the context of a growing national debate on a proposed National Broadband Plan being prepared by the Federal Government, some participants proposed elements of transformation strategies for Brazil that go well beyond such a plan, stressing the positive role ICT can play. One such proposal has been published in both Portuguese and English versions (TelComp 2009), a white paper drawing on the presentations and discussions held during a conference on ICT 2020 – Transformation Strategies for Brazil.[6] The SAE organized a seminar held in Brasília in November 2009 at which the government revealed the general outlines of the National Broadband Plan. This plan was finally launched in May 2010 in the form of a presidential decree[7] creating the National Broadband Program (*Programa Nacional de Banda Larga* – PNBL), discussed further below.

Other participants in this debate presented their views in private to government policy makers and in public during various national and regional conferences. For example, at a high-level seminar organized by Telebrasil, a trade association led by large telecommunications operators, and Brasscom, another trade association representing large ICT equipment and service companies presented a range of quite detailed proposals, with quantified targets for most of them, for accelerating

[5] A Brazilian *município* is the lowest level of government in the federal system. Most include substantial rural areas as well as the city for which the *município* is named, so translating it as municipality is rather misleading.

[6] The conference, held in São Paulo in Sept 2009, was organized by Telcomp – the Brazilian Association of Competitive Telecommunications Providers, Brasscom – The Brazilian Association Information and Communications Technology Companies, and the Faculty of Law of the Getúlio Vargas Foundation.

[7] Decree No. 7175 of 12 May 2010.

Brazilian socioeconomic development through a wide variety of programs. Most of these involved further stages of existing government programs or private sector initiatives, with governments providing new government financing, tax reductions, and other incentives. A major new program would be the PNBL, using Brasscom's preferred approach of tax reductions at both the federal and state levels as a principal means to stimulate demand and encourage private sector investment, one of the approaches also preferred by Telebrasil (Brasscom 2009; Telebrasil 2009).

Within the federal government, different ministries and organs presented competing views regarding the role of the state. Diverse private sector enterprises and interest groups as well as NGOs lobbied for their viewpoints. The Ministry of Communications favored a greater role for the private sector, while groups within the Ministry of Planning, Budget, and Management and the Presidency favored greater public sector involvement, including the ownership and operation of fiber optic backbones and networks for the government's own use, and in some cases sales direct to final customers. As it turned out, to achieve its goals the PNBL is to rely less on tax reductions and the private sector telcos and more on a federal telecommunications enterprise, Telebrás, which had been essentially dormant since the privatization of that sector in 1998. But the private sector will be expected to expand services and engage in greater competition.

A 4-day National Communications Conference (Confecom) was held in Brasília in December 2009 with participation of government, private, and organized civil society sectors. It approved 641 different proposals. It is possible that from the debate centered on the PNBL and the Confecom, some kind of consensus and a more coherent national strategy for e-development may emerge, though as of October 2010 it was still far from clear.

Government Institutions for E-Development

A Presidential decree in June 2000 established the Secretariat for Logistics and Information Technology in the Ministry of Planning, Budget, and Management (SLTI/MP) as the lead agency for developing and implementing an e-government framework. SLTI/MP serves as the secretariat for an interagency e-government committee chaired by the President's Civilian Chief of Staff (*Ministro da Casa Civil*) – the Executive Committee on e-Government (*Comitê Executivo do Governo Eletrônico* – CEGE), to which a number of specialized interagency technical groups report. These formal e-government structures remained in place with only minor changes.

Other ministries and agencies have responsibilities for other aspects of e-development – most importantly the Ministry of Communications and the National Telecommunications Agency (Anatel) for Telecommunications (including radio and television) and their regulation, the Ministry of Science and Technology and its agencies for ICT R&D and innovation (including the development of the important academic and research internet – RNP), the Ministry of Trade and Economic Development for ICT industrial and trade strategy, and the Ministry of Education for formal ICT education and e-learning. Training in ICT skills is the province of specialized agencies in the "S system" (SENAI for industry, SENAC for commerce, SEBRAI for small business, etc.). The private sector and NGOs also play important and complementary roles in shaping e-development strategies.

As digital inclusion became an increasingly important theme during the two governments of President Lula (2003–2010), programs in this area were developed by several different ministries. Despite several attempts at coordination, including through a technical group of the CEGE, it was not until well into the second half of the second Lula government, in August 2009, that a serious effort to coordinate them was undertaken through a Presidential Decree[8] creating the Management Committee for Digital Inclusion (*Comitê Gestor do Programa de Inclusão Digital* – CGPID), this time based in the office of the President.

The CGPID originally had the following five principal responsibilities:

- Establish general directives for the management and application of financial resources for the Digital Inclusion Program and the projects which make it up.
- Approve the annual work program of the Digital Inclusion Program and evaluate its results periodically.
- Accompany and monitor the implementation and performance of the projects in the Digital Inclusion Program.
- Interact with other management committees and interministerial working groups in the Federal Government, the States, and Municipalities having specific objectives linked to digital inclusion programs and projects.
- Undertake studies and proposals related to projects in the Digital Inclusion Program to provide inputs into decisions in the sphere of the Presidency of the Republic relating to digital inclusion projects and programs.

In the decree establishing the PNBL, six additional responsibilities were added:

- Provide assistance and advice to the organs of the Presidency of the Republic related to projects and programs of digital inclusion.
- Define the actions, goals, and priorities of the PNBL.
- Promote and encourage partnerships between public and private entities to achieve the objectives of the PNBL.
- Determine the technical definition of broadband access for the PNBL.
- Accompany and evaluate the actions to implement the PNBL.
- Publish an annual report on the actions, goals, and results of the PNBL.

The CGPID was also broadened from 8 to 12 members in the PNBL decree. Further, CGPID's mandate was expanded with the general objective encouraging and disseminating the use and supply of ICT goods and services to:

- Massify access to broadband Internet connections
- Accelerate economic and social development

[8]Decree 6948 of 25 Aug 2009.

- Promote digital inclusion
- Reduce regional and social inequalities
- Promote the generation of employment and income
- Expand e-government services and facilitate citizen access to State services
- Promote the training of the population in the use of information technologies
- Increase Brazilian technological autonomy and competitiveness

Four members of the CGPID represent organs related to the Presidency of the Republic (President's Civilian Chief of Staff, its chair with a tie-breaking vote; President's Personal Office; Secretariat of Social Communication; and Secretariat for Strategic Affairs) and eight represent ministries (Communications; Science and Technology; Education; Culture; Planning, Budget, and Management; Development, Industry, and Foreign Trade; Health; and Finance). Members of the CGPID are nominated by their respective organizations and approved by the Minister Chief of the President's Civilian Staff (*Ministro Chefe da Casa Civil da Presidência da República*). The CGPID has an Executive Secretariat based in the Personal Office of the President to which a Permanent Technical Advisory Unit is attached. The Executive Secretariat can invite representatives of other public or private organizations to participate, without vote, in meetings of the CGPID. Resolutions of the CGPID are approved by a simple majority vote.

Four Thematic Groups, coordinated by representatives of different Ministries, report to the CGPID: Infrastructure and Telecommunications Services; Applications; Content; and Industrial Policy, Technological Development, and Innovation. Additional Thematic Groups can be created by decision of the CGPID. The overall structure relating to the CGPID is provided in Fig. 2.1.

The decree instituting the PNBL also gave an important role to Telebrás, formerly a federal holding company for state telecommunications companies and largely inactive after their privatization in 1998. Telebrás is to

- Implement the private communications network of the federal public administration.
- Provide support for public policies on broadband Internet connections for universities, research centers, schools, hospitals, health posts, community telecenters, and other points of public interest.
- Provide infrastructure and support networks for telecommunications services supplied by private enterprises, States, the Federal District, Municipalities, and nonprofit entities.
- Provide broadband Internet connections for final users (only in localities where there is no adequate private sector supply of such services).

To carry out its mandate, Telebrás was authorized to use, operate, and maintain the telecommunication networks belonging to the public federal administration or controlled by it, including public and mixed capital enterprises. For those federally owned or controlled enterprises, Telebrás has to enter into formal agreements (*convênios*) – the most important will be with the federal electric distribution companies controlled by Eletrobrás and the federal mixed-capital enterprise,

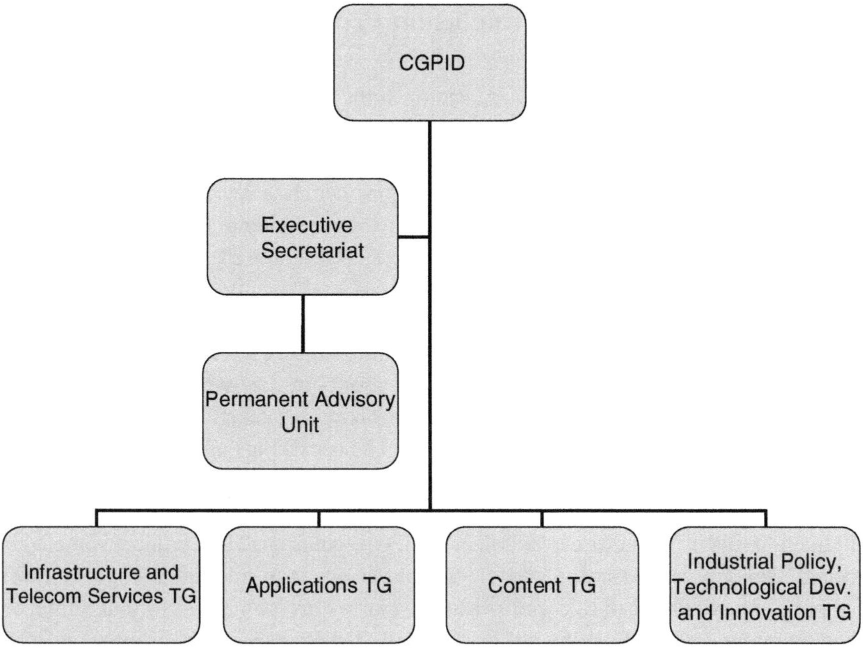

Fig. 2.1 Structure of the management committee for digital inclusion (GGPID)

Petrobrás, that have extensive networks of fiber optic cables linked to their respective high-tension transmission networks and pipelines.

To provide some important inputs to the CGPID, a Connected Brazil Forum composed of some 60 representatives of various federal, state, and municipal government agencies; private sector interest groups; and NGOs was established in June 2010.

As of October 2010, it was not yet clear how effectively CGPID and Telebrás will be able to carry out their important responsibilities.

The new institutional arrangements offer some promise for establishing what had previously been missing in Brazil: an overarching e-development strategy and plan capable of realizing the potential synergies and returns to scale in the use of ICT to accelerate socioeconomic development. Without a whole-of-government approach and effective coordination from near the top of the government providing clear incentives to adhere to the plan and to involve major nongovernment stakeholders (the private sector, academic and research institutions, and NGOs), e-development is unlikely to realize anything like its full potential at any level in Brazil's federal system. The new arrangements were announced just as the campaigns to elect a new President, state governors, and both federal and state legislatures were about to begin. Thus, whether the promise is fulfilled will depend on the priorities of the new federal and state governments to take office in January 2011. It will also depend on the leadership and membership of this inclusive team of stakeholders.

Infostructure and Digital Inclusion Programs

Telecommunications is an important sector in the Brazilian economy, with sales of telecommunication services estimated at US $69 billion and hardware at US $11 billion, totaling 6.9% of GDP in 2008 (Brasscom 2009).

Driven by a technological wave of digitization, there is a clear tendency, worldwide, toward convergence in platforms, equipment, and content. Cable TV networks, previously used for video alone, now offer telephone and Internet, telephone networks also offer Internet and IP video. Television sets and computers are converging in many ways, while mobile terminals increasingly have the capability to access a variety of transmission platforms. And the same or multiple versions of digital content may be sent over different platforms to a variety of receiving devices.

Without telecommunications infrastructure, taking advantage of digital conversion and promoting e-development is impossible. The backbones of the infostructure are provided by submarine and terrestrial fiber optic cables and by communications satellites. In this respect, Brazil is relatively well served. Brazil is also progressing in making this infostructure available to all the population. This requires some additional backbone construction and the use of various last-mile technologies as well as programs whereby public and private resources are combined to make Internet and telephony available to the poorer and more isolated segments of the population that cannot afford commercial access to these services. The PNBL seeks to address this question.

Fiber Optic Cable and Other Terrestrial and Submarine Infostructure

Brazil has multiple submarine cable connections with the USA, some Latin American countries, Europe, and Africa. These provide redundant links to the global Internet.

The incumbent regional operators formed during the privatization of the state-owned Telebrás networks all have their own terrestrial fiber optic networks. At that time, July 1998, Brazil had only 19 million fixed telephone lines and 5.5 million mobile phones in service, a total of 24.5 million lines. Ten years later the number of fixed lines had risen to 40 million, and the number of mobile phones to 133.1 million, for a total of 173 million lines. The number of mobiles continues to rise rapidly – reaching 194.4 million in October 2010, exceeding the population of Brazil in the 2010 census (190.7 million).

Another large fiber optic network is that of Eletronet, conceived in 1999 to operate a reliable system of long-distance lines linked directly to Brazil's power grid. Eletronet has some 16,000 km of high-capacity fiber and entered bankruptcy in 2003, but continues to operate under an administrator. It was essentially a joint venture between the Brazilian subsidiary of the US company AES and electric companies in the Eletrobrás group. Conflicts over its debts to suppliers (principally Furukawa and Alcatel/Lucent) had still not been fully resolved in October 2010. But as mentioned earlier, the presidential decree establishing the PNBL authorized Telebrás to negotiate the use of the fiber optic networks of the companies in the Eletrobrás group and also that of Petrobrás.

Though Brazil's infostructure has developed rapidly over recent years, in November 2007, of the country's 5,654 *municípios*, 3,570 of them still lacked broadband terrestrial connections.[9] However, in April 2008, after over 9 months of negotiations, President Luiz Inácio Lula da Silva signed presidential decree 6.424/2008 governing the so-called "exchange of obligations" whereby the incumbent telecommunications operators agreed that by the end of 2010 they would bring broadband Internet to every Brazilian *município* and connect 56,000 urban schools free of charge through 2025 rather than construct over 8,000 "Telecommunications Services Posts" as required under their concessions.[10] If this goal is met, Brazil will have the basis for universal Internet service, at least in urban areas. Negotiations between the federal government and telecommunications operators were still underway in October 2010 on how to provide connections for schools in rural areas.

Satellites

While connectivity via satellite is more expensive than via landlines, the advantage of satellite connections is that they can be established at any point in Brazil by using what are called VSAT (Very Small Aperture Terminal) antennas and related equipment at quite a low capital cost. In addition, satellite connections can provide important backup (redundancy) connections for terrestrial landlines. There is a wide variety of satellites serving Brazil's telecommunications needs.

Teaching, Research and Community Networks[11]

Scientific and academic networks have long played leading roles in the development of the Internet in the USA, Europe, Russia, and elsewhere, including in Latin

[9] See http://www.anatel.gov.br/Portal/exibirPortalInternet.do, http://extra.globo.com/economia/plantao/2007/11/13/327147047.asp, http://www.mc.gov.br/, and http://www.telesintese.ig.com.br/index.php?option=com_content&task=view&id=7582&Itemid=105, all three pages accessed on 13 Nov 2009.

[10] See the text of the decree at http://legislacao.planalto.gov.br/legisla/legislacao.nsf/fraWeb?OpenFrameSet&Frame=frmWeb2&Src=%2Flegisla%2Flegislacao.nsf%2FViw_Identificacao%2FDEC%25206.424-2008%3FOpenDocument%26AutoFramed , accessed 13 Nov 2009. Data on Redecomep from http://www.redecomep.com.br, accessed 31 Oct 2010.

[11] This section draws heavily on Knight (2008a), pp. 7–9.

America, especially Brazil. In Brazil, the National Education and Research Network (*Rede Nacional de Ensino e Pesquisa* – RNP) was established in 1989, is maintained by the Federal Government and managed by a private company, RNP-OS.[12] In recent years, RNP has been establishing new partnerships that have the potential to greatly expand high-speed Internet access. These partnerships can potentially play a critical role in education at all levels, crucial for Brazil's competitiveness in an ever more knowledge-based global economy, and in Brazil's digital inclusion programs. Combined with the development of interactive digital television, the impact could be impressive, helping create a more equitable and more competitive Brazil.

RNP and the Redecomep Project. RNP's national backbone network, known as the Ipê Network, has points of presence in all Brazilian states and the Federal District, and provides connectivity to the principal universities and research institutions in the country. This fiber optic network is among the most advanced in the world and has connections with foreign academic networks such as RedClara (Latin America), Internet 2 (USA), and Géant (Europe).

A relatively recent initiative of RNP, launched in December 2004, is the program for Community Education and Research Networks (*Redes Comunitárias de Educação e Pesquisa* – Redecomep). Redecomep is supported by the Ministry of Science and Technology and financed by resources from the National Fund for Scientific and Technological Development (*Fundo Nacional de Desenvolvimento Científico e Tecnológico* – FNDCT).[13]

As of October 2010, the Redecomep program had built 21 metropolitan networks, all of which were in operation, and six more were under construction. Some of the Redecomep networks were also making use of WiMAX wireless technologies for parts of their networks.[14]

The unit costs of a fiber optic network are much lower than those for dedicated circuits leased from commercial telecom operators, and building such networks can result in huge savings to universities, research institutes, governments, and other users.[15]

New Partnerships. Two aspects of Redecomep are particularly interesting beyond the immediate objective of linking teaching and research institutions with high-speed Internet connections. The first is that at the Redecomep project, while it provides funding for investment costs, is encouraging a wide variety of partnerships for the construction and financing of operating costs. These partnerships have included

[12] For a good presentation of RNP's development see Stanton and Simões da Silva (2007).

[13] FNDCT was created back in 1969 and receives taxes and other levies on a large number of different goods, services, and transactions, as well as special allocations from federal government budgets.

[14] See http://www.redecomep.rnp.br, accessed 31 Oct 2010.

[15] The total projected government investment for the Metrobel fiber network in the city of Belem in Pará state, with 30 points of presence was R$1.1 million over 5 years, and the maintenance and operating costs on the order of R$200,000 per year. This works out to a cost for a Gigabit connection of about R$13,000 per year, a little more than half the price of a 256-kbp connection for 4,000 times the bandwidth. See http://www.redecomep.rnp.br/modelo/, accessed 13 Nov 2009.

Box 2.2 Partnerships Between the State of Pará, Metrobel, and Eletronorte

The first Redecomep network to enter operation, Metrobel in Belém, led the government of Pará State, of which Belém is the capital, to extend Metrobel by an additional 50 km, and to include 165 additional points of presence, mainly government buildings, including schools and health facilities. Independently, the State of Pará signed an agreement with the federal government-owned electrical utility company, *Centrais Elétricasdo Norte do Brasil* (Eletronorte) that allows the use of 1,800 km of the company's fiber optic cable to link Metrobel with the interior of the state.

In the state of Acre, which borders Bolivia and Peru, the RBMetroNet, another Redecomep project, is being integrated into a broader state-wide network for government offices and general public access. Similar partnerships are moving forward with other electric power distribution companies.[16]

municipal governments, state governments, and both public and private sector enterprises.

The second is that among the enterprises are electric power distribution companies. Most of these (such as pipeline companies, railroads, and other utilities) have fiber optic networks of their own, with a lot of excess capacity given the continual improvements in data transmission technologies for fiber optic cable. By establishing partnerships with such companies, Redecomep networks can greatly expand the reach of their networks at very low cost. Likewise, when Redecomep invests in its own fiber networks, it can offer excess capacity to other users, thus helping reduce current costs to its own users as well as to its partners (Box 2.2).

Redecomep relationships with power companies could be taken to a whole new level if the status of Eletronet were resolved and partnerships established with this 16,000 km network of high-capacity fiber. That possibility has been envisioned by RNP officials at least since 2006 (Simões and Stanton 2006). Under the PNBL the resurrected Telebrás may be able to facilitate such collaboration.

Telecommunications Policy Issues

Brazil's telecommunications legislation – broadly including that governing radio, television, telephony, and the Internet – is fragmented and outdated for the era of

[16] Sources: http://www.navegapara.pa.gov.br/index.php?q=metrobel and http://www.navegapara.pa.gov.br/index.php?q=infovias, both accessed 9 Nov 2009. See http://www.redecomep.rnp.br/, accessed 19 Aug 2010.

digital convergence. That governing radio and television broadcasting dates back to the Brazilian Television Code (*Código Brasileiro de Telecomunicações*) of 1962 and the subject of considerable controversy at the time. Under the military governments (1964–1986), telephony was largely confined to 27 state telecom companies under Telebrás. This system was not changed under the civilian constitution of 1988 until 1998. Radio and television broadcasting remained largely private sector enterprises under concessions awarded by the Ministry of Communications, which also oversaw the Telebrás system. The legal framework for telephony, data transmission, communications satellites, and radio spectrum allocation was established by General Telecommunications Law (*Lei Geral de Telecomunicações* – LGT) of 1997, which also provided the basis for the privatization of the Telebrás system and the establishment of Anatel, the regulatory agency for telecommunications.

In 2003, a presidential decree created the Internet Management Committee (*Comitê Gestor da Internet* – CGI), composed of eight representatives of the federal government ministries and agencies, one representative of the Council of State Secretaries of Science and Technology, one Internet expert appointed by the Ministry of Communications, four private sector representatives each selected from a separate segment (Internet service and content providers, telecommunications infrastructure providers, providers of ICT hardware and software, and users of Internet services), four representatives of organized civilian society, and three representatives of the scientific and research community. The CGI has worked well and been considered a possible model at the international level.

The privatization of the telecommunications sector foreseen in the LGT of 1997 and carried out in 1998 resulted in a rapid expansion of fixed lines and a veritable explosion of mobile telephones. But the cost of telephone service of any kind in Brazil remains high and despite the progress, there are still segments of the population lacking even telephone service, much less broadband Internet connections. These are serious weaknesses in the infostructure for a knowledge economy or information society.

Regarding the first problem, the LGT already foresaw the need for a universal service fund, and in August 2000 a law was passed establishing the Fund for Universalization of Telecommunications Services (*Fundo de Universalização de Serviços de Telecomunicações* – Fust). As written, the law applied only to fixed-line telephone service, and there were a number of other weaknesses. Neither the LGT nor the Fust law foresaw the digital convergence and strategic importance of the broadband connections for voice, data, and video. Furthermore, though the inflows to the Fust, derived mainly from a 1% tax on the gross receipts of telecommunications operators (and explicitly passed on to their customers as indicated in their monthly bills), are on the order of R$1 billion per year, there have been almost no expenditures to universalize any telecommunications service. Rather the resources of Fust have been diverted to the federal treasury and in effect used to build a primary surplus to pay interest on federal government debt.

The Fust law is flawed in many ways, and Fust was evaluated negatively in an audit by the Federal Audit Court (*Tribunal de Contas da União* – TCU). In December 2005, the TCU ordered the regulatory agency, Anatel, and the Ministry of Communications to formulate policies, directives, and priorities for applying Fust resources that should urgently consider the needs for universalizing telecommunications services in Brazil, define which governmental actions to promote digital inclusion should receive Fust resources, actions, and governmental programs in the Multiyear Plan (Plano Plurianual – PPA) for the years 2004–2007 that would receive Fust resources, and carry out a number of detailed studies.[17] While the studies were carried out, no significant spending of Fust funds for any purpose had taken place as of October 2010. Various reasons have been given for this – including ambiguities in the existing legislation, passive resistance on the part of the incumbent telecommunications operators, the need of the Finance Ministry to build a primary surplus to cover public debt service, and perhaps most importantly, the lack of political pressure to resolve the issue.

In June 2008, a number of separate pieces of legislation languishing in the Brazilian Congress were combined into a single unified draft law by a special commission of the Chamber of Deputies and reported out to the Chamber with a unanimous recommendation that it be made law. As of October 2010, the proposed legislation, which would have mandated the use of Fust resources for providing broadband Internet connections to schools, had still not been approved by the full Chamber of Deputies, though the PNBL envisions Fust as an important source of finance.

At the beginning of 2009, President Luis Inácio Lula da Silva announced his intent to convene a National Communication Conference (Confecom) to debate modernization of the regulatory framework of the broadly defined telecommunications sector to take into account digital convergence. Confecom was convoked by a presidential decree in April, and involved the selection of private sector and NGO representatives by state conferences which could also submit proposals to the national conference that took place in December 2009, in which government representatives also participated. Despite approving 461 proposals in 4 days, Confecom could only make recommendations. Some of these were incorporated into the PNBL, but as of October 2010 it remained to be seen what the real impact of Confecom would be.

The high price of telecommunications services in Brazil has been an obstacle to overcome the digital divide. Part of the problem may be due to the oligopolistic nature of the industry, where fixed-line service has been overwhelmingly provided by three incumbent operators – Telefônica, Brasil Telecom, and Oi (the latter two were underwent a merger in 2009) – with Embratel dominant in long distance service. But another major factor is the extraordinarily high taxation levied on telecommunication services in Brazil – the highest of any major sector of the economy (Box 2.3).

In October 2009, the Governor of São Paulo signed a decree instituting a Popular Broadband program whereby telecommunications companies offering basic broadband service at the price of about US $17 per month would not have to pay the 25% state value-added tax. Some federal tax reductions and/or exemptions are included in the PNBL, and states are being encouraged to reduce or eliminate their value-added taxes for basic broadband service. This state policy innovation deserves evaluation.

---

[17]The TCU's decision is recorded in Acórdão 1248/2005 – TCU Plenário issued on 12 Dec 2005.

Box 2.3 Excessive Taxation of Telecommunication Services

No sector of the Brazilian economy is more highly taxed than information services. This high rate of taxation may once have been justifiable on income distribution grounds as only the relatively well-off had telephones; it was also easy to administer. In August 2010, Brazil had over 189 million cell phones for a population of 193 million. Eighty-two percent of these were prepaid, suggesting that they were not used by the rich.

In an ever more globalized, knowledge-based economy, high taxation of information services runs counter to federal, state, and municipal government policies promoting digital inclusion and has become part of the "*custo Brasil*" that reduces Brazil's competitiveness. Communications costs are among those compared by Brazilian and international companies in choosing where to locate and invest. Low-cost connectivity is crucial for continuing education of the labor force via e-learning.

Taxation reaches 57.2% for information services (largely telecommunications) exceeding 42.8% for electricity, gas and water and an average of 24.7% for manufactures. Even for states with the lowest state value-added tax on telecommunications (25%) the total indirect taxes on the gross income of telecommunications operators is 31.2% and there are states with 30% and even 35% state value-added taxes on telecommunications services.[18] And in addition the telecommunications operators must pay a number of other taxes on their payrolls, profits, financial operations, and so forth.[19]

Extraordinarily high taxation of information services runs counter to the principles of tax neutrality between sectors. It is not even neutral among states: the important ICMS varies from 25 to 35% depending on state and has been as high as 40%.

Finally, there is evidence that the income and price elasticities of information services are above one –especially at the lower and middle-income levels – implying that a 1% reduction in price or a 1% increase in incomes would lead to greater than a 1% increase in demand. Reducing rates may therefore not lower revenues much in the short term and could conceivably increase them in the medium and long term if the tax rate reduction leads to a boom in economic activity and investment. The high taxation of information services may therefore be counterproductive.

---

[18] See http://www.teleco.com.br/tributos.asp, accessed 9 Nov 2009.

[19] Indirect taxes include the state value-added tax (ICMS), and the federal Cofins, PIS/PASEP, Fust, Funttel that all incide on the gross value of sales. In addition, there are a variety of other federal taxes paid by telecommunications companies – the corporate income tax (IRPJ), a profits tax (CSSL), the tax on financial transactions (IOF), a levy on fuels (CIDE), a levy to support the regulator (Fistel), and a number of payroll taxes supporting social security health and unemployment benefits of employees. Most of the Fistel revenue is related to active cell phones. There is an installation tax of R$26.83 and an annual tax of R$13.42. Since over 80% of Brazilian mobile phones are prepaid with a low average use, these taxes have a great impact on the cost of using these cell phones. Prepaid phones are used mainly by relatively poor people, and hence these taxes are highly regressive.

Internet Penetration and Usage

Data on Internet penetration in 2009 from the household survey by Brazil's official statistical service[20] show large differences in household Internet access by both region and income class (Table 2.2).

There has been a substantial increase from 13.7 to 27.4% of Brazilian homes having at least one computer with an Internet connection between 2005 and 2009, but that still means that almost three out of four homes lacked one. There were some regional differences for residences having aggregate incomes of over 20 minimum wages (90.7% of these well-off households) in the most industrialized Southeast region had an Internet connection. But even in the relatively isolated North (Amazon), 79.7% of these well-off households had a computer with an Internet connection. The regional differences were much greater for households with up to ten minimum wages of income – ranging from a high of 28.7% in the Southeast to only 9.9% in the North, with an average of 21.6% for the country's 57.6 million homes, reflecting the greater poverty and lesser urbanization in the North and Northeast regions.

Data on Internet use in 2009 by individuals aged 10 and above collected by the Brazilian Network Information Center (the research arm of CGI)[21] show the same general patterns as found in the official household survey data, for regions and income. Fifty-five percent had never used the Internet, though this figure varied sharply by social class, age, education, family income, and, to a lesser extent, gender. Thirty-nine percent of Brazilians in this age group had accessed the Internet from some location within the 3 months prior to the survey. For the top social class (A), the percentage was 85%, and even in the lowest two social classes (D and E) the number was 14%, while only 3% of their homes had a computer with an Internet connection.[22] By far the most important reason for not having an Internet connection given by households (having a computer without an Internet connection) was the high cost of the connection, cited by 48% of such households. Having access to a computer in some other location was cited by 22%.[23]

One of the most striking trends is the important and rapidly growing role of paid public access points called Lan houses or Internet cafés in Brazil, and run as private sector enterprises. In 2009, 45% of all Brazilians who accessed the Internet in the 3 months prior to the survey did so from these private sector establishments, more than accessed the Internet at any other location except home (48%). Access from the homes of others was reported by 26%, at work by 22%, at schools by 14%, at free public telecenters by 4%, and from cellular phones 3%. The percentage using paid public access points was significantly higher for the poorest regions (the Northeast

[20] National Household Sample Survey (*Pesquisa Nacional por Amostra de Domicílios* – PNAD) conducted annually by the Brazilian Institute for Geography and Statistics (*Instituto Brasileiro de Geografia e Estatística* – IBGE). PNAD covers rural as well as urban areas.

[21] Brazilian Network Information Center (2010), Table C2.

[22] Ibid, Tables C2 and A4.

[23] Brazilian Network Information Center (2010), Table A10.

Table 2.2 Residences having a computer with Internet access by level of income, 2009

Region	Total residences (thousands)	% of Brazilian residences	% of residences having an Internet connection (regional)	% Residences with more than 20 minimum wages with Internet connection (regional)	% Residences with 10–20 minimum wages with Internet connection (regional)	% Residences with up to 10 minimum wages with Internet connection (regional)
Brazil	58,577	100.0	27.4	90.7	78.8	21.6
Southeast	25,725	43.9	35.4	92.7	81.5	28.7
South	9,058	15.4	32.8	88.0	79.8	26.6
Center West	4,346	7.4	28.2	89.5	75.4	21.3
Northeast	15,331	26.1	14.4	91.3	75.2	11.3
North	4,117	7.0	13.2	79.7	60.7	9.9

Source: IBGE (2010: Sidra Tabela 2.387). Percentages calculated by the author

and North) those with elementary schooling or less, youths, and the lower social classes. Seventy-four percent of users in classes D and E accessed the Internet from Lan houses and Internet cafés and only 5% from free public telecenters.[24] Lan houses and Internet cafes, however, usually offer only rudimentary instruction, while free public access points (telecenters) usually are financed by governments and provide courses on Internet and computer use, ration computer time, and block access to what they consider socially undesirable sites.

Another recent trend of significance is the rapid rise in the percentage of Class C (lower middle class) homes with Internet connections – it grew from 11% of urban homes of this class in 2005 to 23% in 2009.[25]

Together data from these two surveys reveal the principal factors associated with Internet use in Brazil: geographic location, income, social class, place of access, education, age, and to a lesser extent, gender. Therefore, in designing digital inclusion policies these differences need to be taken into account.

Data collected by IBOPE Net Ratings (a commercial monthly survey) show the number of home Internet users and the average number of hours per month. Between December 2000 and December 2009, the number of active home internets rose from 4.9 million to 28.5 million, or almost sixfold, while the average hours online per month rose from 7 h and 6 min to 29 h and 56 min, or over fourfold.[26]

Digital Inclusion Programs

Brazil's federal government, many state and municipal governments, public and private enterprises, and NGOs have undertaken a wide variety of programs to address the digital divide, or, as it is called in Brazil, the issue of digital inclusion.[27]

While there have been attempts to coordinate these programs at the federal level since 2001, these attempts have not proved particularly effective. Such programs have encouraged experimentation and a wide variety of partnerships at every level of the federation, a positive factor in such a large and diverse country. But the proliferation of different programs has probably not contributed much to efficiency in the use of scarce public resources.

The latest attempt at coordination is being led by the President's Chief of Staff under the presidential decree of August 2009 establishing the CGPID.[28] While this

[24] See Brazilian Network Information Center (2010), Table C4.

[25] Brazilian Network Information Center, 2006 and 2010, Tables C1 and A4, respectively.

[26] Primary Source: Fonte: NetView - IBOPE//NetRatings; Secondary Source: Brazilian Network Information Center (http://www.cetic.br/usuarios/ibope/tab02-01-cons.htm, accessed 22 June 2010).

[27] Many of these are described in Assumpção and Mori (2004), Coelho (2007), Knight (2007), Vedana (2007), and a variety of articles published in recent years in the magazine *A Rede* (http://www.arede.inf.br), accessed 24 June 2010.

[28] See http://www.planalto.gov.br/ccivil_03/_Ato2007-2010/2009/Decreto/D6948.htm, accessed 9 Nov 2009.

initiative appears promising, as of October 2010 it was still unclear how effective it would prove or the magnitude of the resources it would command.

In this section, without any pretense of being inclusive (there are at least 17 such programs), several important programs are discussed, and an effort is made to summarize trends as of November 2009.

Between the January 1, 2003 when President Luis Inácio Lula da Silva took office and August 1, 2008 the US$ fell 56% against the Brazilian real. That made imports of computers and their components cheaper. The availability of free software, especially the Linux operating system and Open Office suite, has also helped to reduce the cost of software, as has the wide availability of pirated proprietary software. While the exchange rate rose sharply during the international financial crisis, by late 2009 it was approaching the precrisis levels and despite some fluctuations since then, this downward trend is expected to continue.

In September 2005, the federal government launched a program called Connected Citizen – Computer for All (*Cidadão Conectado – Computador para Todos*) to facilitate acquisition of low-cost computers assembled in Brazil, with the Linux operating system and packages of free software, and meeting minimum specifications set by the Ministry of Science and Technology.[29] Initially, the price limit was set at R$1,400,[30] but in May 2007 the maximum was lowered to R$1,200 and by mid-2008 it was common to find computers meeting these specifications for under R$1,000.[31] Laptops were also financed, with a maximum price of R$1,800. Financing for purchase of these computers at lower than market rates is provided by public sector banks and provided to customers by retailers.

Parallel to this program, the federal government reduced taxes on computers in November 2005, again as part of its digital inclusion program, for computers costing up to R$4,000. Together with the appreciation of the Brazilian Real, the result of these programs has been a rapid increase in sales of legal (as opposed to "gray market") computers. A large fraction of these computers have been purchased by lower middle class families (Class C). The percentage of class C urban homes with a computer increased from 16% of the total Class C urban households in 2005 to 36% in 2009, and for Classes D and E, the increase was even faster, but was only 7% of the total in 2009. Over the same period, the percentage of class B homes with a computer rose much more slowly and for Class A reached 97% in 2008 but then fell to 94% in 2009 (Table 2.3).

The telecom "exchange of obligations." The "exchange of obligations" of telecommunications operators under their existing concessions granted on the privatization of the former state-owned telcos in 1998, involves bringing broadband Internet backhaul to all Brazilian *municípios* currently lacking it and connecting 56,000 urban schools with a minimum of 1 Mbps by the end of 2010 free of charge

[29] See http://www.computadorparatodos.gov.br/projeto/index_html, accessed 10 Nov 2009.

[30] About US$1,740 at exchange rates prevailing in September 2006.

[31] About US$625 at exchange rates prevailing in June 2008.

Table 2.3 Percentage of Brazilian urban homes with a microcomputer, by social class, 2005–2009

	2005	2006	2007	2008	2009
All homes	17	20	24	28	36
Class A	89	86	88	97	94
Class B	57	63	63	71	78
Class C	16	19	25	26	33
Classes D and E	2	3	4	4	7

Source: Centro de Estudos sobre as Tecnologias da Informação e da Comunicação (CETIC.BR), TIC Domicílios e Usuários, 2005, 2006, 2007, 2008, and 2009, Tables A1, A1, B1, A1, and A1, respectively http://www.cetic.br/indicadores.htm, accessed 22 June 2010

through 2025, with bandwidth increasing over time. This obligation of the telcos was obtained by releasing them from another one, namely to put in place 8,461 Telecommunication Services Posts – (*Postos de Serviços de Telecomunicações* – PSTs). The PSTs were to include several public telephones, a fax machine, and a computer linked to the Internet through a dialup-connection. The PSTs were seen as outmoded and unnecessary in the broadband era. Through this exchange, without spending any public funds, the federal government and the telcos undertook a commitment of strategic importance.

Electronic Government Service to Citizens (*Governo Eletrônico Serviço de Atendimento ao Cidadão* – Gesac) is the largest federal government digital inclusion program. Gesac was initiated during the second government of President Fernando Henrique Cardoso (1999–2002) was continued and improved during the administrations of President Luis Inácio Lula da Silva. In September of 2008, there were approximately 3,400 broadband Gesac connections in the country, mainly in areas having a low Human Development Index (HDI), more than half in schools where the Ministry of Education's computers in schools program (Proinfo) had already provided computers, the remainder in projects of other ministries, military facilities, and NGOs, all of them provided by satellite links. In a few cases, like in the *município* of Rio das Flores in Rio de Janeiro State, the broadband signal is being distributed to the population by municipal governments using wireless technologies, mainly Wi-Fi.

In April 2008, a consortium led by Embratel (and including the three incumbent fixed line operators created after the privatization of Telebrás in 1998 – Brasil Telecom, Oi, and Telefônica) won two separate auctions organized by the Ministry of Communications (MC) to provide 12,000 broadband connections to specific points in Brazil, many of them are given to schools participating in the Proinfo program.[32] According to the terms of reference for the auction and the MC official

[32] The contracts for implementing the 12,000 GESAC points were signed on 26 Aug 2008.

involved, it is possible to relocate planned and existing Gesac connections to rural areas not accessible by landlines.[33]

Under the new Gesac terms of reference, these points of presence can use whatever technology is the cheapest and furthermore, they can be used to extend broadband Internet access via wireless technologies (e.g., Wi-Fi, Wi-Mesh) to areas, and not just to a specific installations (telecenters, schools, military posts, NGOs, etc.).[34] The presence of the fixed-line operators in the winning consortium means that landlines can be used for connections in urban areas, while the majority of connections will be via satellite, principally in poor rural areas.

Telecenters. At the federal, state, and municipal level, alone or in partnerships with NGOs, foundations, and private firms, a movement began in the 1990s to develop public access points where individuals or small businesses can receive digital literacy training and access the Internet without paying a fee.[35] While only 4% of people who used the Internet in the 3 months prior to a 2009 survey accessed it from a free public access point (telecenter) compared with 45% for public access points where a fee is charged (e.g., Lan houses and Internet cafés), publicly financed telecenters have been an important part of official digital inclusion policies as they reach the poorer segment of the population.

One federal attempt to collect data on telecenters is the National Observatory for Digital Inclusion (*Observatório Nacional de Inclusão Digital* – ONID) of the Ministry of Planning. As of August 2010 it had registered 99 digital inclusion programs supporting free telecenters in Brazil, but the number of telecenters in each program actually providing data is often far less than the declared number of telecenters, even among federal government programs.[36]

The Community Telecenter Program, launched by the Ministry of Communications (MC) in 2007, and intended to put at least one telecenter in each of Brazil's 5,564 *municípios* is the largest federal telecenter program. By September 2008, over 5,300 *municípios* had received the needed equipment for at least one telecenter as a grant from the MC. There were also plans to train telecenter managers.

Several other ministries have their own telecenter projects. For example, the Business and information Telecenters (*Telecentros de Informação e Negócios* – TIN – http://www.telecentros.desenvolvimento.gov.br) are a project of the Ministry of Development and International Trade (MDIC) launched in 2001. In October 2008, there were 1,211 TINs located in all but one state of Brazil. Their objective is to bring small and microenterprises into the digital era, training them to use modern

[33] Interview with Heliomar Medeiros de Lima, Director of the Gesac Program, Brasília, 3 July 2008. For the TOR for the auction, see http://www.mc.gov.br/inclusao-digital/gesac/segunda-audencia-publica-1, accessed 13 Nov 2009.

[34] The bidding documents for the competition won by Embratel are available at http://www.mc.gov.br/inclusao-digital/gesac/segunda-audiencia-publica-1, accessed 13 Nov 2009).

[35] See Assumpção and Mori (2007), Assumpção and Falavigna (2004), Baggio and de Luca (2004), Braquehais (2004), Toledo (2004).

[36] See http://onid.org.br/portal/programas, accessed 22 Aug 2010.

Internet tools, introducing them to new business opportunities, and inducing the growth of income and employment. TINs are set up in partnership with various public enterprises, agencies, and banks as well as municipal governments. In the TINs micro and small business personnel receive face-to-face training and take e-learning courses; obtain information on markets, regulations, etc., and in general can seek new markets and enhance their competitiveness.

The federal government's most elaborate digital inclusion project is called Brazil House (*Casa Brasil*) and, in August 2010, was coordinated by the Ministry of Science and Technology.[37] Brazil Houses consist of a building conceived as a community space with free and unrestricted access. They act as a center for technological literacy and dissemination of science and culture, and are intended to promote social inclusion and broaden citizenship. They have a modular construction and include a telecenter, and at least two other modules including popular library, auditorium, multimedia studio, laboratory for disseminating scientific thought, and community radio station. They are usually built in poor communities to reduce social inequality and bring these locations into the knowledge society. This project involves the collaboration of several ministries and public enterprises as well as local partners. Perhaps because of its relatively high cost and complexity, there were only 56 Brazil Houses in operation in August 2010.

In addition to a range of federal government programs, most states and many *municípios* have telecenter programs. In the state of São Paulo, for example, the state government had 638 telecenters (http://www.acessasp.sp.gov.br) with a total of two million registered users and the city of São Paulo had 347 telecenters with 1.7 million users in June 2010.[38] Both of these networks involve partnerships with a wide variety of different government agencies, NGOs, and private sector enterprises and were launched respectively in 2000 and 2001.

Digital municípios and states. A growing number of Brazilian municipal and state governments have decided to go beyond creating telecenters to establish more integrated programs involving expanded connectivity for the population, various kinds of e-government activities, education, promotion of e-business, and new forms of political participation – in short, municipal e-development. The digital city has been defined by Coelho (2007, p. 472) as

> "a new form of organization and integration of a territory, linked by a public network for the transmission of voice, data and images. It is the place where the citizen becomes the principal actor in the production, management and use of new technologies, guaranteeing the right of universal access to information, knowledge, and communication, and assuming a strategic vision of a local information society."

The digital cities and states movement has been facilitated by the development of wireless technologies such as Wi-Fi, Wi-Mesh, and WiMAX. The MC has provided support for building wireless networks in some 20 *municípios*, including Belo

[37] See http://www.inclusaodigital.gov.br/inclusao/links-outros-programas/casa-brasil, accessed 09 Nov 2009.

[38] http://www.telecentros.sp.gov.br/, accessed 22 Aug 2010.

Horizonte and Tiradentes in Minas Gerais, Piraí in Rio de Janeiro, Aparecida in São Paulo, and Santa Cecilia do Pavão (Paraná). Announced plans to greatly expand this program had still not been implemented as of October 2010.

The best known Brazilian digital *município* is Piraí, in the state of Rio de Janiero, which has won a number of national and international awards and served as a model for other *municípios* in the state, throughout Brazil and beyond, though it does not have free public access to the Internet except in a limited number of free public access points.[39] In 2008, the Rio de Janeiro State Government launched a program to build on the success of Piraí and several other *municípios* in the state with the objective of reaching all 92 *municípios* in the state by the end of 2010.

There are also various kinds of state projects in different stages of execution in São Paulo, Rio de Janeiro, Paraná, Minas Gerais, and Ceará, for example. The small state of Acre, in the Amazon bordering Bolivia and Peru, was the first state to decide to build a statewide broadband network linking all government offices and providing the free public access to the Internet to the states entire population, with a target of accomplishing this by the end of 2010.

The CGPID may be able to "articulate with the other management committees and interministerial working groups created in the spheres of the Federal Government, of the States and of the Federal District, and of the *municípios* with specific objectives linked to digital inclusion programs and projects" as specified in the decree establishing it. But this is a massive task and as of October 2010 it was still not clear what resources and incentives will be available to make it effective. It is important, however, for the federal and state governments to take a more active role in bringing down the cost of connectivity. Here, the PNBL and the revived Telebrás may play important roles, to greatly expand and reduce the cost of broadband connectivity, leverage network effects, build shared resources such as digital content, and train telecenter managers.

Brazil's Information Technology Industry

Brazil's information technology (IT) market (hardware, software, and services) almost tripled in size from 2004 to 2009, from US $11 billion to US $30.5 billion, but this was only 1.8% of GDP.[40] Of this total, hardware was US $15.1 billion, software US $5.5 billion, and services US $9.9 billion. In 2009, Brazil's IT market was larger than that of India and Russia, but only 41% of China's (Fig. 2.2).

Compared with countries such as Korea, China, and India, Brazil lagged badly until the mid-1990s, having adopted "market reserve" policies which severely restricted foreign investment and imports. During the last three decades of the

[39] For a comprehensive discussion of the digital *município* movement see Coelho (2007). On Pirái Digital, see http://pt.wikipedia.org/wiki/Pirai_Digital, accessed 13 Nov 2009.

[40] Data from ABES (2005, 2010).

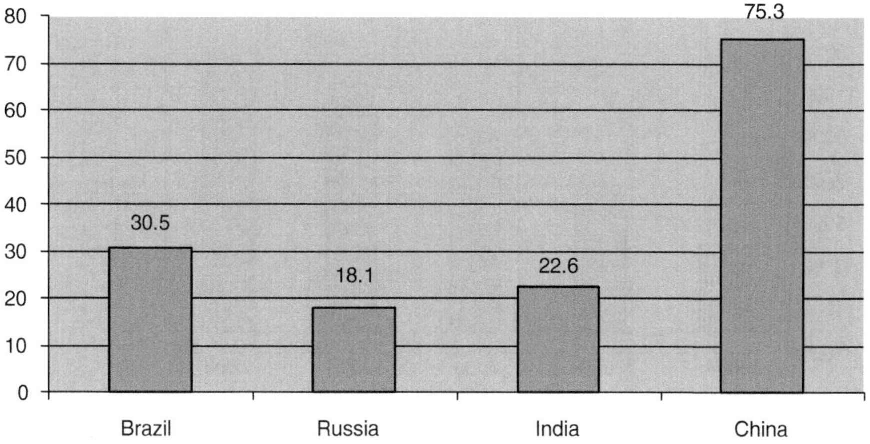

Fig. 2.2 Information technology markets in the BRIC countries, 2009 (billions of US$). Source: Associação Brasileira de Empresas de Software (2010), original data from IDC

twentieth century, Brazil effectively missed the boat, particularly in the area of hardware.[41] Software and services appear to be areas in which Brazil has better opportunities for rapid growth (Scartezini 2007), but most Brazilian companies in these areas are relatively small and federal government policies in support of this sector appear relatively weak compared with those in competitors such as China, India, Ireland, and Israel – total exports of Brazilian software and services in 2009 came to only US $92 and US $271 million, respectively (ABES 2010). However, these numbers probably considerably understate the true value of exports, since many exports of software and IT services may not be registered. One of the objectives of the PNBL is to encourage further development of the IT industry.

Hardware

Most of the high-technology components for the IT industry are imported. Even for personal computers, where sales have boomed, about 85 of the value of production is estimated to come from imported components.

In 2007, the number of PCs sold in Brazil exceeded sales of television sets for the first time. There has been a rapid increase in PC ownership in the country since 2005, especially in the lower middle class (Table 2.3), stimulated by an appreciated

[41] By 2008 Korea was exporting chips, LCD televisions and monitors, and all sorts of sophisticated electronic products; China had become the global manufacturing center for computers and other ICT equipment, and India's software and services industries had become the leading services sector of that country, accounting for some 5.4% of the country's GDP. Brazil, in comparison, lagged badly.

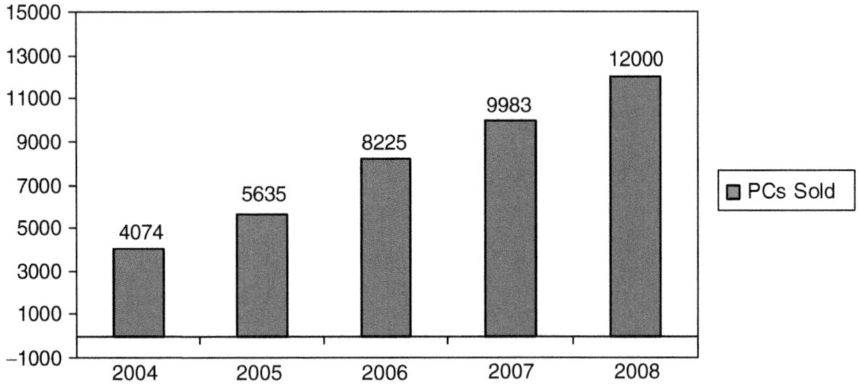

Fig. 2.3 Sales of PCs in Brazil, 2004–2008 (Thousands). Source: Associação Brasileira da Indústria Elétrica e Eletrônica – ABINEE (2009), p. 22

currency, tax incentives, and relatively cheap credit for low-cost computers. Data for 2008 indicate another record, 12 million desktops and laptops, up from 10 million in 2007 or 20% increase (Fig. 2.3).

The Brazilian Association of the Electric and Electronic Industry (*Associação Brasileira da Indústira Elétrica e Eletrônica* – ABINEE) estimates that "official" PC Sales increased even faster, from 1.1 million in 2004 to 7.9 million in 2007, or over sevenfold, as the reduction in taxes on computers took effect and the Federal Police cracked down on the "gray market" for computers assembled using illegal imports. The same source shows that in 2008 the total number of desktops sold (both official and gray market) fell for the first time, while the number of laptops sold jumped 125%, reaching 36% of total PC sales.[42]

Software and Services

Brazil's domestic software and services market ranked as the world's 12th largest in 2009, at US $15.4 billion, slightly less than China's, estimated at US $15.5 billion, but greater than those of India and Russia (ABES 2010). After decades of protectionist policies that insulated Brazil's IT sector from the global economy, in the mid-1990s market liberalization policies directed at opening the large Brazilian market to foreign technology were adopted. These policies led to growth in the software services sector beginning in the mid-1990s, sparked primarily by access to the large domestic outsourcing market, but also the potential for exports.

[42] ABINEE (2009, p. 22).

In the 1990s, the most important government policy specifically directed toward the software sector was the establishment of a government agency called Softex. Softex was established in 1992 to foster software development and raise software exports. Softex's main goals included encouraging the creation of many new software firms for the export sector; developing adequate infrastructure, financing and training for existing software firms; motivating existing firms to operate internationally and not just in the domestic market; and facilitating access to marketing and sales information in major target markets worldwide.

In December 1997, the National Social and Economic Development Bank (*Banco Nacional de Desenvolvimento Econômico e Social* – BNDES) set up the Program for Support of the Software and IT Services Sector (*Programa para o Desenvolvimento da Indústria Nacional de Software e de Serviços de Tecnologia da Informação* – Prosoft), a credit and venture capital program that sought to stimulate and strengthen the national software industry (Gutierrez 2007, p. 38). The program was created in partnership with the Association of Brazilian IT, Software, and Internet Enterprises (*Associação de Empresas Brasileiras de Tecnologia da Informação, Software e Internet* – Assespro) and Softex so that these organizations could support BNDES with their knowledge of the sector as well as the ability to reach the thousands of firms in the sector.

Then in 2003, the Lula Government adopted a new Industrial, Technological, and Foreign Trade Policy (*Política Industrial, Tecnológica e de Comércio Exterior* – PITCE) that included software among the strategic sectors selected to receive incentives for technological innovation coordinated with other agencies of government (especially the Ministry of Development, Industry, and Foreign Trade – MDIC) and other partners in the public and private sectors.[43] In 2004, BNDES revised Prosoft and later, following a positive evaluation of PITCE actions, renewed, and expanded this program that was to have expired at the end of July 2007 (Gutierrez 2007, p. 27).

The Brazilian Software Enterprises Association (*Associação Brasileira de Empresas de Software* – ABES) estimates that the domestic software and services market totaled US $15.4 billion in 2009 (an increase of 157% since 2004), of which US $5.5 billion were software, and US $9.9 billion services (Fig. 2.4). Of the software market (1.7% of the global market), 29% was for software developed in Brazil, the remainder for distribution of imported software. There were 6,495 companies in this market, most of them were micro and small enterprises. Brazilian exports of software licenses was only US $92 million, but growing rapidly. Licensed export statistics probably understate the true value of exports. The larger services market was served by 1,983 companies, also overwhelmingly micro and small enterprises (ABES 2010).

---

[43] The PITCE is the clearest expression of Brazil's technological and scientific priorities. It seeks to develop and disseminate solutions and technological innovations to improve the competitiveness of products and processes of Brazilian firms in both national and international markets (Knight and Marques 2008).

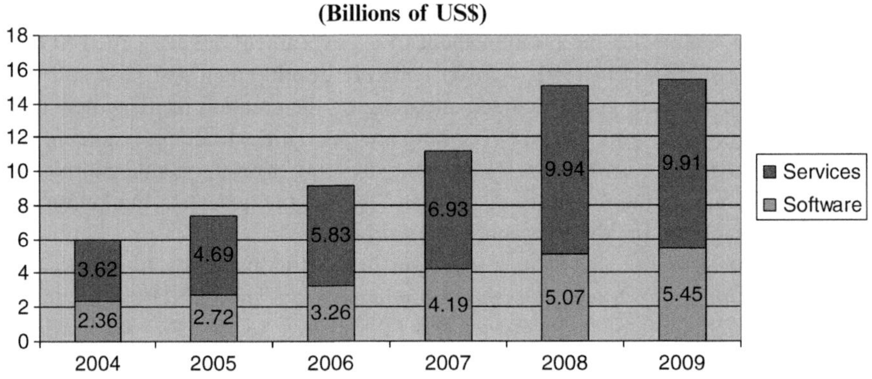

Fig. 2.4 Brazilian market for software and IT services, 2004–2009 (Billions of US$). Source: Associação Brasileira de Empresas de Software – ABES (2007, 2008, 2009, 2010)

The predominance of micro and small enterprises is probably associated with the relatively young age of the software and services industry in Brazil – most of the Brazilian firms were established in the 1990s – and the dynamism of the sector that leads to the continued creation of new firms. Consequently, the process of maturing the business culture and basic management skills of these firms, a number of which grew out of incubators, is still in its early stages.

Among the problems encountered by small Brazilian companies are access to the market, since the youth and fragility of these firms does not inspire confidence on the part of potential purchasers of their products. Incubators and technology parks focused on software and IT services can play a role in improving the environment for the creation and healthy growth of new firms, but there is not much literature available on such specialized incubators and science parks in Brazil. The growth of the domestic market, however, has also encouraged participation of new international players that have sought partners or expand directly into the Brazilian market. A good example is the Indian firm; Tata Consultancy Services. It arrived in Brazil at the end of 2005 through a joint venture and later bought out its Brazilian partner (Gutierrez 2007, p. 36).

A new trade association including some large Brazilian and multinational ICT firms, the Brazilian Association of Information and Communications Technology Companies (Brasscom – http://www.brasscom.com.br) was established in 2004. During 2009 it conducted a strong campaign to develop Brazilian exports of IT and BPO outsourcing services to the world market and undertook proprietary research on the ICT sector in Brazil with the support of the A.T. Kearney. Brasscom does not publish ICT statistics, at least not to nonmembers, but it does say that Brazil exported US $2.2 billion in offshore outsourcing services in 2008, and that Brasscom seeks to help make Brazil one of the three top exporters of IT and BPO services.[44]

[44] http://www.brasscom.com.br/en/content/view/full/1851, accessed 10 Nov 2009.

A major thrust of the two administrations of President Lula was the encouragement of the free and open source software (FOSS) in Brazil in general, and in the federal government in particular. That movement got a big boost in 2003 when one of its most vocal advocates was appointed President of the National Information Technology Institute (*Instituto Nacional de Tecnologia da Informação* – ITI), an organ of the Presidency of Brazil's political advisory unit (*Casa Civil da Presidência da República*).

In October 2003, the Technical Committee on Implementing Free Software of the Federal Government approved 18 directives for implementing free software in the federal government. Though not mandatory, they included giving priority to solutions, programs, and services based on free software to optimize resources and investments in IT; adopting open standards for developing ICT and developing multiplatform services and applications; popularization of free software; expanding services offered to citizens through free software; using free software in digital inclusion programs; and training federal civil servants in the use of free software.

During the second Lula administration, the coordination of this committee was passed to Serpro, a federal government IT company linked to the Ministry of Finance, with a view to increasing cooperation between government institutions. Major objectives were to focus on software of use throughout society and the adoption of plans for migration to free software on the part of public institutions.

The Free Software Portal (http://www.softwarelivre.gov.br) supports this committee and seeks to strengthen government's use of FOSS, collaboration and sharing of information and knowledge, thereby increasing the interaction between government technicians and between them and society. The related Public Software Portal (http://www.softwarepublico.gov.br) serves as a repository of FOSS solutions developed by public institutions. It initiated a new model for licensing and management of software solutions in Brazil, encouraging their improvement through virtual communities of practice. The portal features access to communities of practice for 42 FOSS solutions developed by public institutions as of October 2010, one with over 10,000 participants, and most in the range of 2,000–7,000.

At the World Summit on the Information Society (WSIS), Brazil's chancellor stated the federal government's position:

> "In a society increasingly integrated by the Internet, the universal language that allows the production and sharing of knowledge is called software. Brazil sees the free software as emblematical of the Information Society and of a new culture of solidarity and sharing, an instrument to guarantee the access and domain by every one of this universal language"
>
> (Amadeu da Silveira 2004).

But the federal government's policies in favor of the software industry and its incipient efforts at promoting exports are potentially at odds with the policy in favor of FOSS. A major study on the impact of FOSS on the Brazilian software industry was conducted by Softex (Stefanuto and Salles-Filho 2005). Among its conclusions were

- Free software belongs to the software industry. It develops and transforms itself within the industry. Free software business models are software industry

business models. Thus, FS/OS (free software/open source) has the power to change competitive standards within the industry itself and this is exactly what it has been doing. Its main impact is on segments in which the importance of appropriability (keeping codes closed) is a critical competitive factor and application specificity is lower (more or less specific products).
- Given this combination of competitive characteristics, FS/OS strongly threatens the package model (platforms and operating systems), software components and customizable products, exactly because appropriability is an essential competitive factor for these models. Since the embedded and service models have greater specificity and lower appropriability importance because of closed codes, they are actually models that present the greatest investment opportunities. FS/OS, by definition, speeds up the transition of the software industry from products to services.
- Small software companies (the large majority of companies in the IT sector) as well as the entire IT production sector in Brazil need to address this subject. Likewise, the government – a key player in the free software field – needs to examine more carefully the implications that an open encouragement of FS/OS might cause in the industry and for Brazilian companies. There are opportunities, but also threats. The government actions and policies associated with them need to be more grounded on information and analysis than on voluntary adherence. Free software may be good for Brazilian society for a number of reasons and it is good to explain them in a convincing way. This study – which is far from conclusive, in part because it is the first survey of its kind – suggests a need for caution for permanent and better monitoring of the developments (Stefanuto and Salles-Filho 2005, p. 74).

In any case, FOSS is increasingly used in Brazil's private as well as the public sectors. In November and December 2007, the Institute without Borders (*Instituto Sem Fronteiras* – ISF) –with support from IBM, Intel, Red Hat, and a Itautec – carried out a study on the adoption of free software in Brazil. More than a thousand firms of different sizes, sectors, and geographic regions were interviewed. Among the conclusions of the study is that free software is used to a much greater extent in the largest enterprises, those with more than 1,000 employees, than in smaller firms – 73% of these large enterprises were using free software, whereas only 31% of firms with less than 99 employees were. The principal reason for this appears to be the need to have experienced professionals to install, adapt, and service this software. Of the large enterprises, 53% were using Linux or other free operating systems. Of all the firms interviewed, 56% used free software in servers, though only 7% used free software on all their servers. Among the enterprises using free software, 48% reported using it on mission critical applications (ITData Consultoria 2008a).

Within outsourcing services, the emphasis was on the category management of applications on-site and off-site and outsourcing of printing. These services increased above the average for the market in 2006, especially management of off-site services. CIOs are seeking to slim down their internal IT structures, outsourcing costly areas, and processing to firms with greater expertise and scale, especially datacenters, allowing the firms to concentrate on their core businesses.

But despite the growing concentration of the market for IT services in recent years, the market is still far from concentrated. There are a large number of new small firms contesting the market with established players, even in outsourcing, resulting in a decline in the market share of most of the larger firms (ITData Consultoria 2008b).

To promote the further development of the software and IT services industries, more aggressive public policies are likely to be necessary. Many other countries – including Mexico, the USA, China, Israel, and Korea – have explicit or implicit policies favoring domestic suppliers for government purchases. India, China, Korea, Mexico, and the Philippines have established zones with special fiscal incentives, facilities, and infrastructure. Several Eastern European competitors of Brazil in the European market provide training and employment subsidies using European Union funding. And of course tax incentives are widely practiced (Scartezini 2007, pp. 869–870).

Brazil's high taxes on the software and services sector, like those for telecommunications (and telecommunications account for on the order of a third of the costs of IT services exporters), also cut the county's competitiveness compared with such competitors as India and China. Even with the benefits of incentives, Scartezini (2007, p. 872, Table 39.1) found taxes on Brazil's software exports at 30.7% that were twice those of Chinese software exports and almost four times as high as those of India (for all three competitors, these are the rates with tax incentives). Subsidizing credit to the software sector, as in the BNDES Prosoft program, may mitigate the tax disadvantages, but again shows that government policies lack coordination. Though the federal government encourages drawbacks of the state value-added tax (ICMS), that varies from 15 to 25% on software and services depending on the states, software firms say that many states insist on the payment of the ICMS, which affects competitiveness and causes great uncertainty (Scartezini 2007, p. 874).

In September 2008, a new federal law (Law 11, 774) was passed. It reduced labor taxes for the IT sector in an unprecedented way. The law was further implemented by a presidential Decree (6945) in August 2009. According to Brasscom, this law was the result of a great effort, undertaken mostly under that organization's leadership.[45]

Scartezini (2007, pp. 874, 875) also says that the government has given to other countries, free of charge, e-government software produced in Brazil, thus depriving the country of software export revenues. Further she argues that erroneous interpretation of the free software policy by various government organs has resulted in a wave of internal solutions by government agencies, when commercial solutions are available, often with dubious results and substantial expenditures to contract specialized staff. So rather than encouraging the local software industry through a "buy Brazilian software" campaign, government payrolls may have been inflated with questionable results.

Another area of weakness is the lack of English-speaking technical level staff to work in software and IT services sector. China has massive training programs in English, while India has a large population of English speakers. While Brazilians

[45] http://www.brasscom.com.br/en/content/view/full/1851, accessed 10 Nov 2009.

usually understand Spanish, the principal language of the rest of Latin America, formal training in Spanish is also not very common, which affects competitiveness in the Latin American market.

A positive factor for the development of the software industry may be the rollout of digital television broadcasting in Brazil, which began officially in December 2007 in São Paulo and the transition to digital TV is scheduled to be complete by the end of 2016. Brazil has adopted the Japanese standard (ISDB) and not the US (ASTC) or European (DVB) systems of digital television. The Brazilian system will permit full high definition broadcasts over the air (some 85% of Brazilian homes get their TV via open transmissions rather than by cable or satellite) and also transmission to mobile phones and other mobile devices. With the addition of a Brazilian middleware called Ginga in new digital televisions or set-top boxes to convert the digital signal for viewing on conventional (analog) television sets, the Brazilian system will permit two-way fully interactive TV with great potential for education, government, and e-commerce applications. This two-way interactivity depends on the availability of a return channel – ideally the Internet, though the interaction can be by telephone. Two-way interactivity would be greatly facilitated by a rapid development of free or low-cost wireless Internet connectivity, as advocated by the digital cities movement.

The Ginga middleware and various applications for t-commerce, t-education, t-government, and many others offer great opportunities to the Brazilian software industry, and could also be a source of export revenue, especially if other countries in Latin America and elsewhere adopt the ISCB system. As of August 2010, in addition to Brazil and Japan the Philippines and eight Latin American countries had done so, and the prospects are good for additional adherents, possibly including some in Africa and Asia. And for the management, storage and transmission of digital content are also important opportunities (Stefanuto et al. 2007).

Human Resources

This section focuses on three ways to build the necessary human resources and knowledge necessary to accelerate Brazil's e-development: train e-leaders, disseminate successful experiences, and build digital literacy in the general population.[46]

E-Leaders[47]

An absence of e-leadership at the top of the political system, at least at the federal level since 2003, is notable. However, signs of greater presidential leadership

[46] This is by no means an exhaustive list of all the kinds of programs needed.

[47] This section draws heavily on Reinhard et al. (2008).

have emerged since mid-2009. Without presidential ownership of an e-development or even an e-government program (and at the state and municipal level, strong commitment by governors and mayors), it is very difficult to make substantial progress. A motivating vision and leadership from the top are necessary to break down the natural inertia and turf-consciousness of government agencies, motivate champions in the diverse organs of government and society, and realize potential economies of scale and synergies across the full range of government agencies.

The CGPID, with its Executive Secretariat located in the Personal Office of the President and with four of its members from different organs of the Presidency, may be evolving into a federal institution for exercising e-leadership, but a great deal will depend on whether this trend is continued under Brazil's next President, Dilma Rousseff, elected in October 2010 and taking office on January 1, 2011. But in staffing at this central level and throughout the ministries and agencies of the federal government and for corresponding positions in state and major municipal governments, Brazil faces a problem also encountered in many other countries. Public sector e-leaders normally come either from the ICT specialist stream (often lacking training in public administration, economics, and negotiating skills necessary to carry out their responsibilities, break down traditional ministerial silos, and realize economies of scale and synergies) or from the public administration stream (having insufficient knowledge of ICT and their potential as tools of public administration reform, improving service to citizens and enterprises, etc.).

What can be done about this? Recruitment of future e-leaders for the public sector may come from either the public or the private sectors – indeed it is appropriate to include some emerging leaders from the private sector, especially ICT companies, in the recruitment pool for specialized training. Some rotation of e-leaders between the public and private sector seems desirable to encourage better understanding of the special issues in each sector and more public–private partnerships in an area characterized by rapid technological change.

There are large variations in the intensity and maturity of ICT use between government levels (federal, state, and municipal). The very large systems supporting finance, social security, and other processes at the federal level have historically pioneered the use of ICT and therefore have more competent ICT managers than the smaller states and municipalities, where ICT governance, alignment, and management competences are still lacking. International agencies (the Inter-American Development Bank and others) have in the past sponsored large government modernization programs with significant allowances for ICT investments at the state and municipal levels, where the mentioned competence gaps have been real challenges.

Traditionally, ICT has been seen as an important resource for the modernization of the executive branch of government. At still more incipient stages of ICT use are the legislative and judiciary branches, impacting the effectiveness of democratic processes and institutions. Developing IT awareness and management competence

Box 2.4 E-Leadership Programs

In response to growing needs for e-leaders, in 2007 a special executive masters in public administration (MPA) program was planned for São Paulo State government officials, aiming at narrowing the gap between technical and managerial requirements for ICT professionals. The proposal was developed based on a request from the State Government itself for a proof of concept pilot and stimulus for other similar initiatives, as a way to institutionalize the programs as part of its human resources policies.

The program was proposed to cover three broad competencies (a) managing public organizations, including the topics of economics, public sector management, finance, and accounting and statistics; (b) understanding ICT markets and tendencies; and (c) managing ICT, including the topics of ICT strategic planning, ICT management, project management, information management, ICT governance, electronic government, and specific training for developing managerial competences.

A similar program at an international level was proposed by da Costa (2007) to be implemented in parallel in the BRIC countries (Brazil, Russia, India, and China), and discussions were undertaken in 2008 with academic institutions in these countries and South Africa by Nagy Hanna and Peter Knight regarding the organization and finance of such an international e-leadership training program.

in these branches is therefore of utmost importance. Availability of e-leaders remains the binding constraint.

As a result of growing globalization and expansion of the private sector, ICT issues in government go increasingly beyond execution in the direction of regulation and policy making, requiring even more sophisticated competences in ICT and change management, for which executives have to master additional areas, such as development economics, innovation, international relations, etc. In particular, ICT executives have to be able to interact with and influence highly competent partners from the private sector and other governments and supranational institutions, dealing with complex issues in diversified environments.

Unfortunately, the Brazilian educational system, like that of many other countries, has been slow in adapting its curricula and approaches to this new interdisciplinary and highly political and networked reality, still favoring traditional disciplinary "silos," leaving it mostly to the individuals to develop these new competences. It shall then not come as a surprise that experienced ICT managers are in short supply in Brazil and that often important government decisions and operations are left in the hands of suppliers with their own objectives and agendas (Box 2.4).

Dissemination of Successful Experiences

Another way to promote e-development and develop the needed human resources is to disseminate broadly the most successful experiences at the federal, state, and municipal levels.

Several Brazilian government agencies and NGOs have, for years, been involved in the promotion and diffusion of e-government practices through the distribution of national awards for innovative and effective projects and applications. These awards provide immediate media and political visibility to the initiatives' sponsors and internal legitimacy for the agencies' projects. However, the significant accumulated knowledge contained in reports of these initiatives, complemented by analytical papers and references to related repositories and initiatives in other countries must be organized as a permanent repository in order to become a valuable resource for e-government practitioners and scholars.

This is the objective of the Observatory of Practices of Information and Communication Technology in Public Management (*Observatório de Práticas de Tecnologia da Informação e Comunicação na Gestão Pública* – Observe-gov), a joint initiative of the Foundation for Development of Management of São Paulo State – FUNDAP, the CONIP Institute and the Institute for Management Foundation (FIA) of the University of São Paulo. Observe-gov was created to make public sector IT implementation cases available to the general public. FUNDAP is a public agency linked to the São Paulo State Government that offers consulting and training programs to state agencies and public servants. It maintains a multilingual website (http://www.observe.org.br) and promotes a yearly award, the "Mário Covas Prize," named after a former governor who began a statewide modernizing program in 1996. The award recognizes best practices in public administration in São Paulo.[48]

CONIP is an organization that seeks to disseminate ICT good practice in government. It organizes an annual conference on the subject, and also an annual award (the CONIP Award) for successful cases of ICT innovation in the government sector. Finally, FIA is a business school linked to the School of Economics, Administration, and Accounting at the University of São Paul (FEA/USP) that conducts research in many areas, including public administration and e-government. Observe-gov is therefore a partnership between government, academia, and the private sector. Observe-gov initially published only those innovation cases submitted for consideration for the Mario Covas Prize, the CONIP Award, and a third award offered by the Association of State ICT Entities (*Associação Brasileira de Entidades de Tecnologia da Informação e Comunicação* – ABEP). More recently, Observe-gov has been publishing cases nominated for the Ceará State Electronic Government Prize, awarded by the Government of the State of Ceará in the Northeastern region of Brazil.

The observatory's goals include increasing the visibility of Brazilian e-government initiatives and studies to a larger national and international community and facilitating

---

[48] São Paulo is the wealthiest state in Brazil, with a population of around 40 million (Brazil's total population is about 193 million) and accounts for approximately 32% of the Brazilian GDP.

analytical studies on the subject, as well as serving as a resource center and meeting point for e-government policy makers, practitioners, and scholars. The website also provides local and international funding agencies with valuable information on the state of the art of Brazilian e-government practices. The Portal itself was awarded a national prize for its contribution to the dissemination of e-government practices.

There are, of course, other channels for dissemination and sharing of knowledge. CONIP, for instance, organizes an annual national conference where best practices in ICT in the public area are presented and discussed. This is also the case of ABEP, an association of state-owned ICT companies and parastatals, which organizes a yearly conference and meetings for CIOs and ICT managers from the member organizations and their clients. Both conferences have become references in the public sector in Brazil, and are very important for networking among ICT professionals, besides being a channel for best practices dissemination. In Brazil there are also magazines devoted to public ICT (like the magazine "*Informática Pública*" – IT in Public Administration), published twice a year since 1999 by the municipal ICT company of Belo Horizonte in the state of Minas Gerais. A similar role in the area of digital inclusion has been annual competitions for the best public sector, private sector, and NGO sponsored projects held by the magazine *A Rede*.

Digital Literacy Training

Digital literacy training in Brazil was initially the province of NGOs, the largest and best known is the Committee for Democratization of Information Technology (*Comitê de Democratização da Informática* – CDI),[49] founded in 1995. CDI remained very active in this field as of 2009 (Box 2.5). CDI and other NGOs, such as Sampa.org,[50] the Bradesco Foundation with 108 Centers for Digital Inclusion (*Centros de Inclusão Digital* – CIDs) in low-income communities,[51] and the Embratel Institute's Community Points (*Pontos Comunidade*)[52] have worked both on their own and in association with state and/or municipal governments to provide basic training in computer use, Internet navigation, and software applications and to operate telecenters where such training is provided.

As digital inclusion has become a public policy, the telecenter movement discussed above has played an important role in building digital literacy. Similarly, the explosion of Lan houses and Internet cafés, where users pay for the time they access the Internet, have helped to build digital literacy.

---

[49] See Baggio and di Luca (2004) and the CDI site, http://www.cdi.org.br, accessed 12 Nov 2009.

[50] See Assumpção and Falavigna (2004) and the Sampa.org site at http://www.sampa.org, accessed 13 Nov 2009.

[51] See http://www.fb.org.br/Institucional/AcoesComunitarias/CentrosDeInclusaoDigital/, accessed 13 Nov 2009.

[52] See http://www.bibliotecamultimidia.org.br/interna_projetos.asp?click=proj&id_projeto=1, accessed 13 Nov 2009.

Box 2.5 The Committee for Democracy in Information Technology

The Committee for democracy in information technology (CDI) is a nongovernmental, nonprofit organization which, since 1995, has developed pioneer work in promoting social inclusion by using information technology as a tool for building active citizenship. It was founded and in November 2009 continued to be directed by Rodrigo Baggio, a Brazilian social entrepreneur.

Through its Information Technology and Citizen Rights Schools (*Escolas de Informática and Cidadania* – EICs), created mainly in partnership with community organizations, CDI implements educational programs both in Brazil and abroad, aiming at mobilizing excluded segments of society and helping them to transform their reality. As of July 2008 there were almost 840 EICs in 19 states including the Federal District located in all of Brazil's major regions and six other Latin American countries: Argentina, Chile, Colombia, Ecuador, Mexico, and Uruguay. CDI has received financial support from Brazilian and international companies, foundations, and governments and won a wide range of awards, Brazilian and international, for its work.

The organization develops projects to assist low-income communities, individuals with special needs, the mentally disabled, homeless children, indigenous populations and prison communities, among others.

CDI believes that the expertise in new technologies not only produces job opportunities and generates income, but also enables the access to sources of information and environments intended to foster social interaction, which results in a collective search for solutions to the problems faced by the communities.

CDI's objective is to promote the social appropriation of information technology by different types of audiences, using it as a tool to stimulate active citizenship and entrepreneurship, fostering political, social and economic development in the countries where the organization operates.

In tune with this proposal, CDI encourages freedom of choice, and work with both proprietary and open software, seeking to provide students with the possibility to choose the most suitable tools according to their needs.

Sources: http://www.cdi.org, accessed 18 July 2008 and 13 Nov 2009, Baggio and Di Luca (2004).

ICT Applications

Beginning with e-government, and including e-business and various kinds of civil society organizations and political organizations, applications of ICT are what the policy environment, ICT industry, infostructure, and human resources make possible. It is through the applications that the population receives the benefits that all of these make possible: better government services, lower-cost consumer and producer goods and services, a more vibrant society, and a more participatory political system.

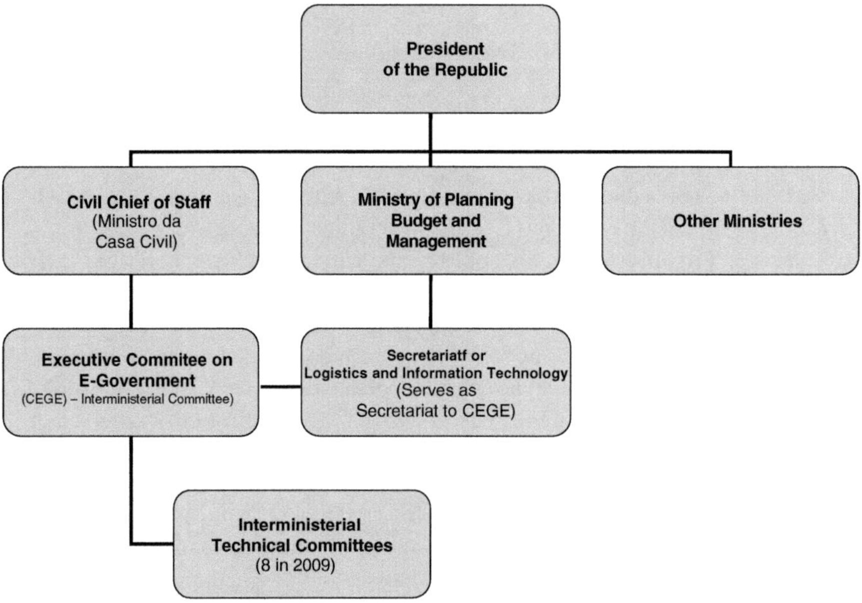

Fig. 2.5 Organization of Brazil's Federal e-Government

E-Government

As indicated in the first section of this chapter, the basic framework for setting strategies and policies for e-government at the federal level was established during the second government of President Fernando Henrique Cardoso in the year 2000 (Fig. 2.5) and has remained constant since then.

Government policy set by the CEGE was oriented by directives on the supply of services and information to the citizen; promotion of the population's access to the Internet; integration of the federal government's diverse information systems, networks, and databases; and use of the government's purchasing power to reduce costs through the focus of activities. Building a legal and normative framework for electronic transactions has been pursued in parallel, with the approval of laws on information security and electronic crimes. Until the end of 2002, the CEGE exercised a strong role due to the activism and leadership of the then Minister Chief of the Presidential Staff (*Casa Civil*).

The official e-government coordination mechanisms deal with the executive branch of the federal government and do not formally embrace the legislative or judicial branches (they have developed their own websites and other programs). This institutional arrangement has remained constant since then. So, following the typology developed by Hanna (2007a, b), in the case of e-government, Brazil really has a hybrid of two models – Policy Coordination Function Under Head of State and Lead Ministry. But the effectiveness of interagency coordination depends on priority given to e-government by the President of Brazil and his Civilian Chief of Staff.

This priority was high in 2000 and 2001, when rapid progress was made in establishing a coherent set of federal e-government policies. But in the federal and state election year of 2002, responsibility for coordinating a national response to the electric energy crisis of that year was given to the Civilian Chief of Staff, and the rate of progress in e-government slowed as he focused his attention on this critical new task and the election campaign. Priority for e-government at the Federal level remained low during the first administration of President Luiz Inácio Lula da Silva (2003–2006), though important progress was made in digital inclusion, development of an interoperability framework and other aspects of e-development. E-government also advanced at lower levels of the federal system, albeit unevenly in the 27 state-level units of the federation (26 states and the Federal District).

Reporting to the CEGE are eight Technical Committees. Since October 2003 they have been: Free Software Implementation; Digital Inclusion; Legacy Systems and Software Licenses; Management of Sites and Online Services, Network Infrastructure, Government to Government (G2G), and Knowledge Management and Information Strategy, established in a presidential decree issued in October 2003. Most are chaired by officials of SLTI/MP. The functions of each committee are spelled out on the federal e-government website.[53]

Under both administrations of President Lula beginning in January 2003, there has been a greater emphasis on the social dimensions of projects, especially digital inclusion, and a new emphasis on the use of FOSS in the public administration and ICT applications funded by it, such as telecenters and computers for use in schools (Fernandes 2007, p. 492). But President Lula's Civilian Chiefs of Staff have not taken an active interest in e-Government per se, and the CEGE has met very rarely since 2002, and certainly not played an activist role. However, the ITI, attached to the Casa Civil, and Serpro, the federal data processing company linked to the Ministry of Finance, have played key roles in promoting FOSS. Some of the results of the increased emphasis on digital inclusion and FOSS have been noted above. Important research has been done that should serve as the basis for a more citizen-oriented e-government in the future (Pessi 2007).

One area in which substantial progress has been made is the development of Interoperability Standards for e-Government (*Padrões de Interoperabilidade para Goveron Eletrônico* – e-Ping), for pursuing greater interoperability among different parts of the federal government and between it and state and municipal governments along the lines of pioneered in the United Kingdom.[54] The issue of interoperability was already flagged in an evaluation of the first 2 years of the federal e-government program made by CEGE in 2002 . The e-Ping architecture, the first version of which was introduced in May 2004, has undergone progressive refinement since then, the

[53] See http://www.governoeletronico.gov.br/o-gov.br/comites/comites-tecnicos-1/comites-tecnicos for functions and for the committee chairs, http://www.governoeletronico.gov.br/o-gov.br/quem-e-quem, both sites accessed 10 Nov 2009.

[54] E-Ping is modeled on the United Kingdom's e-GIF (e-Government Interoperability Framework). Various versions of e-Ping, including some in English are available at http://www.governoeletronico.gov.br/acoes-e-projetos/e-ping-padroes-de-interoperabilidade/versoes-do-documento-da-e-ping, accessed 1 Oct 2010. See also Santanna dos Santos et al. (2007).

latest approved version (through October 2010) being issued in December 2009. It defines a minimum group of premises, policies, and technical specifications that regulate usage of ICT in electronic government services. Areas covered by e-Ping include interconnection, security, means of access, organization and exchange of information, and integration of areas for electronic government (Brazilian Government 2009, p. 4).

E-Ping covers exchange of information between systems within the executive branch of government (for which it is mandatory) and (on a voluntary basis) with other branches of the federal government (legislative, judicial, and the Public Prosecutions Office); other levels of government (state and local); citizens; international organizations; governments of other countries; businesses (in Brazil and abroad); and civil society organizations (NGOs, etc.). For the Federal executive branch – including all its ministries, agencies, and parastatals – application of e-Ping standards is mandatory for

- All of the new information systems to be developed and implemented in the federal government and that are within the scope of interaction, inside the federal government and with society in general.
- Previous information systems that are subject to implementations involving the provision of electronic government services or interactions among systems.
- Other systems that are included in the goal of making electronic government services are available.

All executive branch purchases and hiring directed to development of electronic government services and to upgrading of systems must be consistent with specifications and policies contained in the e-Ping document. (Brazilian Government 2009, p. 8).

Examples of general policies are the use of XML as the primary standard for data exchange, adoption of web browsers as the principal means for accessing all government information systems, market support for solutions (all the specifications of e-Ping have solutions widely supported by the market with the objective of reducing costs and risks in the design and production of services in systems of government information), and preferential use of open standards and, when available, free software (Brazilian Government 2009, p. 9).

Another important initiative of the Lula administrations is portal for transparency, established in 2004 to help fight corruption. Journalists as well as specialized NGOs have made extensive use of this and similar state portals to document dubious expenditures. There is also evidence that exposing corruption has had a favorable impact on elections (Box 2.6).

Box 2.6 Brazil's Transparency Portals

The Transparency Portal (http://www.portaldatransparencia.gov.br), an initiative of the Federal General Controller's Office (*Controladora Geral da União* – CGU) was launched in November of 2004 to help combat

(continued)

Box 2.6 (continued)

corruption. It serves as a channel for citizens to accompany the expenditures for the federal government, both direct expenditures, and transfers to states and municipalities.

Consultations on transfers of public resources can be carried out in four ways: by State, by government programs, by government agency or enterprise, and by persons to whom transfers have been made. Information on direct expenditures of the federal government and its agencies can also be obtained in great detail. Thus, citizens can learn how public resources are being used and exercise social control over politicians and the public administrations involved. The portal uses simple language and has a user-friendly navigation system. It has an online manual explaining how to obtain various types of information, and does not require any passwords. Hence, citizens without any special training, knowledge of public budgets, or familiarity with the labyrinth of Brazil's complex public administrations can hold public officials responsible for their actions.

But to help citizens, journalists and NGOs like Transparency Brasil (http://www.transparencia.org.br) can study the information made available by the portal, including the now well-publicized corporate credit cards issued by the Bank of Brazil to qualified civil servants to use (and sometimes abuse) in carrying out their responsibilities. It was through this portal than abuses of these corporate credit cards, including by officials in the President's Office came to be denounced in Brazil's active mass media.

The federal Transparency Portal has also served as a model that has been emulated by an increasing number of states and even *municipios* – for example, Paraná State, Pernambuco State, Alagoas State, and the *município* of São Carlos in São Paulo State.

One NGO, Open Accounts (*Contas Abertas*) brings together individuals, business people, journalists, students, and anyone interested in learning and contributing to the improvement of public expenditure, especially as to its quality, priority, and legality. It publishes on its site a list of Transparency Portals and similar websites around the country with live links to the same.

In addition to the Transparency Portal, the CGU has, since 2003, been conducting a program to audit the use of federal funds transferred to randomly selected *municípios*. Once reviewed, the reports are published on the Internet and disseminated to the mass media. A recent study (Ferraz and Finan 2007) used data on corruption levels obtained from these audits to look at how public dissemination of these audits affected the results of the municipal elections of 2004. The study showed that mayors in municípios that were audited and had high corruption levels were significantly less likely to be re-elected, whereas those from *municípios* where no corruption were found had

(continued)

Box 2.6 (continued)

significantly better chances of being re-elected. The results were even stronger in *municípios* with local radio stations (newspaper readership is very low in Brazil, especially in small towns).

These results suggest that with the increased availability of broadband Internet in Brazil, tools like the Transparency Portals can be increasingly effective in reducing corruption, and the electorate punishes corrupt politicians and rewards honest ones.

Sources: Corrêa (2007), Rodrigues (2004), Ferraz and Finan (2007) and http://www.portaldatransparencia.gov.br/ and http://contasabertas.uol.com.br, both accessed 10 Nov 2009.

There are other world-class initiatives launched during the governments of Fernando Henrique Cardoso that have been maintained and enhanced under the Lula governments. Examples are the electronic elections at the federal, state and municipal level (Box 2.7); the use of the Internet for filing tax returns (Box 2.8); and e-procurement systems.

Box 2.7 Brazil's Electronic Voting System

In 1986, Brazil's Supreme Electoral Court, that supervises 27 Regional Electoral Courts that in turn run elections in Brazil's 2,886 electoral zones, initiated a process that led to entirely electronic elections throughout Brazil in the 2,000 municipal elections. Since that year, all Brazil's federal, state, and municipal elections have been conducted on electronic voting machines, and the full results of elections have been available on the same day the elections were held, though final certification usually takes a few days more. In the October 2008 elections, the electorate numbered almost 129 million, voting in 400,558 voting sites in 5,563 *municípios*.

The sophisticated system, which has a large number of controls to prevent frauds, has not resulted in any serious questioning of its security and validity by any of Brazil's major political parties. No frauds have been detected in the 12 years since the first electronic urns were introduced. Nevertheless, there have been improvements in the urns in each election, and in the 2008 for municipal elections, for the first time urns with biometric identification (using electronic finger print readers) were tested in three *municípios*. The TSE's objective is to extend this system, which requires previous reregistration of voters to obtain their fingerprints, by 2018. In addition, in 2008 the operational

(continued)

Box 2.7 (continued)

system for the urns is being switched to Linux with a view to further improving security and reducing costs.

The success of the Brazilian electronic voting system owes much to the centralized nature of Brazil's electoral system, subordinated to the Supreme Electoral Court. This has made it possible to realize returns to scale in the purchase of electronic urns and terminals as well as the maintenance of a highly skilled professional staff. The same basic technology is used throughout the system, unlike the system in the USA, where each state and sometimes county maintains its own system.

Sources: http://www.tse.gov.br/internet/eleicoes/votoeletronico/sumario.htm, accessed 10 Nov 2009, Reuters (2008), and Camarão (2004).

Box 2.8 Brazil's Electronic Tax Filing System for the Personal Income Tax

Almost all personal income tax declarations in Brazil are filed online. Even in 2003, 95.6% of declarations were filed electronically, either online or on a diskette. In 2008, 23.9 million declarations for the calendar year 2007, or 98.8% of the total were filed over the Internet, using a programs available for download from the federal tax agency (*Secretaria de Receita Federal*) at http://www.receita.fazenda.gov.br/principal/Informacoes/InfoDeclara/declaraPF.htm. In 2008, 13.7 million homes had computers with access to the Internet, thus as many as 57% of the declarations filed over the Internet could have been filed by taxpayers from their own homes. But many returns probably were filed over the Internet by professional tax preparers, at workplaces, or from public Internet access points.

Sources: For declarations filed in 2003, Receita Federal (2007); for declarations filed in 2008 http://www.receita.fazenda.gov.br/AutomaticoSRFsinot/2008/04/30/2008_04_30_21_36_05_137597168.html, accessed 10 Nov 2009 and for households with computers having an Internet connection in 2008 http://www.sidra.ibge.gov.br/pnad/pnadpb.asp, Table 2,387, accessed 10 Nov 2009.

The centralized nature of Brazil's voting system, and the need of the country to process tax returns quickly, given the county's long experience of high rates of inflation prior to the Real Plan of 1994 are probably the key reasons behind the success of these systems. In the case of e-procurement, there are substantial savings realized by both governments and suppliers submitting bids and reducing opportunities for corruption has become politically popular as well.

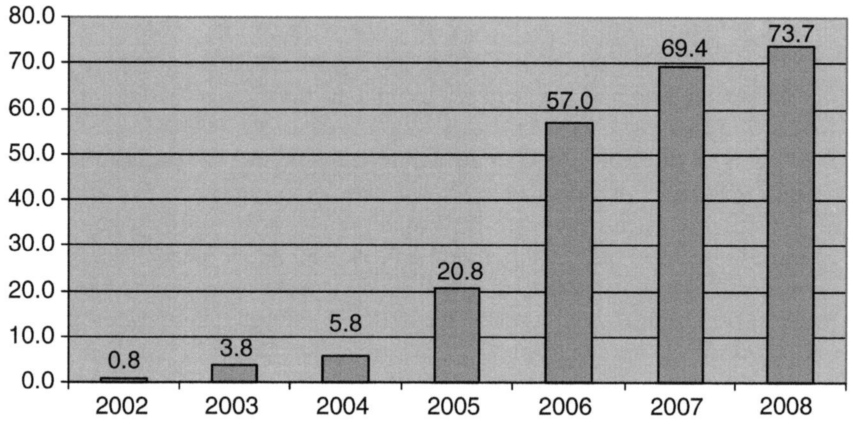

Fig. 2.6 Purchases of common goods and services by comprasnet electronic reverse auctions as a percent of all such goods and services put up for bidding, 2002–2008. Source: Data from http://www.comprasnet.gov.br, accessed 8 Oct 2008 and 10 Nov 2009

The principal federal e-procurement system is Comprasnet (http://www.comprasnet.gov.br), launched in 1999, with reverse electronic auctions (*pregões eletrônicos*) beginning in December 2000, is maintained by SLTI/MP.[55] In 2008, a total of R$12.2 billion in common goods and services were purchased through reverse electronic auctions on Comprasnet, with estimated savings of R$3.8 billion, or 24% compared with reference prices set as the maximum the government was willing to pay, and represented 73.7% of all such purchases.[56] To these gains must be added the reduced costs to suppliers of bidding online.[57] Use of Comprasnet for such government purchases has increased rapidly (Fig. 2.6), especially after the use of auctions for the purchase of common goods and services was made mandatory by a presidential decree in 2005.

The Banco do Brasil, a federal bank, also maintains an e-procurement system (http://www.licitacoes-e.com.br/aop/index.jsp), that can be used by any public or private entity, including state and municipal governments.[58]

But other aspects of e-government do not appear to have been a high priority. An example is the electronic processing for exports. Beginning in 1993 with the creation of the Integrated Foreign Trade System (*Sistema Integrado de Comércio Exterior* – Siscomex), administrative processing of foreign trade operations in

[55] See Fernandes (2004) and Gomes Fernandes (2004) for analyses of the early years of e-procurement in Brazil.

[56] Information from the http://www.comprasnet.gov.br, accessed 10 Nov 2009.

[57] For example, Ferrer and Lima (2007, p. 638) found that the cost of processing bids in São Paulo state's e-procurement system reduced transaction costs for the state government by 51%, and those of suppliers by 93%. Purchasing prices fell by about 25%.

[58] The manual for its system is available at http://www.licitacoes-e.com.br/aop/lct/help/pt_br/site_intro/CartilhaComprador.pdf, accessed 10 Nov 2009.

Brazil has been computerized, but in general it must be said that what has been computerized are outdated and overly bureaucratic processes. All export and import operations are registered through the Siscomex and analyzed online by the federal government foreign trade authorities involved.[59] Tyler (2007) has analyzed Siscomex in detail, and notes that it is a great advance compared with the system it replaced. But it was set up to administer an excessively complicated system, so the Siscomex is also complex and complicated. While it is very useful for the government, it is not that helpful for exporters and importers. Processing of exports can take up to 30 days, which can be a serious problem for perishable goods.

Brazil's foreign trade processes were ranked 100 out of 183 in the 2010 rankings by the International Finance Corporation (IFC) Doing Business Study covering the period June 2008 through May 2009. This was way behind China (44), slightly behind India (94) but way ahead of Russia (162). The world's leader was Singapore, a country with a superb electronic foreign trade system: Finland ranked 4, Korea 8. Even within Latin America and the Caribbean, Brazil ranked only 18 in this category, behind such competitors as Chile and Mexico.[60]

The Siscomex experience demonstrates well the basic point that computerizing bureaucratic processes without process reform reduces the potential benefits of e-government. Transformational e-government uses ICT as a tool for simplifying processes and making them more client-oriented, thereby saving both time and money of citizens and businesses.

Evidence of poor leadership and coordination of e-government programs was found by the Brazilian Audit Court (*Tribunal de Contas da União* – TCU).[61] The TCU sought to determine in what way these programs "contributed toward the provision of electronic public services directly to citizens" as called for in the government's Multiyear Plan (Plano Plurianual – PPA). In 2006, the TCU issued a highly critical report (Brazilian Court of Audit 2006; Tribunal de Contas de União 2006).

Among the TCU's findings were that "one of the main difficulties faced by Program coordinators to ensure the uniform development of all e-government actions at high levels in Federal Public Administration agencies stems from the loss of political interest in the topic in recent years, which led to a loss of effectiveness in the Program's operational framework in relation to what the law originally provided for, namely a framework supported by CEGE and its Technical Committees. Still in the political sphere, the overlapping of roles and power conflicts in implementing the policy, between the Logistics and Information Technology Secretariat of the Ministry of Planning, Budget and Management and the Institutional Communication Secretariat of the President's Office (Secom)," were cited as examples of what has been affecting the e-government program. The report also found a

---

[59] An exception is for export orders that do not exceed US$20,000 and whose weight does not exceed 30 kg. Such orders may be sent through the postal system in a program called Easy Export (*Exporta Fácil*) – see Tyler (2007, p. 845, footnote 11).

[60] The rankings are available at http://www.doingbusiness.org/economyrankings/, accessed 11 Nov 2009.

[61] In an audit of federal e-government programs conducted between August and September 2005.

lack of effective coordination of the program, and noted that the CEGE had not held regular meetings, hence "guidelines and discussions are not being formalized into resolutions, which would be signed off by the Chief of Staff of the President's Office" (Brazilian Court of Audit 2006, p. 16).

The Federal Government's central web portal http://www.brasil.gov.br was visually complex and not easy to navigate for information. But a new greatly improved version was launched in March 2010 implementing a sophisticated modern design including navigation via news, videos, info-graphics, special mini-sites (e.g., on Brazil in the World Cup, Brasília's 50th anniversary, impact of consumption on environment), and services. There is specialized access from the home page for businessmen, students, workers, and journalists with others planned for seniors, children, and civil servants. The home page also offers specialized access for 11 thematic areas including citizenship, culture, education, sports, economics, health, tourism, environment, and Brazil. This portal still offered few transactional services.

The TCU auditors found a lack of monitoring and evaluation activities, and many indications that a relatively low priority was being given to the e-government programs, a lack of performance indicators, poor dissemination of best practices by the program coordinators, unawareness, on the part of managers, of electronic services, of target audience, of citizens' needs and opinions on the quality of these services and programs, a low percentage of citizen-oriented transactional services, and noncompliance with recommendations proposed in documents developed by the e-government program that would have made easier the access to and use of electronic public services by citizens.

The TCU recommended that the institutional model in force should be reviewed; the project for defining e-government performance indicators and evaluating e-government services should be concluded; tools, techniques, and good practices should be identified and disseminated to public managers; and a timeline for implementing the National E-Government Development Plan for 2004–2007 should be defined (Brazilian Court of Audit 2006, pp. 16–38).

An Accenture report reached a similar conclusion:

> Overall, Brazil's service program has shown very little movement. Our survey shows that citizens feel customer service has gotten slightly worse than it was three years ago and that citizens are dissatisfied. To make any real progress now, the Brazilian government actually needs to step back to devise an outcome-focused strategy for delivering real value to citizens through customer service, and then develop a sharp, implementable action plan of realistic targets for moving forward. (Accenture 2007, p. 85)

Perhaps as a consequence of the relatively low priority given to e-government programs and their weak coordination at the federal level, Brazil's ranking in most international comparative studies of e-government, e-readiness, networked readiness, and so forth has slipped since 2002.[62] There has been faster progress in some of the states and *municípios*.

[62] It should be noted that the number of countries compared in most studies has changed over time, and the methodologies vary between study and in some cases between years. Furthermore, such studies look at e-government only at the national level.

State and municipal e-government. All Brazilian state governments and many municipal ones have e-government portals and services, of varying degrees of sophistication. Some of them are quite advanced, make use of the life cycle approach to e-government services for citizens and enterprises, featuring subportals for birth, youth, working life, retirement, and death in the case of individuals, for example. Good examples are the portals for the states of Minas Gerais São Paulo, Rio Grande do Sul, and the *Município* of São Paulo. But in addition there are some interesting uses of G2G (government to government) use of ICT – a good example is Rio de Janeiro state's program for Management of Public Services by Indicators which has been used to improve the quality of education, public safety, and health services in the state (Box 2.9).

Many states, like the federal government, have e-procurement systems of their own, for example, one of the most established is São Paulo's Electronic Purchasing

Box 2.9 Rio de Janeiro State's Program for Management of Public Services by Indicators

Rio de Janeiro State was seeking to improve the quality of key public services – education, health and public safety – to fulfill commitments in Governor Sergio Cabral's program. Under a program known as Management of Public Services by Indicators (*Gestão dos Serviços Públicos por Indicadores* – GESPI), a partnership was established in 2007 between the State ICT Company, Proderj; Modulo, a leading private ICT company; and the Secretariat of Government (that oversees priority State Government programs) to design a system of indicators to monitor conditions in 1,591 schools, 134 police stations, and 33 hospitals with a view to identifying and resolving problems that could affect the quality of the services they provide. The Secretariats of Education, Security, and Health participate in this program as well.

Initially, some 355 inspections per month were carried out on a random basis, unannounced, by teams including a television crew to record the conditions in the units visited and a group of inspectors, who filled out paper forms, and this resulted in reports on each inspection being available to the Secretariat of Government in about 3 days. But then the forms were perfected and incorporated into palmtop computers that could send the completed data as soon as they were entered, with the information going directly to a risk management program on run on Proderj computers in a central datacenter. With this improvement in technology, it was possible to conduct 830 inspections per month, have greater security regarding the data, and have completed reports available to relevant government officials about half a day after the data was entered into the palmtops. On the basis of the reports, action plans for dealing with deficiencies identified are developed and executed with priority depending on the degree of risk assessed by the indicators reported.

(continued)

Box 2.9 (continued)

A second phase of the program, being implemented for the Secretariat of Education's schools in 2008, involved developing an "event manager" to provide real-time management of actions being taken to deal with the problems identified. These can be viewed at various levels of aggregation on a kind of electronic dashboard, by state officials including the Governor. The event manager system involves some 85 staff with notebook computers and/or smart phones, able to access the Internet to respond within 24 h to any event classified as an emergency under a system known as School SOS, or other problems identified (events) and registered in the Workflow Manager in response to the reports of the GESPI system.

In response to each event registered, e-mail messages and/or phone calls are sent to the relevant personnel to carry out a first survey, which is reported back over the Internet. On the basis of this survey, if an emergency situation is confirmed at the central monitoring station staffed by Secretariat of Government and Secretariat of Education personnel, a team from the State Works Company is dispatched to carry out the necessary repairs if the risk requires such, for example, leaking roofs or nonfunctioning toilets. If the problem is administrative (e.g., lack of teachers or equipment) other remedial actions, in this case by the Secretariat of Education, are undertaken. In determining action programs and monitoring their execution, a series of "forums" of the relevant staff are involved and kept informed concerning the actions taken until the event is considered closed, with evidence of the solutions taken submitted.

At the beginning of the Cabral Government in 2007, all the state agencies involved in the project – Proderj and the Secretariats Government, Education, Health and Public Safety – signed an agreement setting goals for the composite "Security Index" obtained using the indicators to be assessed in the inspections. The goal was to reach 60% in 2007, 70% in 2008, 80% in 2009, and 90% in the final year for the Cabral Administration, 2010. The goal for 2007 was surpassed by 8% points, and as of October 2008 the Security Index reached almost 79%, with 1,030 schools, 25 health units, and 40 police stations improving their performance.

The GESPI managers believe that this project demonstrates effective and unannounced on-site evaluations – that take account the population's needs and are supported by both technological resources and decisive political and administrative action – can help government solve problems quickly, bringing dignity and respect to the citizen, the ultimate objectives of the project.

Sources: Interviews and e-mail correspondence with GESPI staff, October 2008.

Exchange (*Bolsa Eletrônica de Compras* – http://www.bec.sp.gov.br) that since 2000 had conducted over R$7 billion in purchases by October 2010 with estimated savings of over R$2 billion. Of course states and municipal governments can use the Banco do Brasil's e-procurement system, and indeed questions have been raised as to whether it makes sense to have as many different e-procurement systems as have sprung up in Brazil (Gomes Fernandes 2004, p. 233). There are fixed costs of establishing and operating such systems, and the larger the number of operations that can be accommodated in a given system, the lower the unit transactions costs.

Alternative channels for delivering e-government services. One of Brazil's most successful uses of ICTs in state and municipal governments is to support integrated citizen service centers (ICSCs), operated by an increasing number of Brazil's states and some municipal governments. The ICSCs responded to concerns of many Brazilian citizens fed up with unresponsive bureaucracies characterized by unnecessary routines, no evaluation of quality of service delivery, low transparency in the relationship of civil servant vs. citizens, hours and locations of service delivery inconvenient for citizens, unpleasant surroundings, long waits, repeated requests by bureaucrats for information the State already has, and an attitude of "create difficulties in order to sell facilities" (corruption).

These ICSCs have different names, depending on the states in which they are implemented – for example, Poupatempo (Timesaver) in São Paulo (Box 2.10), SAC in Bahia, Psiu and more recently UAI in Minas Gerais, Vapt Vupt in Goias, Tudo Fácil (Everything Easy) in Rio Grande do Sul, etc. The objective of the ICSCs is to make available more citizen-oriented services, provided by well-trained, courteous

Box 2.10 São Paulo's Timesaver (Poupatempo) Integrated Citizen Service Centers

The São Paulo State Government established the Timesaver (*Poupatempo*) program in 1996 to bring together in one place, in locations and at hours convenient to citizens, a wide range of public agencies and services. The philosophy adopted was to serve the citizen quickly, with quality and efficiency, thereby saving valuable citizen time and improving the image of the State Government and its civil servants.

In October 2010, there were 17 fixed *Poupatempo* units, seven in the metropolitan São Paulo area and ten in other cities in the state. Some of them were constructed and/or run by private sector companies, under supervision of the state agency responsible for the program. There were also seven mobile *Poupatempo* units installed in large trucks or busses that travel throughout the state, remaining 3–15 days in different locations, depending on the demand for services.

The *Poupatempo* program makes available over 400 services. Of these, the issue of identity cards, police records, work cards, and driver's licenses are the

(continued)

Box 2.10 (continued)

most popular. Information on services offered can be obtained by a free telephone call to the *Poupatempo* call center, or an online guide available at http://domino.sp.gov.br/ug960162.nsf/webframepai?opennavigator. In the first 9 months of 2010, Poupatempo serviced an average of 2.7 million requests per month. With the expansion of the Internet, an *e-Poupatempo* online service was developed beginning in 2002, as the first step toward a virtual *Poupatempo*. The *e-Poupatempos* offer citizens rooms with computers and printers for accessing some 2,000 public services available online from municipal, state, and federal governments, with assistance provided by trained personnel. The e-*Poupatempos* are located within most fixed Poupatempo posts and all the mobile units.

The latest initiative of the *Poupatempo* program is called Ponto SP. It seeks to make available in small and medium cities in the state distant from fixed *Poupatempo* posts the some 2,000 public services available through the state government's website called the *Portal Cidadão SP* (http://www.cidadao.sp.gov.br) in addition to a number of federal services available fully or partially over the Internet. Five Ponto SP posts were in operation as of October 2010. They are set up in partnership with municipal governments and include a number of computers with broadband Internet connections, printers, and attendants who help citizens access the online services.

The *Poupatempo* program has annual evaluations conducted by one of Brazil's leading survey firms, IBOPE. In 2001–2004 the program was approved by 99% of its users. In the latest IBOPE Survey available as of October 2010, conducted with 1,760 users of all fixed and mobile *Poupatempo* units, in November 2009, 97% said that they approved of the service, 95% said that the *Poupatempo* respects people and that it offered good service, and 94% said and that it was something São Paulo could be proud of. The program has won numerous Brazilian and international awards.

Sources: Cunha et al. (2007) and http://www.poupatempo.sp.gov.br/home/.

staff respectful of the citizens, and at locations (e.g., at nodes in the transportation system or in shopping centers) and times (outside normal working hours) that are convenient to citizens, saving them time and effort. In addition, ICSCs provide transparency in public management, bring the state closer to the citizen, and seek continuous improvements in service delivery, debureaucratizing, and simplifying wherever possible without violating existing legislation.

ICSCs usually operate according to guidelines that require

- Continuous training of service providers
- Clear instructions available to citizens
- Personnel able to do multiple tasks

Table 2.4 ICSCs in São Paulo, Bahia, and Goiás, 2007

State	São Paulo	Bahia	Goiás
Year of installation	1997	1995	1999
Fixed units	11	25	19
Mobile units	7	2	1
Services delivered in 2007	27.8 million	11.4 million	6.6 million
Population of state in 2007 (IBGE)	39.8 million	14.1 million	5.6 million

Source: Knight and Annenberg (2008)

- Uniforms and name badges to identify ICSC personnel
- Availability of support services for citizens (photography, Xerox, etc.)
- Call center to provide information on ICSC services pre and postvisit (also online)
- Regular surveys of user satisfaction
- Clear and citizen-friendly ways to provide feedback on services provided to citizens

The construction of ICSCs, and sometimes their operation, can be and often is outsourced to private companies. But the elaboration of strategy and guidelines, finance of construction and most operating costs, and supervision remains with government agencies responsible for these programs. ICSCs, including mobile ones set up in trucks or busses, make heavy use of the Internet to connect to government databases and websites. Often they include a special kind of telecenter oriented toward online government services, and an online version where some services can be obtained over the Internet.

As of May 2008, ICSCs were in operation in 23 of Brazil's 26 states, two more had ICSCs in development. There were also a growing number of municipal-level ICSCs, at least six, mostly in São Paulo State. The best practice for ICSCs in Brazil as of 2008 could be are found in Bahia, São Paulo, and Goiás states. In these states results included: greater acceptance and use by citizens, more units in operation, greater political support and visibility, more involvement of the state agencies and institutions participating the programs, more resources allocated for the ICSCs, and greater continuity in management (Knight and Annenberg 2008). Table 2.4 provides some summary data on ICSCs in these three states for the year 2007.

Looking toward the future, Brazil's ICSCs face some important challenges. First is to integrate various services independent of the parts of Government (federal, state, municipal, and functional parts of government at each level) and of the legacy systems behind them. To date, ICSCs in Brazil not really been "single window government" operations, but rather a collection of services of different government agencies offered under a single roof. This challenge is also one faced by government portals at all levels, many of which simply direct users to separate websites of different government agencies. Others include the following:

- Organize service delivery better using multiple delivery channels (Internet, face-to-face, telephone, digital TV)

- Reduce costs of the ICSCs and find ways to maintain them independent of state and municipal budgets
- Improve and make more agile the delivery of services (redesigning processes and procedures, reducing bureaucracy)
- Find new ways to maintain employee motivation, gradually making them capable of performing multiple services
- Improve relations with citizens (through use of Citizen Relations Management – CRM, a single registry for each citizen, etc.)
- Increasingly value activities related to service delivery, creating appropriate career paths
- Create channels of participation for the population so that the ICSCs become an institutionalized state policy rather than that of a particular government

In August of 2010, the State of Acre was completing a new service center in its capital, Rio Branco, that would implement the concept of single-window services along the lines pioneered by Citizen Stores (*Lojas do Cidadão*) in Portugal.[63] The idea is to go beyond what is currently done in ICSCs in Brazil, where different public services are offered in the same physical location, and allow a citizen in a particular life situation, for example, changing her residence or getting second copies of documents lost or stolen, to get the necessary public services, whether they be municipal, state, or federal, in a single location and presenting all the required documentation at the same time. Under this single-window approach, the citizen does not need to go to each separate agency's counter inside the unit, but deals with a single person, who in the name of the Government, makes all the necessary contacts with specific agencies on behalf of the citizen.[64]

E-Business

The growth of e-business in Brazil has been rapid and by 2008 e-commerce, e-banking, and other business applications had become important in both private and public sector firms. Of course within most large enterprises the use of ICT has been increasing for a long time. But in recent years this has extended to small and medium and even microenterprises, and both business to business (B2B), business to government (B2G), business to consumer (B2C), and even consumer to consumer (C2C) interactions via the Internet have assumed an important role in the economy. The focus in this section will be on B2C applications, which could take on a new importance as full interactive digital television is rolled out in Brazil, permitting what is called t-commerce, t-banking, t-education, etc.

---

[63] See http://www.portaldocidadao.pt, accessed 13 Nov 2010.

[64] This paragraph is based on e-mail correspondence on 27 Oct 2008 with Daniel Annenberg, President of the São Paulo consulting firm Respublica Consultoria and former director of the Poupatempo program.

E-Banking. Brazil is a leader in the use of ICT in the financial sector – both between financial institutions and between them and businesses and individual account holders. This is perhaps one of the few positive legacies of the hypertrophy of Brazil's financial system during decades of high and unstable rates of inflation, and was systematized with the creation of the Brazilian Payments System (*Sistema Brasileiro de Pagamentos* – SPB). The SPB was conceived by the Central Bank of Brazil in 2000 and launched in April of 2002. It integrates, through electronic means, the routines for compensation and liquidation of interbank payments, making them more rapid and agile, as well as guaranteeing the security of all participants in the system – banks, investors, and account holders. Since April 2002 all transactions above R$5,000 are effected the same day they are made, and the Central Bank can monitor online activity throughout the banking system, managing liquidity so as to minimize systemic risk (Knight and Wanderley 2004).

Account holders in most Brazilian banks can monitor their accounts and carry out transfers between accounts in the same bank and between banks online. Banking transactions over the Internet are estimated to cost banks less than 10% of an equivalent transaction in an agency, which is one of the factors encouraging the rapid increase in e-banking, along with the convenience and security it offers to customers. Mobile banking (m-banking), using cell phones, was also growing rapidly with a working group of the Brazilian Federation of Banks (Febraban) developing m-banking without actual individual accounts in banks, using sales of prepaid cards much as for prepaid mobile phones.[65] T-banking (using fully interactive digital TV) is also under development in Brazil.

Use of computers and the Internet in businesses. The use of computers and the Internet in Brazilian businesses was almost universal by 2008 for firms with ten or more employees, with relatively small differences by region or type of economic activity (Table 2.5).

Digital inclusion of smaller firms remains an issue. It is being addressed through the Ministry of Economic Development and Foreign Trade's Business and information Telecenters (TINs) and a variety of programs of the Brazilian Service for Support of Small and Micro Enterprises (*Serviço Brasileiro de Apoio às Micro e Pequenas e Empresas* – SEBRAE). Some are carried out in association with the Brazilian Chamber of e-Commerce (*Câmara Brasileira de Comércio Eletrônico* – Câmara-e.net).

E-commerce.[66] A study commissioned by Visa, showed that the value of goods and services sold via e-commerce in Brazil in 2007 was by far the largest in Latin America. According to that study, 3.7% of the Brazilian population already was accustomed to making online purchases, with total sales reaching US$4.9 billion, a growth of 116% since 2005. It attributed the jump to sustained economic growth,

---

[65] Accountless m-banking techniques have been pioneered in the Philippines and South Africa (Knight 2008b).

[66] Bichara de Oliveira et al. (2007) have documented the development of e-commerce in Brazil, beginning in 1995, when the Brazilian Internet was opened for commercial use.

Table 2.5 Proportion of Brazilian enterprises using the internet, 2008 (percentages of all firms in sample by category[a])

		Yes	No
Total (all firms)		91	3
Size of the firm (number of employees)	10–49	89	3
	50–249	99	1
	250 or more	99	1
Region	North	93	3
	Northeast	91	4
	Southeast	88	3
	South	96	2
	Center West	95	–
Markets in which the firms operate – National Classification of Economic ActivitiesHo	Manufacturing industry	91	2
	Construction	99	–
	Commerce; repair of automotive automotors, personal, and domestic objects	91	4
	Lodging and food	71	6
	Transportation, storage, and communications	96	1
	Real estate, rentals, and services to other businesses	92	2
	Other collective social and personal services[b]	87	2

Notes
[a] Base: 3,500 businesses with ten or more employees, survey conducted in Oct/Nov 2008
[b] Does not include urban cleaning, sewerage, and related services; and associative activities
Source: CETIC.BR – TIC Empresas 2008, Table B1 available at http://www.cetic.br/empresas/2008/c-int-01.htm, accessed 9 Nov 2009

technological advances, and the increase in the use of credit cards by consumers, with about two thirds of online sales being paid for by credit cards (Ipnews 2008). For example, 80% ticket sales by one of Brazil's two top airlines, Gol, were carried out online in 2007.[67] There is even an airline, Webjet that sells tickets only online.

Online sales to consumers reached R$3.8 billion in the first 6 months of 2008, an increase of 45% over the corresponding period of 2007, and were forecast to reach R$8.5 billion for the full year 2008 (Fig. 2.7), or an increase of almost 35% over 2007 with the number of e-consumers reaching 12 million, up over 26% from 2007 (e-Bit 2008). This forecast was made prior to the onset of the global financial crisis, albeit after the Central Bank had begun raising interest rates to control inflation and dampen consumption. M-commerce – the use of mobile phones, palmtops, etc. to make purchases – is also growing rapidly.

---

[67] http://idgnow.uol.com.br/internet/ideia20/archive/2008/08/25/internet-cresce-45-e-passa-tv-por-assinatura-em-receita-publicitria-no-brasil/, accessed 22 Oct 2008.
http://www.valoronline.com.br/valoronline/Geral/empresas/Gol+anuncia+aumento+de+15+nas+vendas+pela+internet+em+2007+para+um+total+de+R$+43+bi,08222,,2,4794775.html (accessed 22 Feb 2008).

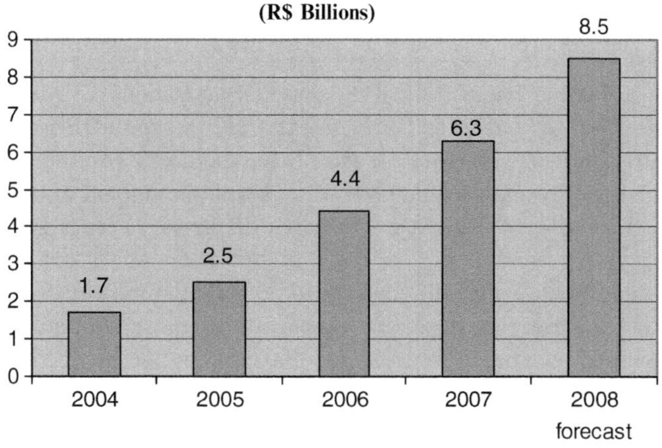

Fig. 2.7 e-Commerce Sales to Consumers in Brazil, 2004–2008 (R$ billions). Source: e-bit Informação (http://www.ebitempresa.com.br) in e-bit (2008)

Interactive digital television. The rollout of digital television broadcasts was begun in São Paulo in December 2007 and had reached 47 cities in 19 states plus the Federal District in June 2010. Beginning in 2013 no new conventional (analogical) channels will be authorized, and at the end of June 2016 analogical transmissions will be completely phased out. Limited interactivity is already possible with one-way transmissions.

But the Brazilian middleware, called Ginga, that allows two-way interaction through a return channel (Internet, telephone, coaxial cable, etc.) is expected to be fully released in 2010 and will then be incorporated in new set-top boxes (converters of the digital signal for use in analogical TV sets) and new fully digital TVs. Once Ginga is available, digital TV rollout in Brazil should stimulate development (already underway) and use of powerful new tools for education (t-learning), interaction with governments (t-government), commerce (t-commerce), and banking (t-banking). This potential is appreciated by government circles (Barbosa Filho and Castro 2007; Bocchino 2007), as well as by the private sector, including the powerful Globo television network (Bittencourt 2007). Given the high cost of telephony and both satellite and cable TV in Brazil, the availability of free or low-cost wireless Internet is likely to be critical in developing interactive applications.

It remains to be seen what incentives for the development of such digital TV-based applications will be provided by government policies and the market. There are issues as to business models which need to be solved if private broadcasters, that command the largest TV audiences, are to make heavy use of the potential in for two-way interactivity. While two-way interactivity has had not developed much in Europe, Japan, and North America as of 2010, the Brazilian system may be very attractive to other developing countries and could provide an important source of export earnings for Brazil.

Box 2.11 Brazil's Information Network for the Third Sector (RITS)

RITS is a Public Interest Civil Society Organization (*Organização da Sociedade Civil de Interesse Público* – OSCIP), a type of Brazilian NGO allowed to contract with governments. It has political, administrative, and financial autonomy and was founded in 1997 with the support of the Dr. Ruth Cardoso, the wife of the then President of Brazil, Fernando Henrique Cardoso.

RITS was created with the mission to be a virtual information network, capable of providing civil society organizations the opportunity to share knowledge and technical resources and encouraging the interaction of their activities through the use of ICT, especially the Internet. RITS contributes to the active participation of such organizations and citizens, leveraging ICT for human development, democracy, and sustainability. It acts in five areas:

1. Analyzing, monitoring, and proposing public policies.
2. Training agents of civilian organizations in communication rights and other online and face-to-face training activities.
3. Support in Internet technologies for civil society organizations.
4. Mobilization of civil society through online information services.
5. Carrying out digital inclusion projects that benefit low-income communities.

In this last line of activity, RITS participated in the installation and maintenance of more than 180 community telecenters and community networks in Brazil.

Since beginning its activities, RITS has acted with the objective of being an instrument for the modernization and strengthening of civil society organizations and has consolidated itself as a leader in the dissemination of information promoting common interests of the third sector.

Source: http://www.rits.org.br, accessed 11 Nov 2009.

E-Society

As discussed above, Brazilian NGOs have been active in the area of digital inclusion. This has been encouraged by SLTI/MP that has taken a leading role in organizing annual National Workshops on Digital Inclusion held in various Brazilian cities since 2001. These are heavily attended by NGOs, and they usually help organize the events.

The Internet has been a vital means of communication between NGOs and between them and society and the government. The Information Network for the Third Sector (*Rede de Informações para o Terceiro Setor* – RITS) has helped other civil society organizations develop this capacity and has also been active in the National Workshops on Digital Inclusion (Box 2.11).

The Road Ahead

Brazil has made substantial progress on the road to e-development. The infostructure necessary to bring Internet access to the whole population of Brazil is being put in place. The ICT sector is growing in importance in the national economy; digital literacy in the population is expanding rapidly, and e-government, e-commerce, and e-society and many other applications not specifically treated in this chapter are advancing.

Making broadband Internet access a right of citizens, financed from federal, state, and local government revenues and through innovative partnerships with the private sector and NGOs is a concept that is gaining political traction and which some states and municipalities are implementing. Such access would not only allow an even more rapid increase in the percentage of Brazilians who access the Internet from computers at home, but also provide a return channel for fully interactive digital television. Whether through computers, handheld devices such as smart phones, or interactive digital television, Internet access in an era of digital convergence offers tremendous opportunities for expanding educational and economic opportunities to the base of Brazil's socioeconomic pyramid (Barbosa et al. 2007). This, in turn, offers powerful tools for reducing socioeconomic inequality, enhancing competitiveness, and perfecting Brazil's democracy.

During 2009, in the context of a debate focused on a federal government proposal being developed for a National Broadband Program and a National Conference on Communications, consensus seemed to be developing on the need for such a program and if not on the precise modes of its execution. But there is a need for a broader e-development strategy as proposed by the *e-Brasil* project (based on research by over sixty contributors) and synthesized in the *e-Brasil* Program.[68] A shorter summary version, called the Ten-Point Program for *e-Brasil* Candidates, was also published, and is summarized below (Box 2.12).

Box 2.12 The Ten-Point Program for E-Brasil Candidates

ICTs are powerful tools for reducing socioeconomic inequality and improving competitiveness. It is hoped that candidates for positions in the federal, state, and municipal governments will commit themselves to a government program that will transform this belief into a reality. The profile of these candidates should be that of a visionary leader, a mobilizer who creates consensus, sells ideas, and obtains a strong mandate that will allow him or her to realize synergies between the work of all ministries or secretariats and reap economies of scale to achieve previously announced goals.

(continued)

[68] See Knight and Fernandes (2006) and Knight et al. (2007).

Box 2.12 (continued)

What we call an *e-Brasil* candidate – whether for President of the Republic, State Governor, or Mayor – knows that with his or her leadership it will be possible to implement public policies, programs, and projects that will not only achieve the goals, but also win recognition from the population and votes in the future. What are the elements that should be in the *e-Brasil* candidate's program? They are different for candidates for President, Governors, and Mayors. For Governors and Mayors these characteristics will vary with the characteristics of the state or *município*. But they will all have ten common elements.

1. *Digital inclusion and e-development.* Without strong public digital inclusion policies it is impossible to achieve the other elements of the *e-Brasil* Program. What is crucial is to accelerate the access of all the population to broadband Internet, using for the less-favored population alternative models of sustainability that exempt them from paying access fees, with remuneration of the supplier through advertising, public budgets, and/or resources from the Fund for Universalization of Telecommunications Services (Fust). Priority should go to schools, telecenters, and other collective access points. It is also very important to encourage competition between providers and broadband technologies (fiber optic cable, satellite, coaxial cable, Wi-Fi, WiMAX, and PLC), hardware and software (including open code software) to lower costs. A national program of digital cities will bring the benefits of e-development to the citizens in *municípios* today unserved.
2. *E-Education and training, lifelong.* Education and training are the highest sectoral priority: they are means for democratizing access to knowledge to improve opportunities for employment, income distribution, and also Brazil's competitiveness in an ever more knowledge-based world economy. Governments should accelerate the computerization of public schools, giving them broadband Internet connections, using all the available alternatives, including government networks; increase the number of computers per school and per student; and encourage the creation of world-class electronic content for teaching. The candidate for President will commit himself to supporting these efforts in the states and *municípios* with the resources of the federal government. Candidates at all levels of the federal system can promote partnerships with the S System (Senai, Senac, Sebrae, etc.), private corporate universities, and public and private universities for permanent education of the labor force. Brazil has to give strategic priority to the question of education and training to position itself as a successful competitor in the global economy.
3. *E-Public safety.* Security is a fundamental right and a necessity to achieve the other objectives. Among the priority actions are the interlinking of the databases of all the public safety agencies: the prison system, the Federal

(continued)

Box 2.12 (continued)

Police, State Civil and Military Polices, the information system of the Ministry of Justice, and civil guards at the municipal level. In addition, it is recommended that the operations centers of the civil and military police and the fire departments of the states be integrated in a single installation in the capital and in large cities in the interior, with facilities to share and coordinate databases and radio communication systems.

4. *E-Health.* Public health is in large part education and can be improved using ICTs. It is also possible to improve the management of both the preventive and curative health systems. Here, a priority is the development of a health portal with subportals for doctors, nurses, pharmacists, and the general population to facilitate education in the areas of health and diagnosis. A health network with broadband connections should be created, interlinking all the health units (federal, state, and municipal), creating an environment conducive to training, medical consultations, making appointments online, obtaining second opinions, practicing telemedicine, etc. It is also fundamental to reserve part of the available development resources (Sectoral Funds, Innovation Law, Informatics Law, Fust, Funtel, etc.) for using ICTs for health, with the objective of reducing the bottleneck generated by the lack of specialized health personnel.
5. *E-Public services and management.* It is possible to greatly improve the delivery of public services to citizens as well as the management of governments. A priority is to develop electronic government, optimizing and interlinking government networks at the federal, state, and municipal levels, promoting the integration and digitalization of all *municípios*, and providing incentives for the participation of municipal governments in public–private sector partnerships (PPPs). Such partnerships can be used for the construction and operation of integrated service centers (one-stop shops) for the population, like the Poupatempo program in São Paulo, the SAC in Bahia, the Vapt Vupt in Goiás, the Super Fácil in Amapá, and the Tudo Fácil in Rio Grande do Sul. It should be a goal to expand the supply, through electronic means, of all public services delivered by the federal, state, and municipal governments, with the revision and simplification of processes, offering, at least, complete and up-to-date information and the electronic making of appointments or scheduling access to services. Other priorities are to promote the integrated management of information in the use of public services, obeying the principle of never asking citizens for information that the state already has.
6. *Government e-procurement of goods and services.* A priority is to establish prefect Internet portals for procurement and computerized systems to support management of bidding and contracts, spreading to all the states the advances already achieved in some electronic bidding and publishing bidding documents and on the Internet, simplification of the suppliers'

(continued)

Box 2.12 (continued)

registry, electronic catalogs of materials and services, registry of prices paid and broad publication of contracts on the Internet. A great achievement of these measures has been the drastic reduction in opportunities for corruption and price cuts on the order of 20% for goods and services purchased using e-procurement. To increase social control of governments, the transparency of public administration should be increased by putting budgets, revenues, expenditures and government accounts on the Internet, in addition to information on the execution of works, projects, and services.

7. *E-Justice*. There seems to be relative consensus on the technical measures that should be adopted, notably those that promote the simplification of procedures for judges and court personnel which result in speeding up the handling of cases. In this context, the use of ICTs is fundamental, because they can reduce the delays and increase transparency in handling of cases. It is a priority to approve a legal framework for electronic judicial processes, greatly reducing the margin for questioning the validity of using electronic documents to support judicial procedures.
8. *E-Commerce*. It is possible to reduce transaction costs in the economy, providing gains for consumers and reducing the so-called Brazil Cost which so reduces the competitiveness of the country. It is necessary to provide incentives for the use of digital certificates in commerce and in relations with the governments, mobilizing the notary publics so that they can participate supplying such certificates. Using digital certificates and computerizing ports and airports can greatly reduce the costs of and obstacles to international transactions.
9. *Encouraging development of the ICT sector*. The software and services subsector in Brazil can grow rapidly with some short- and long-term measures. First, policies for public purchases favoring software provided by Brazilian small- and medium-sized companies. Second, wide-ranging human resource programs for education, training, and retraining of professionals in partnership with the private sector. Third, a revision of the array of taxes to make taxation compatible with the special characteristics of software and informatics service providers. This adaptation would seek to equalize the conditions for competition of Brazilian firms with those of their principal foreign competitors. All this should be included in a general law for the sector, on which Congress has been working for some years.
10. *Strategy, coordination, and leadership*. Electronic government policy should enter the priority agenda of the federal, state, and municipal governments and be aligned with other e-development policies. Leadership is

(continued)

Box 2.12 (continued)

fundamental, and should begin at the highest level of the executive branch, the President of the Republic for the federal government, the governors for the states, and the mayors for the *municípios*. Under the chief executive's leadership it is necessary to strengthen a coordinating unit in his or her office, headed by a person who has his or her confidence and a combination of political and technological skills sufficient to develop and implement strategic programs which cut across the ministries or secretariats and agencies. These are programs that demand coordinated action of diverse public sector agencies and partnerships between these and the private sector, universities, research institutes, and civil society organizations, and also relations with the media. The public ICT firms and administrative units dealing with ICTs in the agencies and entities of public administration should act aligned with the e-government and e-development policies and be restructured to update their technologies and ways of doing business.

Source: Author's translation from Knight et al. (2007), pp. 26–29.

The issue of *strategy, coordination, and leadership* is a continuous challenge on the road to e-transformation. As suggested earlier, a whole-of-government approach and effective coordination from near the top of the government (at the federal level, probably in the President's office) with strong leadership and support from the chief executive is crucial. The CGPID could develop into a key institution for exercising this leadership at the federal level. These institutional and political arrangements are necessary to provide clear incentives to adhere to a well-articulated strategy, to involve major nongovernment stakeholders (the private sector, academic and research institutions, and NGOs), and to realize both synergies and economies of scale. Without them e-development is unlikely to realize anything like its full potential at any level in Brazil's federal system.

A *shared vision* of a desired ICT-enabled future would give a more central role to the use of ICTs to realize Brazil's goals. Since there are already plenty of good examples of how to do this within Brazil and around the world, and these have been amply documented in the publications of the *e-Brasil* project and elsewhere (e.g., Telebrasil 2009; Telcomp 2009; Brasscom 2009; Booz and Company 2009; Hanna 2010), the key now is to draw on this intellectual capital to build public understanding and support for such a strategy.

A *strategic communication program*, would greatly facilitate this support and make intensive use of the mass media, both electronic (radio, television, and the Internet) and print (newspapers, magazines, and technical–professional journals). Among all the media, in Brazil, television is perhaps the most important (Bittencourt 2007; Bocchino 2007; Barbosa Filho and Castro 2007). Even before digital TV is more broadly disseminated, television should play a central role in helping build awareness in the Brazilian population of what is possible. To that extent, all popular program formats: news, talk shows, "magazines" (examples are programs like Friday evening program *Globo Reporter* and the Sunday afternoon *Fantástico* on the leading network, Globo), and even the highly popular dramatic serials, *telenovelas*, can be enlisted (Knight and Schiavo 2007).

Telenovelas are a particularly powerful tool for showing how ICT can positively affect the daily lives of Brazilians. These dramatic serials have been effective in spreading knowledge of family planning, environmental issues, public health questions, and the fight against corruption. It is not difficult to imagine how to incorporate the effective use of e-learning, e-government, e-health, e-commerce Internet banking, telecenters, and Lan houses into such dramatic programs which get from 35 to 60% of the TV audience during prime time. Seeing popular characters in *telenovelas* improving their lives by taking advantage of these applications of ICT can be a powerful motivator. Supplemented by news programs, magazines, and talk show presentations of similar topics, television programming can make a great difference. Radio can play an important supplemental role. Print media is more effective in reaching a more elite audience – again there is a need to have more articles focusing on e-development-related topics.

Thought leadership and national consensus on e-development must be also developed. To reach decision-makers, intensive 2-week seminars for parliamentarians, leading civil servants, business people, and leaders from labor unions, the media, and NGOs such as were run for over 20 years in Finland could be extremely effective. Shorter seminars (1–3 days) focusing on such elites have been organized in Brazil since 1988 to focus on key development issues by the National Forum, an organization led by former Planning Minister João Paulo dos Reis Velloso.[69] Normally several hundred people participate in the seminars, which have a series of contributed papers and discussions in a series of panels, but little participation on the discussions by the participants.

The Finnish national management seminars involve smaller groups of participants over a longer period of time. They played an important part in building a national consensus on development strategy in that country (Dahlman et al. 2006). Such seminars could be organized in Brazil, building on the experience of the National Forum.

To help develop more effective e-leaders for both governments and the private sector in Brazil, developing executive MPA programs could make effective contributions. If 25–50 future leaders were to be trained in such a program each year over a period of 5 years, Brazil would have a cadre of skilled leaders with training in e-transformation, ICT trends, knowledge economy, political economy, and public administration that could contribute greatly to the execution of a successful e-development strategy.

[69] See Knight and Schiavo (2007) and the National Forum site, http://www.inae.org.br, accessed 24 June 2010.

Finally, it is necessary to identify politicians at all government levels who are motivated and to draw on their support. Political leadership is critical to implement successful e-development projects at the municipal, state, and federal levels that can provide further evidence of what it is possible to accomplish by pursuing such a strategy. This, in turn, will help build further support for a more focused and aggressive pursuit of the strategy at all levels of Brazil's federal system.

Developing these kinds of strategic communication campaigns and educational programs to build national consensus and capacity will require substantial funding and commitment. But they could play a critical role in Brazil's future e-development.

Acknowledgments The author wishes to thank Ciro Campos Christo Fernandes and Maria Alexandra Cunha, coeditors and authors of Knight et al. (2007) and the other 58 authors of the 40 chapters in that book, a number of which are cited in this chapter (see summary references in footnotes and full references at the end of the chapter). This chapter draws heavily on the *e-Brasil* project's publications to analyze Brazil's e-development through October 2010 and prospects for the future.

References

Accenture, 2007. *Leadership in Customer Service: Delivering on the Promise*. Government Executive Series. Accenture, no city given.

Amadeu da Silveira, Sergio. 2004 "SoftwareLivre.Gov.Br. Presentation [apparently] made at UNCTAD XI Conference São Paulo, 13–18 June. Available at http://r0.unctad.org/ecommerce/event_docs/fossem/amadeu.pdf. Accessed 17 October 2008.

Araújo, Wagner Frederico Gomes de. 2007. "e-Legislativo e as possibilidades democrátiocas da internet no Brasil. Chapter 32 in Knight, Fernandes and Cunha (2007), pp. 703–723.

Associação Brasileira da Indústria Elétrica e Eletrônica – ABINEE. 2009. *Panorama Econômico e Desempenho Setorial, 2009*. São Paulo: ABINEE, 2008. Available at www.abinee.org.br/abinee/decon/decon40.htm Accessed 10 November 2009.

Associação Brasileira de Software (ABES). 2005. *Mercado Brasileiro de Software: Panorama e Tendências - 2005*. São Paulo: ABES. Available at www.abes.org.br/templ2.aspx?id=306&sub=306. Accessed 9 November 2009.

Associação Brasileira de Software (ABES). 2007. Brazilian Software Market: Scenario and Trends – 2007. São Paulo: ABES. Available at www.abes.org.br/templ2.aspx?id=306&sub=306. Accessed 9 November 2009.

Associação Brasileira de Software (ABES). 2008. Brazilian Software Market: Scenario and Trends – 2008. São Paulo: ABES. Available at www.abes.org.br/templ2.aspx?id=306&sub=306. Accessed 9 November 2009.

Associação Brasileira de Software (ABES). 2009. Brazilian Software Market: Scenario and Trends – 2009. São Paulo: ABES. Available at www.abes.org.br/templ2.aspx?id=306&sub=306. Accessed 9 November 2009.

Associação Brasileira de Software (ABES). 2010. Brazilian Software Market: Scenario and Trends – 2010. São Paulo: ABES. Available at www.abes.org.br/templ2.aspx?id=306&sub=306. Accessed 27 October 2010.

Assumpção, Rodrigo and Maurício Falavigna. 2004. "Sampa.org: Um projeto de inclusão digital", Chapter 9.1 in Chahin et al. (2004) pp 254–260.

Assumpção, Rodrigo and Cristina Mori. 2007. "Inclusão Digital: discursios, práticas e um longo caminho a percorrer", Chapter 19 in Knight, Fernandes and Cunha (2007), pp 431–442.

Baggio, Rodrigo and Cristina di Luca. 2004. "Escolas de Informática e Cidadania e Inclusão Digital", Chapter 9.2 in Chahin et al. (2004), pp 261–268.

Barbosa, Alexandre Fernandes, Fernando Inácio de Faria and Sólon Lemos Pinto. 2007/ "Governança eletrônica no setor público." Chapter 23 in Knight, Fernandes and Cunha (2007), pp 512–537.

Barbosa Filho, André and Cosette Castro. 2007. "Convergência digital analisada sob o prisma da Nova Ordem Tecnológica". Chapter 14 in Knight, Fernandes and Cunha (2007), pp 332–344.

Bichara de Oliveira, Claudine, Daniel Domeneghetti and Cid Torquao. 2007. "Mercado Brasileiro em rede: uma visão do comércio eletrônico no Brasil", Chapter 37 in Knight, Fernandes and Cunha (2007), pp 795–834.

Bittencourt, Fernando. 2007. "Televisão aberta brasileira: rumo ao digital". Chapter 18 in Knight, Fernandes and Cunha (2007), pp 413–430.

Bocchino, Elizabeth Veloso. 2007. "Papel da comunicação eletrônica de massa na construção do e-Brasil". Chapter 12 in Knight, Fernandes and Cunha, 2007, pp 292–317.

Booz and Company. 2009. "Brasil Digital – Alavancando TIC para Estímulo Econômico". Background slides for Brasscom presentation at 53° Painel Telebrasil, Guarajá, São Paulo, 27 August. Available at www.telebrasil.org.br/painel/53/index.asp?m=capa.htm#Resumo%20do%20Painel, accessed 13 November 2009.

Braquehais, Antonio de Paula. 2004. "CorreiosNet: O papel dos Correios na era digital", Chapter 9.4 in Chahin et al (2004), pp 278–285.

Brasscom (Associação Brasileira de Companhias de Tecnologias de Informação e Comunicação). 2009. Presentation at 53° Painel Telebrasil, Guarujá, São Paulo, 27 August. Available at www.telebrasil.org.br/painel/53/index.asp?m=capa.htm#Resumo%20do%20Painel, accessed 13 November 2009.

Brazilian Court of Audit. 2006. *Electronic Government Program Evaluation*. Executive Summaries. New series. Brasília: Brazilian Court of Audit (*Tribunal das Contas da União* – TCU).

Brazilian Government. 2009. *e-PING: Electronic Government Interoperability Standards, Version 2010*. Brasília: Executive Committee for Electronic Government, 11 December. Available at www.governoeletronico.gov.br/acoes-e-projetos/e-ping-padroes-de-interoperabilidade/versoes-do-documento-da-e-ping (accessed 24 June 2010).

Brazilian Network Information Center (CETIC.BR). 2010. *Survey on the Use of Information and Communication Technologies in Brazil: ICT Households and ICT Enterprises 2009*. Brazilian Internet Steering Committee. Available in both English and Portuguese at http://www.cetic.br/usuarios/index.htm (accessed 24 June 2010). in pdf files which can be downloaded, as are the surveys for the years 2005–2008. All tables for these publications are available in html as well.

Camarão, Paulo. 2004. "e-Eleições". Chapter 7.4 in Chahin et al. (2004), pp 204–216.

CBEC-EAESP/FVG. *e-Brasil. Tecnologia da Informação para o Desenvolvimento.*Câmara Brasileira de e-Comércio e Escola de Administração de Empresas de São Paulo. São Paulo: Fundação Getulio Vargas. 2002. Available at: www.camara-e.net/_upload/ebrasil.pdf, accessed 13 November 2009.

Chahin. Ali. Maria Alexandra Cunha, Peter T. Knight, and Solon Lemos Pinto. (eds.). 2004. *E-gov.br – A Próxima Revolução Brasileira*. São Paulo: Prentice Hall/Financial Times. 2004. Exerpts available in Portuguese and English at: www.tedbr.com/projetos/e-dem.br/e-dem.br.htm, accessed 13 November 2009.

Coelho, Franklin Dias. 2007. "Cidades digitais: caminhos de um programa nacional de inclusão digital", chapter 21 in Knight, Fernandes and Cunha (2007), pp 460–488.

Corrêa, Isabel Moreira (2007). "A política de incremento da transparência do governo federal brasileiro", XII Congreso Internacional del CLAD sobre la Reforma del Estado y de la Administración Pública, Santo Domingo, República Dominicana, 2007.

Cunha, Maria Alexandra, Daniel Annenberg, and Roberto Meizi Agune. 2007. "Prestação de serviços públicos eletrônicos aio cidadão." Chapter 25 in Knight, Fernandes, and Cunha (2007), pp 559–584.

da Costa, Eduardo Moreira. 2007. "Formação de e-lideranças no Bric para promover a sociedade em rede." Chapter 13 in Knight, Fernandes and Cunha (2007), pp 318–330.

Dahlman, Carl J, Jorma Routti and Pekka Yä Anttila. 2006. *Finland as a Knowledge Economy: Elements of Success and Lessons Learned.* Washington, DC: World Bank Institute.

Diniz, Vagner and Álvario Gregório. 2007. "Do e-Governo Eletrônico para o m-Gov Cidadania Móvel." Chapter 31 in Knight, Fernandes, and Cunha (2007), pp 688–702.
e-Bit. 2008. *Web Shopppers 18a edição*. (first semester 2008). Available at http://www.webshoppers.com.br/webshoppers.asp (accessed 22 October 2008).
Economist Intelligence Unit. 2008. *E-readiness rankings 2008 – maintaining momentum*. Available at http://a330.g.akamai.net/7/330/25828/20080331202303/graphics.eiu.com/upload/ibm_ereadiness_2008.pdf, accessed 13 November 2009.
Eira, Luiz Antonio Souza da and Luciano Alberto Rocha. 2004. "Sileg: Sistema de Informações Legislativas". Chapter 7.5 in Chahin et al. (2004), pp 217–233.
Fernandes, Ciro Campos Christo and Pinto, Solon Lemos. 2003. "Sociedad de la Información en Brasil: balance y perspectivas", *Nueva Sociedad* 187, Caracas, Venezuela, September/October, pp. 153–168.
Fernandes, Ciro Campos Christo, 2004. "Impactos dos sistemas de compras eletrônicas na administração pútlica: O caso de Sisag/Comprasnet". Chapter 8.2 in Chahin, et al, (2004), pp 234–252.
Fernandes, Ciro Campos Christo. 2007. "Organização do governo eletrônico no Brasil: situação atuyal, problemas e propostas". Chapter 22 in Knight, Fernandes, and Cunha (2007), pp 490–511.
Ferraz, Claudio e Frederico Frederico Finan. 2007. "Exposing Corrupt Politicians: The effects of Brazil's Publicly-Released Audits on Electoral Outcomes" September. Available at www.econ.ucla.edu/ffinan/Finan_Audit.pdf. Accessed 21 October 2008.
Ferrer. Florência Ferrer and Paula Santos. 2004. e-Government: o governo eletrônico no Brasil. São Paulo. Saraiva.
Ferrer, Florencia and Christian Lima. 2007. "Introdução de mudanças tecnológicas no setor público: por onde começar?" Chapter 27 in Knight, Fernandes and Cunha (2007), pp 626–638.
Gomes Fernandes, Andréa Campos. 2004. Negócios eletrônicos e compras públicasz: A experiência brasilieira em G2B". Capítulo 8.1 in Chahin et al. (2004), pp 224–233.
Gutierrez, Regina Maria Vinhais. 2007. "Complexo eletrônico : O setor de software brasileiro e o Prosoft", *BNDES Setorial, Rio de Janeiro, n. 26* (September), p. 25–62.
Hanna, Nagy K. 2007a. *E-Leadership Institutions for the Knowledge Economy*. Washington, D.C.: World Bank Institute.
Hanna, Nagy. 2007b. "Instituições de e-liderança: opções, inovações e lições da experiência". Chapter 9 in Knight, Fernandes and Cunha (2007), pp 194–220.
Hanna, Nagy K. 2010. e-Transformation: Enabling New Development Strategies. Springer, New York.
Instituto Brasileiro de Geografia e Estatística (IBGE). 2010. *Pesquisa Nacional por Amostra de Domicílios - 2009*. Rio de Janeiro: IBGE. Tables may be prepared by consulting www.sidra.ibge.gov.br/pnad/pnadpb.asp. Accessed 20 August 2010.
Ipnews. 2008. "Sete milhões de brasileiros fazem compras pela Internet". 15 September 2008. Available at www.ipnews.com.br/voip/pesquisas/pesquisas/sete-milhoes-de-brasileiros-fazem-compras-pela-internet.html. Accessed 22 October 2008.
ITData Consultoria. 2008a "Mercado Brasileiro de Serviços Profissionais em 2007", press release, 25 June 2008, available at www.itdata.com.br/prs/index.php?location=prs&id=21. Accessed 12 Ocober 2008.
ITData Consultoria. 2008b. "Software Livre é utilizado por 73% das maiores empresas do país" web press release, 25 June., available at www.itdata.com.br/prs/index.php?location=prs&id=18 (accessed 12 October 2008).
Knight, Peter T. and Carlos Alberto Wanderley. "O Sistema de Pagamentos Brasileiro (SPB)", Chapter 4.4 in Chahin et. al (2004), pp 103–115.
Knight. Peter. *Rumo ao e-Brasil*. 2006. Rio de Janeiro: Garamond. 2006.
Knight, Peter Titcomb. 2007. "BR-e: estradas digitais via satélite para a interiorização do desenvolvimento", Chapter 17 in Knight, Fernandes and Cunha (2007), pp 394–412.
Knight. Peter Titcomb and Ciro Campos Christo Fernandes (Eds.). 2006. *e-Brasil: Um programa para acelerar o desenvolvimento socioeconômico aproveitando a convergência digital*. São Caetano do Sul. São Paulo: Yendis.
Knight. Peter Titcomb. Ciro Campos Christo Fernandes. and Maria Alexandra Cunha (eds.). 2007. *e-Desenvolvimento no Brasil e no mundo: subsídios e Programa e-Brasil*. São Caetano do Sul. São Paulo: Yendis.

Knight, Peter Titcomb and Marcio Ruiz Schiavo. 2007. "Desenvolvimento de um consenso nacional", Chapter 11 in Knight, Fernandes and Cunha (2007), pp. 273–291.
Knight, Peter and Daniel Annenberg. 2008. "Brazil's Experience with Integrated Citizen Service Centers. PowerPoint Presentation at Zelenograd Prefecture, Moscow, Russian Federation, 28 May.
Knight, Peter T. and Rosane Marques. (2008). "Closing the Technology Gap". Chapter in Jerry Haar and John Price, *Can Latin America Compete? Confronting the Challenges of Globalization*. New York: Palgrave McMillan.
Knight, Peter T. 2008a. "Teaching, research and community networks in Brazil", *Connect World*, Latin American Edition, pp 7–9 Available at http://www.connect-world.com/PDFs/magazines/2008/LA_2008.pdf (Accessed 17 October 2008).
Knight, Peter T. 2008b. "Novas parcerias para a inclusão bancária" *Banco Hoje*, March 2008, p. 20. Available at www.tedbr.com/publicacoes/bancohoje2008/bancohoje03-08.htm. Accessed 25 October 2008.
Núcleo de Assuntos Estratégicos. 2005. O projeto Brasil em Três Tempos – 2007/2015/2022. Cadernos NAE n. 1. Núcleo de Assuntos Estratégicos: Brasília.
Pessi, Patrícia. 2007. "Serviços públicos por meios eletrônicos – uma visão orientado ao cidadão. Chapter 24 in Knight, Fernandes and Cunha, 2007, pp. 538–558.
Receita Federal. 2007. *Consolidação da Declaração do Imposto de Renda das \Pessoas Físicas – 2003*. Estatísticas Tributárias 12. Brasília: Receita Federal, January. Available at www.receita.fazenda.gov.br/Publico/estudotributarios/estatisticas/ConsolidaDirpf2003.pdf. Accessed 21 October 2008.
Reinhard, Nicolau, Peter T. Knight and Cesar Souza. 2008. "Developing ICT Management Competence in Brazilian Public Administration". Unpublished paper, September.
Reuters. 2008. "Urnas eletrônicas terão Linux e biometria em 2008" 17 September. Available at http://tecnologia.terra.com.br/interna/0,,OI3190147-EI4801,00.html Accessed 21 October 2008.
Rodrigues, José Geraldo Loureiro. 2004. "Controle, transparência e acesso a informação no governo federal do Brasil: o portal da transparência". X Congreso Internacional del CLAD sobre la Reforma del Estado y de la Administración Pública, Santiago, Chile, 18–21 October.
Santanna dos Santos, Rogério, Leandro Corte, and Leonardo Boselli da Motta. 2007. "Padrões de interoperabilidade de governo eletrônico – e-Ping e a prestação de serviços ao cidadão". Chapter 30 in Knight, Fernandes and Cunha, 2007, pp. 668–687.
Scartezini, Vanda. 2007 "Software e serviços no Brasil visão crítica e propostas". Chapter 39 in Knight, Fernandes and Cunha (2007), pp. 865–892.
Simões, Nelson and Stanton, Michael (2006), "Optical Networking for Brazil's Higher Education and Research Community", presentation at Customer Empowered Fibre Networks Workshop, Prague, May.
Stanton, Michael A and Nelson Simões da Silva. (2007). "Optical Networking for Brazil's Higher Education and Research Community". Paper presented at Interworking 2006, conference organized by the Engineering School of the Universidad de Chile, 15–17 January 2007,Santiago, Chile. Santiago, Chile. Available at http://www.ic.uff.br/~michael/pubs/interworking2006-nova-rnp.pdf. Accessed 15 September 2008.
Stefanuto, Giancarlo Nuti and Sergio Salles-Filho (Coordinators). 2005. *Impact of the Free Software and Open Source on the Software Industry in Brazil*. Campinas: Softex.
Stefanuto, Giancarlo Nuti, Paulo Bastos Tigre, Ana Maria Carneiro, and Felipe Silveira Marques. 2007. "Tecnologias de visualização na indústria de broadcasting digital: potencial econômico e tecnológico para a indústria brasileira de software. Chapter 40 in Knight, Fernandes and Cunha (2007), pp. 893–914.
Takahashi. Tadao (ed.). 2000. *Sociedade da Informação no Brasil: Livro Verde*. Brasília. Ministério da Ciência e Tecnologia. September. Available in pdf format at www.mct.gov.br/index.php/content/view/18878.html, accessed 13 November 2009.
Takahashi, Tadao. "Rumo a um e-Brasil: pontos a ponderar". Chapter 10 in Knight, Fernandes and Cunha (2007), pp 222–262.
Telcomp (Associação Brasileira das Prestadoras de Serviços de Telecomunicações Competitivas). 2009. *ICT 2020: Transformation Strategies for Brazil: Proposal for a Broadband National*

Plan. (October). Also published in Portuguese. Both versions available in pdf at http://www.telcomp.org.br/Documentos/TIC2020.pdf (accessed 12 November 2009).

Telebrasil (Associação Brasileira de Telecomunicações). 2009. "Carta de Guarujá". Document prepared at 53º Painel Telebrasil, Guarajá, São Paulo, 27 August. Available at www.telebrasil.org.br/painel/53/index.asp?m=capa.htm#Resumo%20do%20Painel, accessed 13 November 2009.

Toledo, Paulo. 2004. "Inclusão Digital: Uma proposta empreendedorista", Chapter 9.3 in Chahin et al. (2004), pp 269–277.

Tribunal de Contas da União. 2005a. Relatório de Auditoria Operacional realizada no Fundo de Universalização de Serviços de Telecomunicações – Fust". TC-010.889/2005-5. Brasília, Tribunal de Contas da União.

Tribunal de Contas da União. 2005b. " Acórdão No 2.148/2005 TCU – Plenário. Brasília: Tribunal de Contas da União, 12 December.

Tribunal de Contas de União. 2006. "Avaliação do Programa Governo Eletrônico: Recomendações. Acórdão 1386/2006 – Plenário". Brasília: Tribunal de Contas da União, 2006.

Tyler, William. 2007. "Aplicação de métodos de e-governo às transaç~oes comerciais internacionais: o caso do Brasil". Chapter 38 in Knight, Cunha and Fernandes (2007), pp 835–864.

Vedana, Vilson. 2007. "O futuro é a internet gratuita", Chapter 20 in Knight, Fernandes and Cunha (2007), pp 443–457.

World Bank. 2005. *World Development Indicators. 2005.* Washington: The World Bank. 2005.

World Bank. 2010. *World Development Indicators. 2010.* Washington: The World Bank.

Chapter 3
China's Evolving Informatization Strategy

Nagy K. Hanna and Christine Zhen-Wei Qiang

Since the mid-1990s China has devoted considerable resources to developing its informatization strategy and conducted extensive research to determine the appropriate framework and goals for building an information society.[1] Strong leadership at the national, provincial, and municipal levels, combined with a sustained, long-term focus from the highest levels of the Chinese government on developing information and communication technology (ICT), have given ICT a prominent role in sustainable development strategies and ensured its application to core economic and social goals.

China's recent economic growth has expanded industrialization and urbanization, upgraded consumption, increased social mobility, and initiated a shift from an economy based on agriculture to one based on industry and services. Still, more than half of China's people still live in rural areas – where average income per capita is less than a third of the urban average,[2] a gap that is among the largest in the world. Reducing these differences is critical to building a harmonious, inclusive society.

In its 11th Five-Year Plan (covering 2006–2010), China has adopted a new development paradigm that emphasizes the building of a Harmonious Society (*he xie she hui*) with more balanced development across regions. The new development paradigm adopts a "scientific view of the development process" that emphasizes sustainable growth and "people-centered development." Accordingly, the government has substantially increased its commitment to propoor, prorural programs. This new approach is reflected in numerous official statements and many new programs introduced in recent years. However, the growth dynamics unleashed by economic liberalization and fast technological development will make such paradigm shift very

[1] This chapter uses the Chinese government's terminology of informatization, defined as the transformation of an economy and society driven by information and communications technology, and uses it interchangeably with the terms information society, knowledge economy, and e-development.

[2] China urban–rural income gap continues to widen http://in.reuters.com/article/asiaCompanyAndMarkets/idINPEK1715020080124.

N.K. Hanna and P.T. Knight (eds.), *Seeking Transformation Through Information Technology*, Innovation, Technology, and Knowledge Management,
DOI 10.1007/978-1-4614-0353-1_3, © Springer Science+Business Media, LLC 2011

challenging, and will require coherent integration of ICT with poverty reduction and regional strategies to help the lagging regions.

This chapter examines the long-term focus on China on leveraging ICT for development, competitiveness, and social harmony. It has two parts. The first part takes a holistic view of China's informatization (e-development, e-transformation) strategy. It describes the status of China's Informatization strategy in terms of key ICT enablers and application areas. The second part identifies future sources of growth and systemic problems underlying poverty and inequities. The challenge of rural informatization is examined because the digital divide persists between urban and rural, and more than half of China's population lives in rural areas. The broad thrusts for ICT applications across sectors are then identified. They are used, in turn, to guide the development of informatization enablers and building blocks. This e-development framework is used to identify key gaps and weaknesses in each enabler as well as synergies and cross-cutting coordination issues that need to be managed to support ICT application priorities and achieve national development goals. The latter cross-cutting issues are also examined relative to rural informatization.

Assessment of Past Achievements

An overall assessment of China's informatization efforts and achievements would cover the institutions leading these efforts, the legal and regulatory reforms necessary to create an ICT-enabled economy, the massive development of the telecommunications infrastructure, the promotion of the IT industry as a key engine for export, and the diverse application of ICT in government, business, and rural development. Progress on all these fronts was motivated by a shared belief among Chinese leaders that ICT can transform the economy and society. Yet, China lacked a coherent overarching informatization strategy and coordinating mechanisms to tap the potential synergies and ensure optimal sequencing of investments on these interdependent fronts.

Institutional Leadership

In 1993, China's State Council established a high-level National Economic Information Joint Committee. The committee launched the first-tier and second-tier Golden Projects to promote informatization focused on economic goals. These projects were designed to facilitate China's transition from strictly administrative use of ICT applications to more public service-oriented uses; in 1997 the Outline of the National Informatization Development Plan established a framework for promoting informatization, supporting the development of related policies and regulations, information resources (content), network infrastructure, applications, the information technology (IT) industry, and human resources.

In 2000, the Fifth Plenary Session of the 15th Central Committee of the Communist Party of China established a strategy of "promoting industrialization through informatization" (Qu 2005). In 2001 the State Council Informatization Office, headed by the premier, was created to generate policy proposals, coordinate strategy implementation, draft laws and regulations, set standards, and develop plans for China's information society. Guidelines to promote e-government and support the development of China's software industry were also issued.

Over time, China's e-leadership institutional framework has moved from one of shared responsibility without clear policy coordination to one of improved policy coordination but still widely diffused responsibility for e-development program coordination and implementation. For a country as large and diverse as China, governance of the informatization agenda and leadership in implementing it are major, ongoing challenges. Top-down, authoritarian visions must compete with bottom-up, liberal visions. Key players and a wide range of institutions have to bargain intensely over how to restructure the rules of the game.

Whether called the information industry, Internet, digitalization, or informatization, political elites have viewed these new technologies as resources for enhancing China's advancement while maintaining their influence and political stability. As the knowledge economy and Internet activity have quickly grown, ministries and agencies have tried to carve out bigger pieces of these processes for themselves. Sectoral Golden Projects have proliferated since 2002, ranging from internal automation to online transactions and applications for trade and customs, payment systems, government portals, Internet and government intranets, tax administration, and sector-specific applications involving agriculture, health, insurance, and tourism, among others. These projects have involved one or more leading ministry, numerous other participants, or both. Much of this action has been driven by institutional entrepreneurship, social connections, and extensive networks.

This context has made it difficult to develop an overarching institutional framework for informatization. A key challenge has been to address the complexity and uncertainty of the division of legal and regulatory responsibilities and their lack of coordination in the ICT sector. The absence of a legal framework stipulating the principles and scope of informatization has made regulations unclear. Cooperation among regulatory departments is weak, and China's myriad agencies have different and sometimes overlapping responsibilities. As a result many agencies often regulate the same area – yet accountability is lacking and the resulting regulations are inconsistent, making implementation and execution of laws and regulations problematic.

In addition, China lacks a coordinating authority that can prioritize ICT investments and help facilitate project implementation at the national level. Weak coordination and persistent interagency conflicts have contributed to redundant and overlapping initiatives. Although institutional mechanisms for coordinating ICT use in government are emerging, their functions remain limited. An e-government unit in the Ministry of Finance controls a small part of the budget for e-government proposals. The State Council Informatization Office, a specialized body, provides guidelines for overall e-government development and technical assessments of aspects such as ranking government Websites.

Informatization in rural areas is a special case where institutional leadership and coordination are most needed but lacking. Many ministries and government agencies at all levels (from central to local) are involved in rural informatization projects with similar goals, but with individual mandates and limited coordination. Every ministry has initiated its own informatization program, such as the Golden Agriculture (Jing Nong) Project under the Ministry of Agriculture and the National Cultural Information Resources Sharing Project under the Ministry of Culture. Other key players include the Ministries of Information Industry, Commerce, Education, and Science and Technology.

Agencies with primary policy and coordination functions have also engaged in national and provincial pilot projects. These agencies include the National Development and Reform Commission, Central Committee of Communist Party of China, State Council Leading Group Office of Poverty Alleviation and Development, and Ministry of Finance. Centrally driven but fragmented programs and administrative silos impede horizontal resource sharing and network integration.

In addition to centrally driven programs, every province considers rural informatization an important part of local socioeconomic development plans. Collaboration practices vary among provinces. In one province, for instance, a government department in charge of monitoring the safety of roads and bridges as well as utility infrastructure had to pay another department a considerable amount of money to acquire the latter's electronic maps and the updates that form the basis of its information management systems.

This contrasts with a case in another province where the Department of Industry and Commerce, in charge of issuing business licenses and registration, and the Tax Bureau decided to share information on registered companies. Better enterprise management and extra tax collection were achieved as a result. This collaboration was based on a good relationship between these two departmental units, not as part of a structured process established at all levels of government. In addition to the establishment of a cross-functional department that promotes collaborative actions, policies that address access to government and public information are urgently needed to ensure the proper sharing of information among government departments for the interests of the general public.

Institutional leadership issues are also critical for enhancing telecommunications infrastructure and exploiting the rapid technological convergence of telecommunications, broadcasting, and the Internet. The division of responsibility remains vague (Fig. 3.1). The Ministry of Information Industry has been the main regulator of telecommunications and e-commerce. The State Administration of Radio, Film, and Television regulates broadcasting networks and television administration. Several bodies under the State Council also contribute to ICT and e-commerce regulation. For example, the State Council Informatization Leading Group formulates national ICT policies, coordinates ministries and bureaus, and settles disputes among them

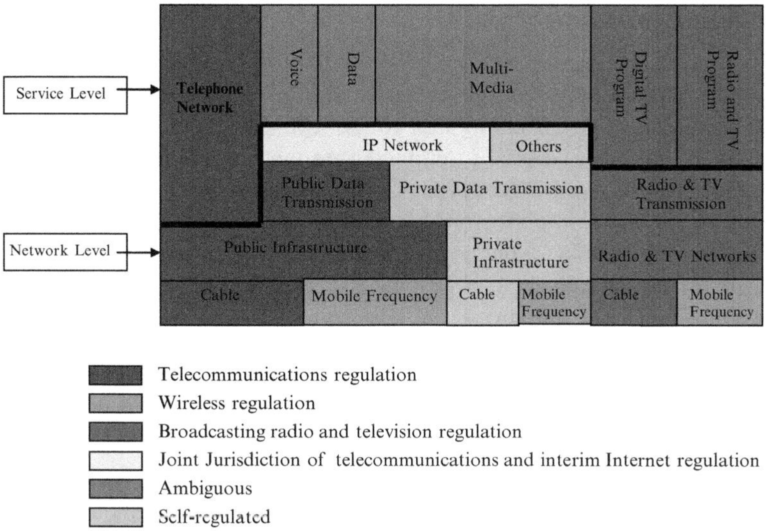

Fig. 3.1 Regulatory jurisdictions for China's ICT services and networks. Source: Qiang (2007)

on ICT policies. The National Development and Reform Commission and the State Economic and Trade Commission oversee funding and operations of state enterprises, influencing the diffusion of e-commerce.

Given China's size and diversity, and the multiplicity of stakeholders, duplications and inconsistencies are bound to arise. But having different ministries and agencies each doing things their own way has led to duplicated efforts and wasted resources. Redundant investments and scattered resources raise serious problems of affordability, sustainability, and scalability. No policy and institutional mechanisms are in place to raise awareness, overcome interdepartmental rivalry, and foster close coordination, collaboration, and synergy at any level of administration.

The March 2008 People's Congress approved establishing a Ministry of Industry and Informatization, incorporating the Ministry of Information Industry, parts of the National Development and Reform Commission, the State Council Informatization Office, most of the Commission of Science and Technology for National Defense, and the State Tobacco Monopoly Administration. The new ministry's main duties include implementing industrial planning, setting industry policies and standards, supervising the daily operation of industry enterprises, pushing the development and self-innovation of major technology equipment manufacturers, managing the communications industry, guiding the construction of informatization, and protecting national information safety (China TechNews 2008). This reform aimed to eliminate overlapping responsibilities in China's vast bureaucracy and increase efficiency. Only the passing of time will determine whether the new ministry can achieve those goals.

Enabling Environment

Given the complex and cross-cutting nature of ICT, creating the right environment for its development is a daunting task for policymakers. China's policy and legal environment has been adapted to promote informatization. The E-Signature Law went into effect in April 2005 (Letner 2005). Regulations on publicizing government information came into effect on May 1, 2008.[3] The draft new Telecommunications Law was made available for public review and comments in early 2009. In addition, many provincial and municipal governments have dedicated resources to coordinating and managing ICT initiatives.

Despite progress in developing the enabling environment, China's legal and regulatory framework for informatization faces several challenges. The legal framework for the enabling environment is quite complex – contributing to the institutional and regulatory competition and overlap – and, in some cases, underdeveloped.

Several areas of the legal framework will require high-level legislation in the short and medium term. The government has sometimes taken a bottom-up approach to legislation – allowing precedence and practices to take hold first, then legislating practices. This approach is useful for legal reform, because it provides rich experiences based on current legal practices and ensures a smooth legislative transition. But it carries greater risks because it is not systematic and often creates conflicts among departmental jurisdictions.

Major Areas of Reform

Major areas of legal and regulatory reform in support of China's informatization include telecommunications, network security, Internet content, data protection and privacy, open access to government Information, stronger protection of intellectual property rights, and cyber crime. The following seven areas are the top priorities for improving the enabling environment for ICT in China:

- *Telecommunications.*[4] China's telecommunications sector has experienced rapid technological advancement and growth in new services. Market entry requirements need to be reconsidered to support further competition and innovation. In addition, the market involves a host of new players, creating interconnection issues that should be addressed by the legal system. With increasing competition and more foreign service providers entering the domestic market, new legal and regulatory issues are expected to emerge. Finally, the provision and framework of universal service obligations need to be addressed.

---

[3] http://www.law.yale.edu/intellectuallife/openinformation.htm.

[4] China's draft new Telecommunications Law was made available for public review and comments early 2009. But it is still not issued after being in the drafting status for 30 years.

- *Network security.* Information network security law focuses on ensuring the stability of China's computer networks, which are under constant threat from viruses and other menaces as well as from hackers trying to access government and private networks and data. Accordingly, China needs stronger policies, laws, and consultative processes to ensure the security of networks.
- *Internet content.* China's Internet content regulators determine whether content is consistent with social values and focus on preventing dissemination of information that the government considers illegal. Unlike information network security, which mainly deals with data and network protection, Internet content regulation involves placing regulations on what Chinese people can read, see, and hear on the Internet. Although regulation occurs at different levels and the existing legal framework largely results in self-censorship, technological advances make Internet content regulation an increasingly costly undertaking for the government.
- *Data protection and privacy.* Abuse of personal information has become an issue in China's developed urban areas, yet there is no specific law protecting consumers. Releasing personal information that does not infringe on the reputation of the subject is not considered illegal. To avoid harassment, consumers often provide false information or refuse to give personal information online – hampering the development of China's credit reporting system.
- *Open access to government information.* The Chinese government is interested in providing the public with more information and considers increased transparency and accountability crucial to eliminating corruption. Still, despite efforts to introduce freedom of information programs, China does not have a specific law requiring the government to provide information. Moreover, the cost of accessing information is still relatively high. Although the government has built its capacity to provide information to the public, further legal reform is needed to make information administration more open and effective. A government information access law would provide a legal basis to support the free flow of information and the development of e-government.
- *Stronger protection of intellectual property rights.* One of the main remaining causes for concern in the protection of intellectual property rights is piracy, which poses an obstacle to conducting business in China for both domestic and foreign investors. Even though China relies heavily on open source software (e.g., to circumvent piracy issues related to proprietary software and reduce dependence on foreign proprietary code), the essence of the "openness" of open source software relies on robust copyright protection. China recognizes that it is in its interest to address these issues. The government has recently taken steps in the computing and software areas, adopting directives to safeguard software copyrights.
- *Cyber crime.* The main issues to be addressed in legislation dealing with cyber crime are illegal data interception, data interference, system interference and access, and other crimes facilitated by computers. The Criminal Code already makes unauthorized access to computer systems illegal. It should also be clarified that other criminal matters in the physical world (forgery, fraud, copyright

infringement, and production and distribution of obscene or pornographic material) apply equally to the virtual world of the Internet as they do to the physical world. Some of these may be dealt with through amendments to existing laws; others may require new laws.

The structure of the legal system remains unbalanced in terms of rights and obligations. Many laws and regulations are designed for administrative convenience, which is often considered more important than individual or enterprise rights. Among enacted laws and regulations, there are far more restrictive provisions than provisions for other measures, such as self-regulation and dispute resolution. Obligations are given more weight than the legal rights of subjects. An emphasis on processes and procedures (such as licensing) has overlooked protection of privacy and individual rights. Inadequate attention is paid to protect copyrights and personal data. An enabling legal and regulatory system should focus on encouraging innovation and avoid restrictive provisions on research and development (R&D) that hinder technological change and economic development.

Information Infrastructure

Over the past decade China has made enormous progress in developing its telecommunications infrastructure. In the context of liberalization in 2002, basic telecom licenses were issued to five state-owned operators – China Telecom, China Netcom, China Unicom, China Mobile, and China Railcom – with each focusing on different market segments (Table 3.1). This approach has introduced competition among fixed and mobile telephone and Internet service providers (ISPs). But the government's entry policy allows only network-based competition, which explains the limited entry observed in China's telecommunications market.

The government's goal was to balance concerns about excess investment and effective competition, and to nurture three or four large state-owned operators before China's telecommunications market was fully opened to foreign investors, in compliance with the country's World Trade Organization (WTO) commitments. Since then, foreign operators such as Telefónica (Spain) and Vodafone (United Kingdom) have achieved some minority ownership in the sector.

As of June 2010, China had more than one billion fixed and mobile telephones, making it the world's largest telecommunications market in terms of subscribers (BMI 2010). Overall telephone penetration rate reached 80%. According to BMI analysis, the number of prepaid mobile phone subscribers has been growing (from 74% of total subscribers in 2009 to 76% in 2010), especially in rural areas.[5]

There were 25 million 3G subscribers at the end of June 2010, according to data published by the country's three mobile operators. This represented 14.8 million net additions since 2009. The number is expected to reach 40 million, or close to 5% of

[5] Business Monitor International (BMI). China Telecommunications Report Q4 (2010).

Table 3.1 China's main telecom providers, by market segment

Provider	Owners	Market segment	Market share
China Telecom[a]	Government (70.89%), Guangdong Rising Assets Management (6.94%), Zhejiang Financial Development Company (2.64%), Fujian State-owned Assets (1.2%), Jiangau Guoxin Investment (1.18%), others (17.15%)	Fixed-line telephony (local – southern China, DLD, ILD), data, Internet and mobile (CDMA)	10% of the mobile market share, 50% of the broadband market share
China Mobile (Hong Kong)[b]	China Mobile (74.25%), public (25.75%)	Fixed-line telephony (local, ILD), data, Internet and mobile (GSM)	(GSM) 70% of the mobile market share
China Unicom[c]	China Unicom (40.92%), China Netcom Group (24.49%), Telefónica Internacional (5.38%), SK Telecom (3.79%), other public share holders (20.42%)	Fixed-line telephony (local northern China, DLD, ILD), data, Internet, mobile (GSM)	(GSM) 20% of the mobile market share; 40% of the broadband market share

Source: BMI (2010)
Note: *DLD* domestic long distance, *ILD* international long distance
[a]Acquired CDMA mobile unit from China Unicom under market restructure
[b]Nationwide coverage via 31 regional subsidiaries, acquired China Railcom (Tietong) fixed-line assets under market restructure
[c]Coverage via 30 regional subsidiaries (nationwide except Guizhou), acquired China Netcom fixed-line assets under market restructure

the total mobile base, by end of 2010 (BMI 2010). Growth of the 3G subscriber base is being led by 3G investments including network deployments, the procurement of 3G handsets, growth in smart phones as well as the growing popularity of mobile broadband services offered over data cards connected to laptops and PCs.

China is also the world's largest Internet and broadband market. Its Internet market is migrating from narrowband to broadband access. As of June 2010, there were 420 million Internet users in China, and about 90% of them connected through broadband. The mobile Internet is another growing trend in China. There were 277 million mobile Internet users as of June 2010, an increase by 18.6% from the previous year. Now 11.7% of the Internet user only use mobile device to access to the Internet (CNNIC 2010). The price for the broadband connection services varies across the providers and the geographical locations, but in general the price has been declining over time. For instance, broadband monthly ARPU by China Telecom dropped from RMB83.8 in 2008 to RMB80 in 2009.[6] The expansion of network and

[6] Telegeography. GlobalComms Database China. http://www.telegeography.com/.

price reduction attracted the lower income people to access the Internet. According to CNNIC, there was a 20% increase in Internet users over the past year whose monthly income is below 500 yuan (about US $75).

IT Industry

China's IT industry has been an engine of economic growth, expanding two to three times faster than GDP over the past 10 years. The industry now accounts for more than 15% of GDP growth – in 2004 it represented 7.5% of GDP, up from 4% in 2001 (Qu 2005). According to the Organization for Economic Cooperation and Development (OECD), China led the world with $180 billion of ICT exports in 2004, surpassing the USA (Qiang 2007). In 2009, IT products account for 25% of China's exports[7] – electronics companies such as Huawei and ZTE are now major multinationals.

The Chinese hardware (IT products and electronics manufacturing) industry was estimated at $320 billion in sales revenues in 2004, more than 40 times larger than India's (Gregory et al. 2009, p. 142). By 2006, the Chinese hardware industry had increased dramatically – to $580 billion. The main product lines in Chinese hardware industry were computers and telecommunications equipment.

Some of the key factors to China's performance in hardware, compared to India's, are: capital is important input into hardware production while labor constitutes a much smaller share than it does in software; Chinese firms had access to capital at lower interest rates and foreign investors supplied much capital; they spent more on R&D; more foreign ownership and management control of Chinese hardware firms thus supplying latest technologies and connections to supply chains; government proactive support and incentives including stronger marketing support, R&D support, and income tax concessions; easier access to land and electric power; access to more mobile skilled labor and less restrictive labor laws; and Chinese managers took advantage of national culture traits that fit with hardware manufacturing requirements for structure, order, control, and discipline in the workplace (Gregory et al. 2009).

Sales revenues for Chinese software industry were $29 billion in 2004, $64 billion in 2006, and $90 billion in the first half of 2010.[8] This compares well with sales revenues for India's well-known software industry: which stood at $40 billion for 2006 (Gregory et al. 2009, p. 56) and $60 billion in 2009.[9] But there are significant

---

[7] Source: US–China Business Council Statistics Website: http://www.uschina.org/statistics/tradetable.html.

[8] http://www.prlog.org/10937057-statistics-and-operation-of-chinese-information-technology-industry.html.

[9] http://www.nasscom.in/upload/SR10/ExecutiveSummary.pdf; http://www.thaindian.com/newsportal/uncategorized/revenues-of-indian-software-industry-to-top-60-billion-nasscom_100150945.html.

differences in the service–product mix between the Chinese and Indian software industries. India's software industry concentrates on software services, with software consulting services and BPO the fastest growing segments, and about 70% of Indian software revenue was generated offshore in 2004. China's industry is much more oriented to software products than India's. A majority of Chinese products and services consists of low-skilled entry-level work. But high domestic demand resulted in substantial systems integration work requiring higher skills.

Again contrasting China with India's software industry performance, some of the distinct factors for growth are rapid expansion of software-using industries as Chinese software industry grew by serving the domestic market, which was growing close to 10% for more than two decades; the need for adaptation to local practices and language provided a ready market for domestic software firms; FDI facilitating international links and packaged software products; and active government promotion through public procurement, for example, encouraging state-owned enterprises to use Chinese software vendors and foreign-owned software companies to use Chinese suppliers. However, in China, and in contrast to India, software firms did not benefit from the same export incentives and hence had grown mainly to serve the domestic market, while hardware manufacturing has been export oriented (Gregory et al. 2009).

China's IT market also features several paradoxes:

- Although China is a leading exporter of semiconductors, it still has to import chips to meet domestic needs.
- Although Chinese firms export third-generation (3G) mobile technologies, these same technologies have yet to be commercialized on the mainland.
- Although Lenovo, China's leading personal computer (PC) firm, is the third largest in the world, there were only 56 million computers in a country with a population of well over one billion people (2008).

The PC industry has followed the same pattern as other technology markets in China. Foreign firms dominated the market until domestic companies became competitive, at which point foreign firms abandoned the low-end market and tried to shift into higher value products. Although foreign firms have fared well in the market for servers, China Langchao is the market leader, and Lenovo is targeting the market.

A major challenge for China's PC industry will be to expand beyond production of machines for the domestic market and low-value peripherals and components for the global market. Given the country's strong technical skills and ability to attract foreign investment and technology, it has a reasonable chance of meeting this challenge. Lenovo is moving into software, Internet services, and information appliances; other hardware makers are expanding their scope as well.

Software is viewed as a key pillar of China's IT industry. Both the central and local governments (such as Beijing and Shanghai) are promoting the industry by facilitating funding for software startups and incubators. For example, Chinese software companies do not have to pay taxes during their first 2 years of operation and receive a 50% tax break in their third and fourth years. The industry also benefits from simplified administrative procedures and relatively fast approval of foreign investment.

In addition, preferential treatment is given to research facilities that successfully commercialize their research, and local governments have provided financial support for the construction of software parks.

In addition, several aspects of the Chinese economy lend themselves to the software industry's growth, such as the manufacturing sector (which uses software in computer and telecommunications equipment) and widespread use of consumer electronic products and automated machinery, all of which require software bundling. The country's 20 million small and medium-sized enterprises provide a substantial business user base for software.

But China's IT services industry faces several problems. Key among them is the industry's fragmented structure. Three-quarters of China's software firms have fewer than 50 employees. Without adequate scale, such companies are unlikely to attract top international clients, secure adequate quality and process controls, attract and provide training and challenging opportunities for talented software engineers, and invest in R&D.

Chinese IT service firms also face extensive challenges involving piracy and intellectual property rights. The government has enacted tough antipiracy laws and conducted publicized crackdowns. There has been some progress in gradually reducing piracy rates. In 2003, about 92% of software in China was pirated (IDC/BSA 2003). According to the China Daily, the piracy rate was reported as 45% in 2009 based on the survey conducted by the State Intellectual Property Office.[10] However, this rate is still high, giving firms little incentive to invest significant R&D resources in creating new products. This is a serious concern for China's software vendors and a major barrier to the development of a packaged software industry.

China aims to develop an IT services industry, like India's, that works for foreign firms. It has even attracted a few Indian IT companies to help build its market. But many Chinese companies lack English language skills, undermining the value of the country's large engineering workforce. In addition, Chinese firms have little or no experience in USA or other foreign markets and so have not worked with clients on the front end – writing business process requirements and creating system architecture and design. The country must develop the long-term human capital required to expand these industries.

Foreign companies moving their software development operations to China have recently become a key driver in China's outsourcing market. Whether such development centers are performing software outsourcing in the traditional sense is debatable, since their main customers may be their corporate parents in their home markets rather than third-party customers. Still, such centers create new software export markets and make China a major link in the global software value chain. Expertise developed at these centers will ultimately diffuse into the broader Chinese market, improving the technical capabilities of domestic software outsourcing firms, which foreign companies may make greater use of in the future. According to a report released in November 2010 by XMG Global, a Canadian-based ICT research

[10] http://www.chinadaily.com.cn/china/2010-05/11/content_9831976.htm.

and advisory firm, China's outsourcing industry is steadily closing the gap with the market leaders. By the end of 2010, the outsourcing industry in China would account for $36 billion, or 28.7% of the global outsourcing market while India maintains its lead capturing $54 billion, or 43.7% of the total.[11]

China has mastered the use of joint ventures and R&D to promote technological capabilities and innovation. It has been encouraging global companies to establish a research institute, center, or laboratory for joint R&D in order to get approval for joint ventures. It has used different approaches to promote technology transfer through collaboration in production, research, and training. At times, market access is made conditional on technology transfer.

Two promising developments may reshape the Chinese software industry: the increasing foreign direct investment (FDI) in China by Indian software companies, and the trend of exporting customized software services to Japanese clients. For customized software services, the Chinese weakness in project management is being overcome by expatriate Indians. In 2006, more than 60% of all Japanese software outsourcing was supplied by Chinese software firms (Gregory et al. 2009).

Human Resources

Human capital is the driving force of an information society. Three levels of ICT human resources are critical to informatization:

- A general public able to use ICT applications at work and home.
- Informatization managers who lead ICT development in government and business.
- ICT professionals experienced in network design, software development, and R&D.

China's compulsory basic education has dramatically increased literacy. Primary completion rate reached more than 96% in 2008. Gross enrollment in secondary and tertiary education has also risen substantially over the past two decades, though it remains lower than in developed countries, Brazil and Russia. For informatization, China's competitive edge will be determined by its population's willingness and ability to acquire information, share knowledge, and use information and communication effectively. As informatization accelerates and the public becomes more aware of its importance for China's economic transformation, the country will need more ICT experts as well as a labor force with adequate ICT skills. It has become a pressing task to improve and expand skills to meet the demand for China's ICT development.

China has enormous demand for ICT skills but faces several challenges in providing the education and training needed to develop them. First, limited awareness

[11] http://english.people.com.cn/90001/90778/90861/7197674.html.

of informatization undermines the general public's interest in and ability to use ICT. The public's ICT capacity is important because it affects the absorption rate of ICT applications. The main reason that Chinese people do not use the Internet is because they do not understand computer and Internet technologies. Another factor contributing to low public awareness is that access to ICT – especially broadband – remains limited in many parts of the country. Public awareness is also critical to building support for China's informatization policies and allocation of investment resources.

Second, as e-government and e-business develop, ICT management expertise has become increasingly crucial. Yet many Chinese firms and government agencies lack the managerial understanding and skills required to integrate ICT applications. Managers may not know their options for ICT solutions and often do not have the information they need to make decisions about allocating resources and efforts on ICT equipment and human resources.

In many organizations IT divisions or information centers are the main source of ICT skills and knowledge. Managers of these units provide technology solutions and supervision but are often not involved in strategic decision making. Mid-level managers do not have authority over other divisions, making informatization planning and coordination and resource allocation and promotion extremely difficult. In addition, most of these IT managers are engineers who have technical knowledge but no timely experience with business or public administration. As a result some e-government and e-business projects in China over the past decade did not have clear impacts – despite huge investments in information systems and business reengineering applications.

Recent initiatives, such as that of the China Information Association, are targeting the creation of chief information officer (CIO) structures in both the public and private sectors. Related on-the-job training in areas such as e-government, informatization planning, and project management is being provided to government leaders, members of the State Council Informatization Leading Group, and IT managers. The main goal of the training is to build recognition among decision makers of the key role of CIOs in optimizing resource use and processes and enhancing efficiency and competitiveness. Another goal is to develop a pipeline of potential CIOs and other ICT managers among university graduates, combining technical skills with business and public administration skills.

Information suggests that a large gap exists between the supply of and demand for ICT workers. According to the China Statistical Book 2009,[12] there are about 1.44 million workers in IT, computer science, and software sector in 2008, which accounted for only 1.2% of China's labor force. This number seems small compared to many developed countries. For instance, according to the national census, the IT, computer science, and software sector employed 2.5% of the total labor force in the USA in 2009.[13]

---

[12] http://www.stats.gov.cn/tjsj/ndsj/2009/indexeh.htm.

[13] United States Department of Labor, Occupational Employment Statistics. http://www.bls.gov/oes/current/oes_nat.htm#00-0000.

Moreover, an internal brain drain from rural to urban areas is a major issue in China. Successful informatization requires a trained and skilled workforce – precisely the types of workers who tend to emigrate. Not only are residents of more developed regions unwilling to work in underdeveloped areas, but also few graduates return to rural areas once they get urban residency. One reason for the migration of skilled labor from China's rural areas is that awareness of the significance of informatization for economic development is not yet well established in underdeveloped areas. Low awareness leads to low investment in ICT infrastructure, impeding further investment in ICT programs. All these factors drive away educated, technologically savvy residents from underdeveloped areas.

E-Government and E-Community

Coordinating the development of e-government in China is a massive undertaking. China is transforming from an agricultural to industrial economy, from a rural to urban society, and from a centrally planned to market economy. Government's role is shifting from micromanagement to macrocoordination. Globalization and membership in the WTO are accelerating this transformation, with major implications for ICT's role in making the government more efficient, effective, and transparent.

Like many countries, China has an entrenched tradition of government secrecy. Chinese scholars estimate that some 80% of useful information in China languishes in government files (Horsley 2004). This culture of secrecy has meant that the government acts as a bottleneck to the free flow of economic, social, and other information that would facilitate continued dynamic growth and development. The lack of transparency also contributes to corruption, misallocation of resources, and distrust of public institutions. Also, this culture could become a binding constraint on practicing open government, using the new tools of social networking in government, and tapping the vast potential for innovation arising from sharing government data (in useable electronic form) with the private sector and civil society.

China's progress on informatization is evident from e-government applications in both central and local governments. The Golden Projects, most of which were introduced in the late 1990s, have facilitated China's transition from a strictly administrative to a more public service-oriented use of ICT applications (Table 3.2). The scope of the projects varies, from automating internal processes to creating interactive Websites allowing online transactions.

Implementation of these projects has been widespread, and some have achieved impressive results. For instance, the e-government system developed for public revenues and expenditures – known as the Golden Tax (e-taxation) project – has enabled value added taxes to be processed and tax invoices audited through Web-based applications, improving tax collection and increasing tax revenues by more than 30% in 2002 relative to 2000. Tax administration authorities in medium-size and large cities now allow enterprises to pay taxes online. In addition, the Golden Gate (e-customs and foreign trade) project has helped reduce smuggling and fraud by

Table 3.2 China's golden projects

Project	Stakeholders	Goal
Tier one (highest profile)		
Golden Gate	Ministry of Foreign Trade, Customs, Jitong Co.	Develop an information network of foreign trade activities to expedite customs clearance and enhance authorities' ability to detect and prevent illegal activities, and collect taxes and duties
Golden Bridge	Ministry of Electronics, State Information Center	Create an infrastructure backbone for the first national economic information network
Golden Card	People's Bank of China, Ministry of Electronics, Ministry of Internal Trade, Great Wall Computer Co.	Create a unified payment settlement system enabling broad use of credit and debit cards
Tier two (designed to apply information networks to expedite economic reform)		
Golden Macro	China Export–Import Bank, Ministry of Finance, State Information Center	Strengthen the central government's (Central Economic and Financial Leading Group) macroeconomic control over national economic activities and analysis capacity
Golden Tax	Ministry of Finance, Ministry of Electronics, National Tax Bureau, Great Wall Computer Co.	Computerize tax collection, prevent tax evasion and fraud, reduce tax losses, and allow customs departments to verify a range of data to facilitate customs management
Golden Wealth	Ministry of Finance	Construct a government financial management information system to support budgeting, payment, and accounting
Tier three (sector-specific IT applications)		
Golden Agriculture	Ministry of Agriculture	Build a databank service network providing agricultural information, weather reports, and market information
Golden Audit	National Audit Office	Transform the reactive audit system to a more proactive one by having a secure platform for information sharing and for tracking, and checking accounts
Golden Quality	Various government departments	Enhance regulation, quality, transparency, and service orientation of government units that conduct quality control activities such as certification of products and services
Golden Social Security	Ministry of Labor and Social Security	Better manage the growing workforce covered by the national insurance system and offer information on retirement and medical services information to the insured
Golden Shield	Ministry of Public Security	Strengthen central police control, responsiveness, and crime-fighting capacity
Golden Water	Ministry of Water Resources	Harness technology for the collection, transfer, storage, and management of water resources; also encompass a system to better manage floods and droughts in the country

Source: Authors' analysis; Yong (2005)

curtailing false customs declarations from 0.227% in early 2001 to 0.004% in late 2003. Because of the Golden Wealth (e-fiscal management) project, nearly 85% of government agencies now use electronic payment management, and have increased the capacity of the treasury payments system to supervise the use of public funds (Qiang 2007).

China's e-government efforts have also contributed to the spread of ICT, particularly in urban areas. Society has increasingly higher demand for public services, including individuals and businesses in a dynamic and competitive environment, disadvantaged populations in cities who want government assistance, and migrant workers requiring diverse, effectively managed services. More than 90% of municipal governments have established websites, and many large cities have developed integrated e-community service platforms in response to growing demand for information services. Examples include Beijing's "review and approval" system, Shanghai's social security card system, Guangzhou's community service platform, and the integrated emergency response system of Nanning city in Guangxi province.

Government-run ICT applications and infrastructure have also supported rural development. A website has been established that collects and provides daily price information for 280 large wholesale agricultural markets and more than 300 agricultural products. In addition, 9,000 villages and towns have been connected to the Internet, raising village coverage to 23%.

Still, some local government officials fail to realize that e-government is not about technological networks, but rather about applying technology for reengineering processes and improving public services. The resulting applications have been driven by technology instead of citizen demand – leading to a structural imbalance between supply and demand. ICT vendors tend to build networks, databases, hardware, and software based on existing technologies and products. Many do not have the capacity to analyze the types of services that are in demand and, as a result, cannot provide mature solutions to the problems the government urgently needs to resolve. Hence, the supply and demand of e-government applications need to be carefully matched.

E-Business

E-enabled enterprise transformation is a long-term and continuous process involving deep changes and innovations in internal processes, external relationships with clients and suppliers, and in the products and services themselves (Hanna 2009b). These changes are interdependent and increasingly overlapping, but for simplification purposes we define informatization at the enterprise level in terms of two broad categories:

- *Internal informatization applications, providing firms with opportunities to enhance productivity and efficiency.* These mainly consist of ICT applications for basic management and operational functions (such as office automation and management information systems) as well as applications within and across the

structures of firms (such as encouraging email communications internally and externally, including through Websites).
- *External linkages or e-commerce applications, allowing firms to conduct contractual transactions with other businesses (B2B) as well as individual consumers (B2C), typically over the Internet.* E-commerce will allow Chinese firms to become part of complex integrated networks of players involving various online business processes (such as supply chains) and to contract, buy, and sell online, as well as allow firms to conduct business-to-government transactions (B2G) in the context of public procurement and public service delivery through public–private partnerships (PPPs).

A 2004 survey by the Ministry of Commerce indicated that the two main goals of Chinese firms for informatization are to increase efficiency (such as in supply chain management) and to reduce sales costs (such as by automating transactions and conducting them online) (Ministry of Commerce 2004). Other objectives indicate that ICT use be viewed as a way to strengthen links with suppliers and customers and to improve management capacity. These are all important elements for firms to stay competitive in rapidly evolving markets.

Thus, Chinese firms' investments in informatization have grown steadily in recent years. Different ICT investment levels across industries show that, beyond a basic level of connectivity (computer use, Internet access, online information, and marketing), some firms in China may choose to stay with traditional business processes, either because more sophisticated ICT applications are unsuitable for their sector or because expected returns are too small. Any supporting role played by ICT is crucially dependent on the business processes required by a firm and its broader industry environment (Qiang et al. 2006). Thus, it is important for firms to decide how much informatization is needed for their operations, and what kinds of ICT applications are best suited to help improve performance. While the path and pace of e-transformation may vary by industry and enterprise, it is clear that ICT diffusion and impact will continue to spread and ultimately lead to structural transformation of almost all industries and services (Hanna 2010).

As Chinese firms evolve, they require increasingly sophisticated ICT applications, such as business process management (BPM), customer resource management (CRM), enterprise resource planning (ERP), and materials requirements planning (MRP). Most medium-size and large Chinese firms have automated one or more of their office operations. These applications have significantly improved production and management systems in China's industrial firms and play an increasingly important role in supporting their growth. A survey of Chinese firms conducted by the Ministry of Commerce found that among firms that had adopted specific ICT applications, most found that the impact on their operations met or exceeded expectations (Ministry of Commerce 2004).

Many Chinese firms have started to move beyond informatization of internal information and processes to enter the arena of e-commerce. Models such as B2B (sometimes B2G, when the buyer is government) and B2C have started to emerge as profitable activities. According to the iResearch Consulting Group, the e-commerce trade revenues reached one trillion yuan (about $150 billion) in the first quarter of 2010, of which close to 90% was B2B. Most of these revenues came from B2B transactions among small and medium-sized enterprises as opposed to those by large firms, and almost half of the transactions were made through Alibaba's AliPay platform.[14]

In 2005 the country's e-commerce market grew by 42% to $84.2 billion, of which 95% was B2B (CCID 2005). A few large companies in the automobile, iron and steel, and electronics industries have led the way in developing B2B e-commerce and incorporating ICT into their purchasing, advertising, and marketing. B2B e-commerce has become a key element in improving the efficiency of supply chain management of many large Chinese firms.

But many Chinese firms – especially the small and medium-sized enterprises – still find it difficult to participate in B2B e-commerce. The reasons mainly have to do with their lack of expertise with ICT applications and lack of knowledge in dealing with online transactions and e-contracts. Many small and medium-sized enterprises have difficulty finding the funds and IT expertise to integrate their internal operations with online business transactions and functions.

In response to these constraints, off-the-shelf B2B platforms have become popular, providing an intermediary step where businesses can join and search for potential clients and suppliers in a sort of commercial information exchange. Common platforms provide a global base that enables firms to search for business opportunities in parts of the world where they otherwise would not have the necessary contacts. They also allow smaller firms to access commercial information and bid for business projects and deals with larger, established firms. Firms can also lower costs by conducting logistical and operational transactions online. Alibaba China, for example, is the largest online marketplace for domestic small and medium-sized enterprises to advertise their products and find trade opportunities.

B2B e-commerce platforms based on a specific industry or niche market have great potential in China. For example, the China Chemical Network (chinachem info.com) is an influential Website for facilitating international trade in the chemical industry, providing exporting domestic firms with information such as business regulations of other countries and price quotations.

B2C e-commerce is a key aspect of informatization for Chinese firms that sell their end products to consumers. B2C has been growing since 2001; in 2010 B2C revenue totaled about 100 billion yuan, or $15 billion.[15] The number of online shoppers has been growing rapidly. A June 2010 survey by CNNIC found that over one-third of the country's 420 million Internet users made purchase online, jumped from 22% in 2008 (CNNIC 2010).

Many large and established firms in China offer a wide range of products online. They conduct the entire operation on their own, from setting up their B2C Websites to marketing and distributing their products to online consumers. Some may already have

[14] http://www.chinadaily.com.cn/bizchina/2010-05/14/content_9849975.htm.

[15] http://www.chinadaily.com.cn/bizchina/2010-05/14/content_9849975.htm.

a working logistics and distribution system across China – an advantage if they are able to integrate logistics IT applications with the new B2C platform and train managers to adapt to the new system and perhaps handle increased product distribution.[16]

Although larger players in the market may benefit from their own B2C platforms and logistics and distribution channels, profit margins can be limited due to high operating costs and intense price competition. In some cases the firms that are doing exceptionally well are those that have focused on a market niche and limited distribution area. Small and medium-sized enterprises, on the other hand, often rely on intermediaries to provide their B2C platforms, using third-party delivery channels such as China Post, EMS, and Eastern Express to deliver products to consumers.

Moreover, there is much room for improvement in the services that accompany online purchases, such as after-sale services, e-security, and return and credit policies. But as e-commerce matures, the market for Internet user profiles will grow, enabling advertisers and marketing firms to tailor their promotional programs to targeted audiences. Progress will require a more holistic view, for example, to protect consumers' data and privacy as they surf the Web.

E-Rural[17]

The gap between China's economically more advanced eastern coastal provinces and the rest of the country persists, and in some cases has widened. The digital divide between rural and urban populations within provinces has also grown, leading to imbalances in development prospects and poverty burdens. These imbalances demand effective policies to ensure equitable, sustainable development throughout the country.

China has identified rural informatization as key to achieving nationwide growth and improving people's capacity for participating in new economic domains. In addition to specific informatization goals in the 11th Five Year Plan, the related deployment of strategies such as the State Informatization Development Strategy, 2006–2020 underscore the importance the government has accorded to rural informatization. Thus, the growing digital gap between rural and urban areas has been a mounting area of concern, encouraging the development of numerous policies and initiatives to promote rural informatization and better equip all citizens for participation in the new global order.

[16] Distribution channels for B2C e-commerce are different in that there are many more destinations for products sold online. The distribution center can be considered the last link between the product and the customer, so the management and operation of the distribution become critical when dealing with individual orders and addresses. Delays in delivering products and mistakes in orders will create customer dissatisfaction, which is an important determinant for online shoppers.

[17] This section draws on Qiang et al. (2009).

Key development objectives of rural informatization in China include:

- *Catching up with more advanced regions.* Informatization could facilitate contacts and exchanges between China's central and western regions and more developed regions, allowing farmers and agro-businesses to obtain technologies and market information that enable them to make full use of their comparative advantages in developing new products and increasing trade, market share, and ultimately incomes. Furthermore, leading agro-businesses in developed regions can show small and low-value industries in less advanced regions how to improve their management and technological skills and market competitiveness, reducing regional gaps.
- *Integrating and modernizing the rural market economy.* Most rural enterprises in China are small and private. Given their isolation and weak financial foundation, the market economy in rural areas remains underdeveloped. Better rural information infrastructure can provide market information, communication channels, and financial resources to farmers and rural enterprises, enabling these key players in the rural economy to enter markets and increase their diversification and competitiveness. Such infrastructure can do so by facilitating better farming techniques, helping to choose crops to plant in response to market information, improving production and resource management (for example, through geographic information systems), and reducing marketing costs and exploitation by intermediaries.
- *Strengthening delivery of social and public services.* Government information support systems should aim to capture timely, accurate, comprehensive data on local economies and social activities. One approach to improving public service delivery is to integrate information on rural economies, science and technology, education, health, social protection, and other areas. The resulting common infrastructure and databases can then be shared across ministries and regions in support of rural service delivery.
- *Augmenting income and nonagricultural employment through diversification and increased productivity.* With information, farmers are better equipped to make important decisions and learn about diversified employment opportunities. With the growing dependence on the services sector, rural economies could benefit from diversifying into providing local ICT-enabled extension services.
- *Increasing the quality and relevance of information and the human capacity of the rural population.* Access to relevant information can transform economic opportunities and improve livelihoods for rural households – especially poor and young people. Rural informatization not only directly affects economic development, but it also brings in modern ideas and forward-looking mindsets from more advanced regions. This can pave the way for transformative ideas and beliefs, increasing rural, social, and cultural capacities in rural areas.
- *Enabling participation in formulating agricultural policies and strategies.* National development strategies and policies try to involve key stakeholders and the broader public. But it is not easy to involve organizations that represent the rural poor. In recent years, ICT has been used to engage thousands of rural people

in developing countries to deliberate policies. The spread of ICT in rural areas makes this type of participatory approach more feasible for dialog on agricultural policy.

The Chinese government has been promoting rural informatization since the mid-1970s. This process has fallen into three stages. During the first, from the mid-1970s to the early 1990s, the initial concept of agricultural informatization emerged from the planned economy's requirements for agricultural statistics. In the 1980s computers began to be introduced, but it was not until the early 1990s that informatization grew.

During the second stage, from the early 1990s to 2000, computerization of agricultural data was introduced and several systems were developed as part of efforts to establish and improve the socialist market economic system. In 1992, the Ministry of Agriculture issued a plan to strengthen the rural economy's information system. In addition to promoting rural economic development, construction began on an agricultural information system. Networks developed rapidly and agriculture entered a fast track for informatization, with scattered information becoming more networked. In 1994, a new department was set up through the institutional reform of the Ministry of Agriculture, and every province created an information department for agriculture.

During the third stage, since 2001, the government has attached even more importance to informatization, taking it to a new level (Box 3.1). Rapid progress has been made in improving services (from simple one-way delivery of government information or services to two-way, interactive delivery), content (from the production of basic statistics to comprehensive information on production, markets, and technology), and service models (from simple, traditional service models delivered by individual government departments to innovative partnerships cutting across departments, the private sector, and civil society). With opening markets, nascent efforts are being made to expedite informatization, supported by partnerships and greater investments by the government, telecommunications companies, and the domestic private sector.

A growing range of actors have been involved in rural informatization. But the government plays a dominant role here. The Chinese government wants to ensure that farmers do not bear the brunt of the financial burden for accessing needed information. Central government agencies also hold major information resources that can be of major benefit for rural areas. In addition to centrally driven programs, every province considers rural informatization an important part of local socioeconomic development plans.

Many government ministries and agencies at all levels (from central to local) are involved in rural informatization projects and are pursuing similar goals. But these efforts are pursued under each organization's individual mandate and with little apparent coordination (Table 3.3). Every ministry has initiated its own rural informatization program, such as the Ministry of Agriculture's Golden Agriculture Project and the Ministry of Culture's National Cultural Information Resources Sharing Project. Other key players include the Ministries of Commerce, Education,

Box 3.1 Central Government Strategies for Rural Informatization, 2001–Present

- In 2001, implementation began on the 10th Five-Year Plan of Action for rural market information services. In 2003, a "rural economic information release calendar" was introduced as the main system for disseminating agricultural information, supported by two national conferences. These initiatives had positive impacts inside and outside the agricultural system, leading to a surge in the provision of information systems.
- In 2006, the 11th National Economic and Social Development 5-Year Plan proposed to "integrate agriculture-related information resources, strengthen the rural economic information application system construction, promote agriculture service organization and mechanism innovation, encourage and guide farmers to develop different types of specialized cooperative economic organizations, and improve the organization of agriculture."
- The related deployment of agriculture informatization in the State Informatization Development Strategy, 2006–2020 (issued in 2006 by General Office of the CPC Central Committee and General Office of the State Council[18]) aims "to use the public network with a variety of access methods and affordable prices for farmers, improve rural network coverage, integrate agricultural information resources, standardize and complete the public information intermediary services, build the urban–rural information service system in a concerted manner, provide farmers with appropriate information applications such as market, science and technology, education, healthcare, etc. and advocate a reasonable and orderly flow of surplus rural labor."
- In 2007, the Ministry of Agriculture proposed the Overall Framework for National Agriculture and Rural Informatization Construction, 2007–2015. The strategic goal of this framework is to greatly improve agricultural and rural integrated information infrastructure; enhance modern agriculture, rural public services, and social management; fully develop information service organizations at the township and village levels; and gradually complete a sustainable development mechanism for agricultural and rural informatization – which would fulfill the development needs of modern agriculture and the construction of a new socialist countryside.

Source: Ministry of Agriculture websites
[http://agri.gov.cn/gdxw/t20071207_933887.htm]
[http://www.agri.gov.cn/xztz/t20071129_929804.htm]

Information Industry, and Science and Technology. Agencies with primary policy and coordination functions have also engaged in national and provincial pilot projects, including the Central Committee of the Communist Party of China, National

[18] http://www.china-embassy.org/eng/xw/t251756.htm.

Table 3.3 Rural informatization initiatives by central ministries and agencies

Ministry/Agency	Mandate	Key projects	Year(s)
Central Committee of the Communist Party of China (CCCPC)	China's central strategic body, with members selected by election. The committee's main focus is improving agricultural productivity and increasing the income of farmers	Modern Distance Learning of National Party Cadres in Rural Areas Project	2003–06
Ministry of Agriculture	First player to launch rural informatization projects to improve the agricultural and rural integrated information platform, and adopt informatization to support modern agriculture, rural public service and social management	Overall Framework of National Agriculture and Rural Informatization, 2007–2015, and pilot projects[a]	2007
		Golden Agriculture Project	2007
		Three in One (Telephone, Television, and Computer) Agriculture Information Services Project[b]	2005
Ministry of Commerce	Responsible for formulating development strategies, guidelines and policies of domestic and foreign trade, investment, and international economic cooperation[c]	Xinfu Project (Commercial information services system for the countryside)	2006
		Thousands of Villages and Townships Project	2005
Ministry of Culture	In charge of public libraries and overall culture activities	Comprehensive Culture Station Project	2006–2010
		National Cultural Information Resources Sharing Project	2002
Ministry of Education	Central government agency under the State Council, responsible for China's educational undertakings and language work[d]	Distance Learning Project in Rural Primary and Secondary Schools	2003
Ministry of Finance	Formulates and implements strategies, policies and medium- and long-term development plans and reform programs of public finance and taxation; participates in macroeconomic policy making; provides policy advice on macroeconomic regulation[e]	National Cultural Information Resources Sharing Project (In collaboration with Ministry of Culture)	2002
		Distance Learning Project in Rural Primary and Secondary Schools (In collaboration with Ministry of Education)	2003
Ministry of Information Industry	Focuses on building network infrastructure, expanding telecommunications coverage in rural areas, and promoting information technology applications in agriculture	Extend Telephone Coverage to Every Village Project[f]	2004–2005
		Rural Comprehensive Agriculture Informatization Service Pilot Project	2006

(continued)

Table 3.3 (continued)

Ministry/Agency	Mandate	Key projects	Year(s)
Ministry of Science and Technology	Provides science and technology information for rural residents	State Agricultural Science and Technology Park Development Program	2007
		"Spark" Agricultural Science and Technology 110 Information Services Project[g]	2005–2010
National Development Reform Commission	Macroeconomic management agency under the State Council, which studies and formulates policies for economic and social development, maintains a balance of economic aggregates and guides the overall economic system restructuring[h]	Pilot Project for Rural Informatization	Under development
State Administration of Radio, Film, and Television	In charge of regulating the broadcasting industry and administering radio spectrum for broadcasting	Extend Broadcasting (TV, and Radio) Coverage to Every Village Project[i]	2006–2010 (phase 2)
State Council Leading Group Office of Poverty Alleviation and Development	A deliberative and coordinating organ, tasked with organizing investigation and subsequent research; formulating guidelines, policies and plans for developing the economy in backward areas; coordinating the efforts to tackle the key issues arising from development initiatives; supervising, inspecting development projects, and facilitating the exchange of lessons acquired[j]	Pilot Project for Rural Informatization in 1,000 Villages	Under development

Source: Qiang et al. (2009)

[a] http://www.agri.gov.cn/jhgb/t20080321_1029943.htm

[b] http://www.agri.gov.cn/jhgb/t20080321_1029944.htm

[c] http://english.mofcom.gov.cn/mission.shtml

[d] http://www.moe.edu.cn/english/ministry_f.htm

[e] http://www.mof.gov.cn/english/english.htm#

[f] http://www.miit.gov.cn/col/col4586/

[g] http://www.most.gov.cn/zfwj/zfwj2004/zf04wj/zf04bfw/200412/t20041228_31393.htm

[h] http://en.ndrc.gov.cn/brief/default.htm

[i] http://news.xinhuanet.com/misc/2007-03/06/content_5806935.htm

[j] http://en.cpad.gov.cn/organ/index.html

Table 3.4 Rural informatization problems and attempted solutions

Problem	Attempted solutions
Poor residents and limited affordability of ICT access	Shared usage and service access points such as telecenters – for example, information stations that serve large numbers of potential users at low or no access cost
Limited sustainability of funding and excess reliance on government support	Diversified funding, with a mix of government, private sector, telecom carrier, and other sources
Low ICT penetration	Varied connectivity options to address last mile needs and user preferences
Unmet local information needs (such as agricultural information for farmers, education for youth, and healthcare guidance)	Efforts to develop and integrate domestic and international information resources, improve information gathering channels, and increase timely content supply
Poor maintenance of ICT initiatives, limiting their sustainability	Better operation, management, and maintenance
Limited ICT skills, experience, or awareness	Public awareness initiatives and efforts to generate community acceptance – for example, through information agents and training of information service teams to form rural information service networks and extend coverage of information services to grassroots levels
Inadequate efforts to tailor initiatives to user needs, often top-down in nature	Efforts to collect user feedback and evaluations of initiatives to make offerings more relevant

Development Reform Commission, State Administration of Radio, Film, and Television, State Council Leading Group Office of Poverty Alleviation and Development, and Ministry of Finance.

A growing number of pilot projects have also emerged in recent years under the direction of various actors. Province-level pilots range from fully government-initiated and -financed initiatives to those involving partnerships with schools, culture centers, and rural cooperatives. These actors are working – individually or in partnership with other members engaged in rural ICT development efforts – to address the problems of rural informatization in China using innovative service offerings and business models. Key elements of the business models for these pilot projects are described in Table 3.4 and Fig. 3.2.

Many of the business models used to deliver content and services are heavily reliant on government subsidies. Thus the long-term operation of such services in towns and villages often depends on continued financial support from local governments – an unsustainable financial burden (Qiang et al. 2009).

Accordingly, business models using more innovative leadership patterns, sustainable ownership, and funding models are needed to support the government's long-term informatization goals. Government agencies are exploring new options for providing information services, with the goal of providing some overall support rather than heavy subsidies. Partnerships with domestic enterprises are being attempted. China's large telecom providers are keen to increase their coverage in

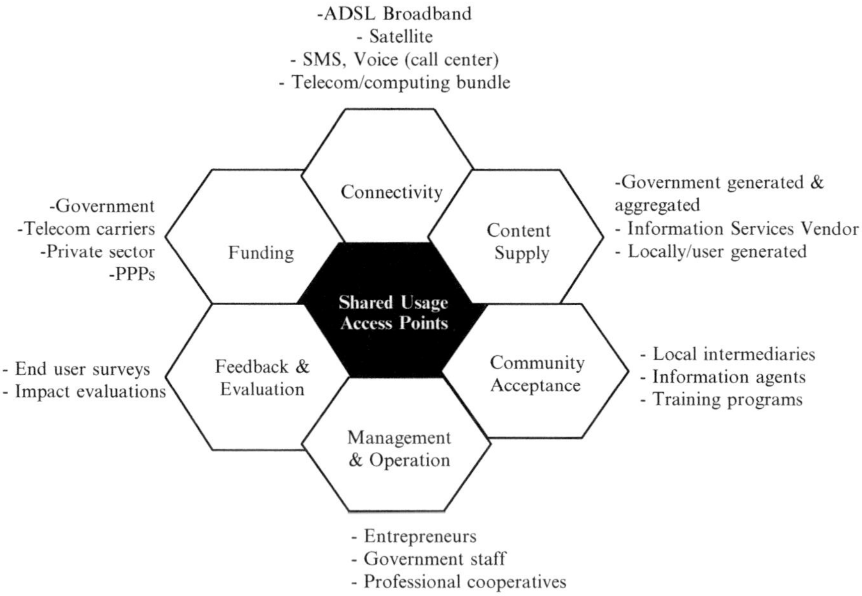

Fig. 3.2 Key elements of rural informatization pilot initiatives

rural areas as urban markets reach saturation. An example is in Chongqing, where a partnership with the government gave rise to a profit sharing arrangement with 40% of profits going to the telecom carrier and 60% to the Ministry of Agriculture.

Rural informatization initiatives often have a narrow focus, usually on agriculture. Most information services are low-level and cannot satisfy the practical needs of farmers and directly affect the overall sustainability of the initiative. Examples from other countries, such as e-Choupal (India), Grameen (Bangladesh), and n-Logue (India), are enlightening as they leverage existing telecommunications networks and maximize their efficiency by providing a wide range of services. The additional public and social services that can be delivered through informatization that would otherwise not be possible (such as distance education) make an economic case for deploying ICT networks in rural areas possible and more compelling.

Maintenance and upkeep of services have also proven problematic. In many projects, local governments have provided startup investments for hardware and equipment, but without adequate arrangements for maintenance. Pilot projects supported by foreign aid agencies and multinational corporations suffer from similar lack of attention to regular upgrading and maintenance. The challenge is to consider the lifecycle of ICT products – if a sustainable mechanism for regular upgrading of systems does not exist, initial investments are wasted.

Content has been another key problem for rural informatization. Though many information resources have been developed in recent years, farmers often cannot find urgently needed and locally relevant information. Problems include:

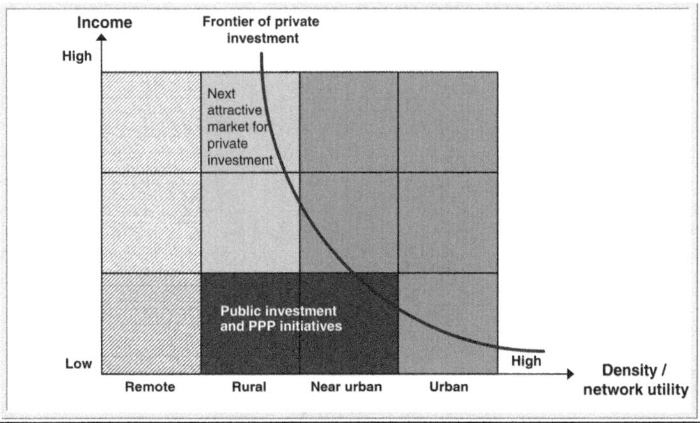

Fig. 3.3 ICT segmentation of rural and urban populations in China. Source: World Bank (2006)

- Lack of practical, localized, contextualized online content that is relevant for farmers. With no substantive discussion of specific local examples, farmers do not believe in abstract solutions and have little motivation to adopt them.
- Weak capacity for collecting and disseminating information resources and developing original, region-specific, customized information services.
- Disorderly distribution of information and lack of working mechanisms for integrating agricultural information resources, which are scattered among departments and enterprises at the city and provincial levels.
- Narrowly focused agricultural content, with little diversification to other ICT-enabled rural services such as education and finance.
- Weak integration of informatization programs with locally driven community development initiatives.

Overall, rural informatization lacks a coherent strategy and an integrated approach across ministries. Centrally funded programs do not take into account the diverse geographic and socioeconomic conditions of China's rural areas. Diversified geographic conditions in many rural areas pose a challenge to uniform standards and regionally undifferentiated programs. It is important to segment the rural market and take different implementation approaches for each segment.

For example, the frontier line covers segments – urban high- and medium-income, and increasingly rural high- and medium-income – that could be attractive for private investment or innovative public–private initiatives (Fig. 3.3). At the same time, a national strategy needs to direct public resources to financially less viable rural and near urban low-income segments, where low population densities, nonexistent infrastructure, and low literacy may not result in financially sustainable service centers.

Future Directions for Informatization

What is the likely future of China's informatization strategy? How should ICT be leveraged to support likely sources of sustainable growth, accelerate poverty reduction, and address other systemic economic problems? What are the implications for the building blocks of e-development? What priorities and challenges should be addressed in using ICT to transform government, empower communities, and foster innovation? And what should be done to tap synergies and manage cross-cutting issues for a holistic approach to informatization?

Informatization and Economic Development

After China's economic opening over 30 years ago, the country's economic development entered a new stage – and today requires a new informatization strategy. Informatization and economic development are mutually reinforcing: China's successful economic development has laid the material and technological foundations for informatization and greatly expanded the demand for it. Urbanization, industrialization, increased consumption, and expanded social mobility have created unprecedented opportunities as well as new challenges for e-transformation. China's future economic growth will likely come from three main sources:

- Encouraging the development of services and domestic demand for them.
- Increasing firm competitiveness, particularly through ICT and FDI participation.
- Facilitating the movement of workers out of agriculture and to cities.

To sustain the momentum of economic growth, China started to address three interwoven factors during the 11th Five-Year Plan (2006–2010) and is expected to do so well beyond.

First, industrialization has resulted in continuous changes to China's economic structure. Many workers are moving from agricultural to industrial and service jobs with higher value added. Electronic communications, real estate, and social services are among the fastest growing sectors in terms of both value added and employment.

Second, productivity has increased considerably in industries that produce ICT equipment as well as among ICT-using providers of wholesale, retail, financial, and logistics services (World Bank 2004). These increases suggest that the economy will continue to shift toward information- and technology-intensive manufacturing and service sectors. Moreover, the use of ICT in service sectors to meet a fast growing domestic demand for improved services can substantially transform the currently very low productivity levels in these sectors. Facilitating the adoption of ICT in traditional industries and services will be crucial to reduce the growing disparities of a dual economy, sustain global competitiveness, and reduce reliance on exporting sectors as the sole drivers of growth.

Finally, FDI continues to flow into China at a growing rate, mainly to develop manufacturing capacity for exports but increasingly to service domestic demand. From January to September in 2010 China attracted $74.3 billion in FDI.[19] The total FDI amount China received between 2000 and 2009 was more than $755 billion (IMF 2010).

Foreign firms used to invest in China primarily to take advantage of its low labor costs. An increasingly important benefit for China is the opportunity to adopt advanced technologies, through new technology embedded in equipment and processes, demonstration effects, circulation of managers and workers, competitive pressures, and technological links among foreign firms and their suppliers and subsidiaries. All these effects provide incentives for businesses to adopt ICT. Aside from contributing to productivity, the spread of ICT has the potential to accelerate innovation in a broad range of products and processes. Foreign firms also use ICT to penetrate the domestic market.

Productivity and innovation at the firm level are functions of ICT use and FDI. Companies that use ICT grow faster, employ more skilled workers, and are more productive and profitable than those that do not (Qiang et al. 2006; Hanna 2010). Among Chinese firms, joint ventures and firms linked to international production networks invest most heavily in IT, highlighting the significance of FDI (Yusuf and Evenett 2002).

Since the 1980s China's growth has been driven by urban areas and their industrial activities. Accordingly, the country has experienced rapid urbanization, with the urban share of the population reaching nearly 44% in 2009,[20] up from 30% in the 1990s. Rural emigration has accounted for nearly 70% of the increase in the urban population. The fastest growing industries are in major cities on the coast as well as a few along main inland waterways.

Because of these changes, the income gap between urban and rural populations has widened. In 2008, the average per capita urban income was 3.3 times that in rural areas.[21] The growing gap is partly a result of China's development strategy focusing on industrialization, which tends to be urban-centered.

The evolving needs of firms based in coastal areas – and of the growing middle-class concentrated in cities in those areas – are increasing the demand for informatization. To support informatization and sustain growth, coastal areas need to develop high-quality infrastructure – including access to ICT facilities and services – for the growing urban centers that drive economic performance and serve as the locus of innovation. On the other hand, provinces seeking to catch up also need to harness ICT to avoid increasing urban–rural economic and social gaps.

[19] Ministry of Commerce: http://english.mofcom.gov.cn/aarticle/statistic/foreigninvestment/201011/20101107222134.html.

[20] Source: United Nations, World Urbanization Prospects.

[21] Source: National Bureau of Statistics. http://www.stats.gov.cn/tjsj/ndsj/2009/indexeh.htm.

A Framework for China's Informatization Strategy and Challenges

China's informatization strategy has been more closely linked to goals for increasing economic growth, but not equally focused on alleviating poverty. Moreover, China's ICT strategy suffers from a lack of coordinated management, monitoring and evaluation mechanisms, and coordinated efforts to narrow the digital divide. Given China's vast size and population, an effective implementation strategy will be critical to ensure that its informatization strategy serves its development goals.

The overarching, long-term goal of informatization is to support China's efforts to achieve rapid, sustainable economic growth that benefits all of its citizens. Over time China will shift from a growth pattern that favors capital-intensive industry to one that is less resource-intensive, more efficient, and more equitably shared. That will involve rebalancing growth to sectors that require less capital, energy, and resources, and that generate more employment. To that end, informatization could support thc following goals:

- Institutional changes that make government functions more service-oriented, efficient, and transparent, contributing enormously to efficient markets and resource allocations.
- Growth of IT services and IT-enabled services and related employment opportunities.
- ICT use to grow and transform all service sectors and improve access to financial resources.
- ICT use to transform the manufacturing and energy industries, and increase the value added of Chinese products.
- Efforts to increase Chinese enterprises' productivity, international competitiveness, and capacity for technological and business innovation.

For the overall informatization strategy to progress, the framework in Fig. 3.4 links these priorities and goals to drivers and enablers. These enablers, with the support of solid leadership, should aim to transform government and business processes into agile, streamlined, and intelligent processes that deploy ICT applications in governments, communities, and businesses.

Developing E-Leadership Institutions

China's leaders are more unified than their counterparts in most emerging markets and western nations embracing technology as a strategic tool for national development. They are building a talent base with much expanded higher technical education, and attracting Chinese expats with experience in technology hothouses such as Silicon Valley. This commitment and proactive government measures have served the country well in advancing ICT as a sector, particularly in manufacturing. Yet the future will require more diffused leadership at all levels to adopt ICT as a tool for transformation across all sectors. And in the ICT sector, leadership and entrepreneurship will be

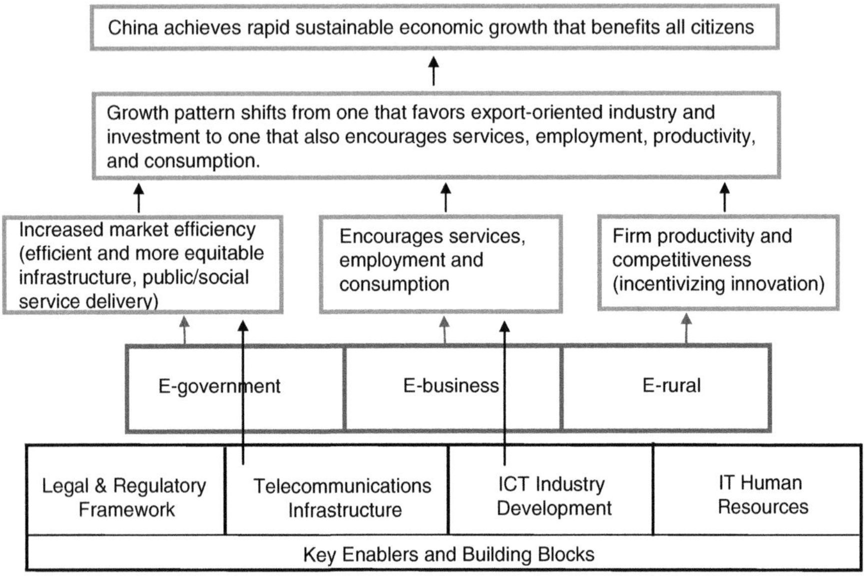

Fig. 3.4 Framework for China's informatization

needed to promote more bottom-up and collaborative innovation, and to move China from low-margin, high-volume hardware manufacturing into high-margin innovative products, high-margin software, IT services, and the use of ICT to move other industries and services to higher productivity and up the value chain.

The next phase of e-transformation will require a multistakeholder approach that encourages wider use of ICT to foster economic and social development. Progress will depend heavily on modifying China's enabling environment and tapping the synergies among key elements of e-transformation.

To pursue ICT-enabled transformation of government, China needs to develop an e-leadership institutional model capable of promoting enterprise architecture, interoperability, PPPs, effective outsourcing and contract management, exchange of experience, process and service innovation, information sharing, and prioritization across e-development and e-services. An enterprise architecture and interoperability framework would facilitate information sharing, and coordination across and different levels of government. Policy and institutional frameworks for PPPs at the central, provincial, and local levels would mobilize the vast resources and expertise of the private sector while protecting the interests of government and citizens. A leading institution for such partnerships would set standards for demand analysis, process reengineering, and monitoring and evaluation of e-government services and thus reduce excess technology and vendor-driven investments.

Institutional mechanisms are also needed to promote cross-regional sharing of information resources and collaboration on e-government applications at all levels of government. Top political leaders and administrators could also lead the process of moving toward an open government and motivate government agencies to share information with the public. They may create and lead organizational cultures that are tolerant to change and risk taking, and supportive of innovation at all levels. Finally, e-leadership is needed to prioritize e-government infrastructure and applications for maximum development impact. To date, investment has focused on telecommunications, networks, databases, and back-office e-government (G2G) applications, while G2C and G2B services have lagged far behind.

Leadership cannot come only from government, as exclusive government involvement can be a mixed blessing. The experience of China, as well as other countries, suggests that ICT sector successes as well as broad-based e-transformation are seldom the result of laissez-faire government. While improving overall supply of critical inputs for the sector, and the overall investment climate for business, governments often also create microclimates for the short term through industry-specific interventions (Gregory et al. 2009). But excessive interventions can lead to uncertainties, distortions, and corruption. For example, the Chinese military and several large cities like Shanghai own hundreds of large enterprises in the ICT sector. China's recent announcement that it will create its own government-controlled search engine, in an apparent bid to extend its control over the Internet, could distort the country's ICT sector, potentially diminishing the productivity potential for other sectors of the economy. Also much of e-transformation will require leadership from outside the government: private sector, academia, media, and civil society. E-leadership institutions need to engage all actors and stakeholders for broad-based transformation.

Creating an Enabling Environment

A more enabling environment for ICT development is needed, with a host of changes in policies and regulations as well as a reorganization of government agencies involved in ICT policymaking. Informatization requires a legal system that can protect identities, intellectual property, and online transactions.

ICT applications can be used to promote government consultation and participation by citizens and businesses in shaping legal and policymaking processes. The government has developed several ways to encourage cooperation with businesses and civil society on legal matters, but there is considerable room for improvement. Due to the lack of a freedom of information act, the private sector and civil society are often unaware of government deliberations on policy. Without public participation, it is difficult to build a sense of legitimacy and representation of proper rights. An open approach could be used to formulate informatization policies. Furthermore, e-government applications could be used to increase public participation in policymaking.

China's legal and regulatory framework can provide certainty and predictability to help the country realize its informatization strategy by fostering a business-friendly climate where competition can flourish, foreign and domestic sponsors can invest with confidence, and ICT development can take root. Developing the enabling environment for e-transformation would require addressing key issues: issuance of third-generation (3G) network licenses, restructuring of state operators, development of local technology standards, opening of markets to foreign players, development of systems for universal service obligations, and control and censorship of content and applications over telecommunications networks.

Building the Information Infrastructure

Different approaches have been suggested for achieving the twin goals of upgrading to an advanced ICT infrastructure and increasing access. On the one hand, broadband access is a clear strategic direction for China and a prerequisite for further advancing e-transformation. Many of China's informatization projects in areas such as digital media, e-commerce, and e-government are dependent on a broadband platform to achieve high levels of functionality and usage. Broadband infrastructure must be widely accessible to narrow the digital divide and benefit economic and social development through the availability of multimedia applications in fields such as education and health. A key step is to intensify intermodal competition among fixed-line providers, cable television companies, and wireless operators, to reduce broadband costs and make service affordable to more consumers and enterprises. This includes waiving existing restrictions that prohibit operators from providing "triple-play" services (voice, Internet, and broadcasting) over their broadband infrastructure.

On the other hand, expanding rural access to ICT is critical to equitable economic and social development. There are many ways to increase rural penetration of telecommunications services – such as establishing a universal service policy, a fund to finance infrastructure expansion to underserved populations, subsidies to maintain lower service charges, and competitive bidding among operators for subsidized contracts. The best practice is to adopt an open policy to allow for technology-neutral ways of implementing universal access obligations.

Investment in China's telecommunications networks totaled about $30 billion in 2007 (ITU 2010) – the eighth straight year with investment exceeding $25 billion. While investment has been sustained, network development has been hardware-intensive, focusing on infrastructure and equipment. Less attention has been paid to operations management and support systems, customer service, and network optimization.

On network technology, the Chinese government faces the challenge of promoting its home-grown third generation (3G) wireless technology that may in the long run achieve economies of scale and hence lower investment costs versus accepting technology-neutral solutions that could rapidly promote the development of broadband infrastructure. In April 2008, China started trials in its homegrown 3G networks in Beijing, Shanghai, and six other cities, with the aim to bring affordable video and web services and experiment with various packages and prices (see http://shanghaiist.com/2008/04/01/china_rolls_out.php). In January 2009, China awarded long-awaited licenses for 3G mobile networks to three telephone operators, paving the way for substantial investments in network upgrading and expansion.

These operators have since been keen to boost 3G subscriber figures through demand stimulation. China Telecom announced that it had begun selling a locally produced tablet computer, the LifePad, in an attempt to stimulate extra demand for its 3G mobile services. The device, which includes a number of preinstalled applications such as email, e-book reader, stock trading, and navigation, is similar in functionality to the Apple iPad, which China Telecom is also considering as an incentive for prospective 3G customers. However, operators are realizing that such devices can only help grow 3G subscriber bases if they are affordable. Demand for Apple's iPhone, for instance, has been slow in the country. China Unicom announced, in May 2010, that it had decided to increase subsidies for iPhone and planned to invest up to US$735 million in subsidies in 2010 (BMI 2010), a move expected to help attract new 3G subscribers.

Large-scale adoption of 3G technology would spur enormous network infrastructure development, enable telecom and other service providers to offer a wide range of new applications and content services, provide another option for broadband access, and help ensure that China's mobile networks do not fall behind in technical sophistication. The government may want to consider leaving which type of 3G system to implement to operators, with the government awarding the necessary spectrum. To help offset high investment costs in 3G networks, the government could encourage infrastructure sharing – a policy adopted in countries such as Australia and Sweden. A more open entry policy is crucial to mitigate potentially significant risks in 3G network deployment and to promote rapid development.

While supporting its own industry has some merits, the government could rely more on market forces when choosing technologies, both for 3G deployment and universal access implementation. Upgrading telecommunications infrastructure and expanding access will require significant investment in the coming years. It is uncertain that existing domestic operators will have the resources necessary to fully fund the needed investment. Thus, the government may encourage greater competition and participation by foreign operators to attract more investment in the sector.

To support network convergence, policy and regulatory issues that prevent broadcast, broadband, and telecom providers from accessing one another's networks should be addressed. Many countries are starting to combine regulation of telecommunications networks with information technology and broadcasting. Similarly, in China a new law for telecommunications (and, perhaps more broadly, electronic communications) could support the development of a level playing field and a fair, open market. But contrary to market expectations, the government restructuring announced in March 2008 did not integrate the State Administration of Radio, Film, and Television with the new Ministry of Information Industry. As a result the progress of network convergence will almost certainly be delayed.

Promoting the ICT Industry

The demand from China's large domestic market and foreign export markets offers huge opportunities for the country's ICT industry. China's performance in ICT hardware manufacturing and export has been remarkable. For the next phase of industrial development, innovation and R&D capacities will be increasingly critical to attract investment, maintain high growth, and become globally competitive in higher value activities. Barriers to more effective innovation may be addressed by introducing regulatory and policy reforms, encouraging collaboration, and increasing government support. China needs a robust national innovation system fueled by an ICT-enabled innovation ecosystem.

The government has an important role in facilitating an environment that incubates innovations in products, processes, and practices. This role includes ensuring that the legal framework protects intellectual property rights and relaxing restrictions that may inhibit innovation. Eliminating entry barriers and allowing more FDI and joint ventures in the ICT market are fundamental to stimulating domestic innovations. Similarly, by removing highly restrictive regulations on digital content, digital media could become a significant industry of its own and could help build synergies with other elements of e-development.

China is expected to continue to establish strategic directions around technologies critical to its industrial development and future competitiveness. To make best use of its resources and competencies, China should focus R&D efforts on core technologies, products, and services that have been identified as important for informatization, necessitate extensive customization, or are unique to the Chinese market or where it has strategic advantages. These include areas such as integrated circuits, network security software, telecommunications equipment, and mobile data applications. China's huge customer base of mobile phones also provides a unique opportunity for building technological competence and leadership in mobile Internet-based applications.

In addition, China needs to further integrate enterprises, universities, and scientific research institutes to stimulate innovation and connect skills development and R&D with industrial development, so that technologies can be commercialized and turned into practical and relevant applications. Industry–university collaboration brings benefits for both: enterprises can provide additional funding for targeted research for universities and research institutes, while universities and research institutes have a pool of highly skilled human resources from which to draw. Government is advised to strengthen financial incentives for academic and business collaborations. Measures may include outright funding support and tax holidays. Such measures could create incentives for commercializing and disseminating technology, while contributing to the funding of R&D in universities and research institutes.

In terms of the R&D investment amount, China's overall investment in R&D has increased, but still remains low against GDP. In 2009, China spent $87 billion on R&D in total, and $20 billion out of the total came from the government. The total amount jumped 4.5 times from 2000, and now it is ranked fourth highest in the world after the USA, Japan, and Germany.[22] Some of top IT companies have been keen to spend the money on R&D. For example, Huawei Technologies has spent 27% of its revenue for R&D in 2009 (OECD 2010). However, against GDP, it is still 1.7% of GDP in 2009 – much less than other leading countries which is around 3% of GDP for R&D.[23]

The ICT market is extremely dynamic and internationally integrated. China should be cautious about encouraging too strong an involvement in driving the selection of technologies that would be inconsistent with global standards. Efforts should be made to continue to work with international standard-setting bodies to get the country's technologies recognized and resist the temptation to go independent routes. When it comes to standards, strategic engagement is likely to be more successful than isolationism.

Developing IT Human Resources

As informatization accelerates, China will need more ICT experts as well as workers with adequate ICT skills. It has become a pressing task to improve and expand the human resource base to meet the demand for the country's ICT development. The various stakeholders – governments, enterprises, schools, research institutes, individuals – need to work together to build up the human resources needed to maximize the economic and social benefits from ICT development. It is also important to create a shared vision among stakeholders to coordinate plans for e-education.

A nationwide strategic communications and awareness raising program is needed to build domestic demand and e-literacy, including how ICT can be accessed and used and its role in economic and social development. Efforts are needed to promote e-government, to encourage citizen use of online public services and participation in decision making. One way of achieving this is by putting popular public administration applications online. Public awareness of ICT can also be increased through media campaigns on the radio, television, and Internet.

Programs also need to be established to provide widespread ICT training to the general population. This is particularly critical for people unlikely to be exposed to ICT through the educational system or work, including homemakers and the unemployed, disabled, or elderly. Educating and training China's vast population is a challenge. ICT diversifies the range of learning opportunities. It helps overcome physical shortages of teachers and classrooms through online education delivery. ICT also provides new and innovative ways of teaching that can make learning more interesting while offering students an opportunity to enhance computer skills.

---

[22] http://www.upi.com/Science_News/2010/12/02/China-ranks-fourth-in-RD-spending/UPI-89181291310006/.

[23] http://www.upi.com/Science_News/2010/12/02/China-ranks-fourth-in-RD-spending/UPI-89181291310006/.

Requiring ICT classes in primary and secondary schools is essential for building basic skills among the population. Often too much emphasis is placed on connecting schools to the Internet, and not enough on teaching ICT skills and the use of ICT tools to enhance pedagogy and learning in all subject. Schools need to provide teachers with ICT training – including general competency in ICT use and, more important, appreciation of when and how to mix ICT and other media into standard pedagogies. Incentives and programs could be designed to mobilize private participation in education investment and improve school infrastructure for ICT-supported learning (e.g., by providing and maintaining equipment).

Over the medium and long term, China needs to add ICT-related majors in higher education – or even launch specialized, world-class ICT institutes – to bridge the quantitative and qualitative gap between supply of and demand for ICT-skilled labor. The guiding principles of modern ICT education include multiple levels tailored to different audiences, responsiveness to industry trends and market demand, flexible teaching materials easily customized to student needs, and emphasis on applicable skills. In addition to mainstreaming ICT in the formal education system, it is important to normalize and expand training and certification programs to enable people of all ages to enjoy ICT education, customized to their demand. Enterprises should play a growing role in upgrading the workforce with ICT skills through on-the-job training, vocational training, and online courses.

University–enterprise partnerships provide a win–win relationship for promoting ICT skill development. Links between universities and firms could be strengthened by providing institutional foundations such as the establishment of intermediary institutions and encouraging ICT multinationals to invest in local centers of excellence in ICT education.

Leveraging ICT for Government and Community

Efforts to apply ICT to transform government and empower communities may be strategically guided by a few key principles and priorities. Given the vast needs and challenges facing China, these principles and priorities are particularly critical to ensuring agility and flexibility, scaling up and consolidating e-government initiatives, and securing interoperability and information sharing. These principles should aim to manage a unified e-government architecture, promote PPPs, take advantage of cloud computing whenever possible, enhance quality standards, improve returns on investment in e-government projects, promote information disclosure and sharing, and support bottom-up local initiatives.

It will be important for China to embrace technology architecture for the successful deployment of e-government services. When defining its IT architecture, the government needs to revisit organizational structures for guiding ICT development. Such an approach to e-government can help China's central and local governments coordinate departments and institutions at different levels, planning both vertically and horizontally, and connecting information "islands" at all government levels.

The continuous process of generating, updating, absorbing, and exchanging information resources as part of a well-defined IT architecture remains key to achieving its huge economic and social benefits.

China has made limited use of PPPs in e-government. While PPPs are not a panacea for all the challenges involved in implementing e-government, they can provide distinct value for a range of e-government applications and offer relevant, cost-effective, sustainable solutions and accelerated implementation. The challenge will be to entrust the private sector to participate in government transformation initiatives while creating incentives for the country's application providers to develop the capacity to support such complex tasks. To encourage greater adoption of PPPs, it will be necessary to develop a framework for e-government PPPs at the central, provincial, and local levels, and to train key government staff on the planning, design, development, implementation, and monitoring of PPP projects.

The government can increase the returns on its investments in e-government by prioritizing e-government investments, adopting advanced project management methodologies, integrating process reengineering into large ICT-enabled modernization efforts, and pursuing demand analysis and user involvement. Third-party supervision should help ensure the quality of e-government projects. It would be desirable to create capabilities for defining and monitoring standards for application and process design in e-government. Leading universities and quality standards organizations would be natural partners for such initiatives. Monitoring and evaluation should be enhanced to ensure effective project management, learning, and accountability. Recent technological advances and business models such as cloud computing also offer new options for government to access up-to-date ICT facilities and applications more flexibly and cost-effectively than has been possible in recent past.

The provisions on open government information that came into effect in 2008 have established a presumption of disclosure, making secrecy the exception rather than the rule. Citizens, legal persons, and other organizations have the right to request government information. They impose a legal obligation on government agencies to disclose all information not covered by a specified exemption.[24] In addition, such information must be posted on the government's Website. It would be useful to emphasize the performance of different government departments and agencies in achieving transparency in annual e-government website rankings and to widely publicize the findings, to motivate government entities to be more transparent. The US Open Government Directive and DATA.Gov offer promising models to change the culture of information sharing, institutionalizing a preference for making federal data more widely available in more accessible formats.

[24] All government information is to be accessible by the public unless it falls in one of six areas exempted from disclosure: a state secret, a commercial secret, an individual's private information, information related to a matter being investigated, discussed, or processed, information related to an administrative enforcement action that might influence the enforcement activity or endanger an individual's life or safety, or information otherwise exempted from disclosure by law or regulation. All but the state secrets exemption may be subject to a balancing test.

Mechanisms are also needed to support local governments and communities in bottom-up efforts to use ICT. There are huge gaps among regions in applying ICT and developing local information resources. Institutional and funding mechanisms can help reduce these gaps through shared application development, common support services, and exchanges of information among local governments. E-community applications at the local government level, such as call centers and websites, can provide citizens with improved information flows and strengthen interactions between local officials and citizens. Rural areas are most in need of these support measures.

Fostering E-Business

In China's highly dynamic environment, the government has a large range of responsibilities to fulfill in promoting enterprise informatization. Key actions include improving the policy environment for e-commerce, modernizing the logistics and distribution system, incubating ICT-enabled service enterprises, and harmonizing laws and regulations for e-commerce.

New regulatory measures are needed to help standardize the e-commerce marketplace, lower barriers inhibiting e-commerce, and foster market growth. Building on the E-Signature Law, the government's further support for a regulatory framework that builds trust and security and combats cyber crime is essential in encouraging business use of ICT applications. Encryption technologies must be made more widely available to enable secure online transactions. Although the E-Signature Law did much to support e-commerce and online financial transactions, authentication mechanisms and antifraud measures – combined with privacy and consumer protection protocols – are crucial for making more Chinese feel safe shopping online.

The growth of e-commerce in China is increasing the requirements for the development of logistics and distribution systems, as well as offering significant new opportunities. Because logistics in e-commerce is characterized by widely distributed consumers – small volume, multiple batch, and short cycle – traditional logistics have had to make significant progress in speed, stock control, and service quality. Given the current low levels of productivity in logistics and distribution in China, there is substantial room for enhancing productivity of these functions, with the help of ICT.

Logistics and distribution systems should thus adopt informatization themselves, using advanced technologies such as barcode readers, electronic ordering systems, package tracking systems, customer relationship management systems, and global positioning systems. These systems would integrate traditional distribution and financial systems with modern information networks, and would improve business intelligence, understanding of customers' behavior, and enable personalization of products and services. Upgrading logistics and distribution may also include the modernization of the postal system, as well as the opening of specific postal and delivery services to competition.

Firms that want to pursue e-commerce but lack the means to do so can be aided by government-sponsored B2B and B2C platforms and incubation initiatives. Such initiatives could be coupled with promotional programs and e-commerce trade-shows that demonstrate how e-commerce works and the steps needed for online transactions. Promotional programs could also encourage small and medium-sized enterprises that do not currently export to do so through e-commerce.

The Chinese government continues to encourage domestic companies to buy and sell goods and services from and to both domestic and foreign businesses operating online, to reap the rewards of reaching global suppliers and consumers. In the near future, China will likely be the regional leader in the volume of e-commerce transactions and number of e-commerce trade partners. Thus, China could play a lead role in furthering international e-commerce standards. A harmonized legal and regulatory framework would benefit the region, instilling trust in this new mode of trade and cooperation.

Making Rural Informatization More Sustainable

China is poised to draw on its extensive experience and that of the global community to scale up and maximize informatization's impact on rural development. As a first priority, China needs to take stock of its experience and devise a shared vision and strategy for the next phase. Such a strategy should start by segmenting rural markets in terms of e-readiness and connectivity, remoteness, e-literacy, and socioeconomic development. Assistance (subsidy and training) levels and business models can then be tailored to the different segments and types of local environments. The success or failure of various business models and informatization initiatives are critically dependent on local contexts, so these assessments are essential to tailoring national programs, service models, and subsidies to these local contexts.

A key issue that the ICT strategy must address is the measures used to reach poor people in rural areas. Using ICT for rural development is not the same as using ICT for poverty reduction. If inappropriately designed, rural informatization efforts may even widen the digital divide among the rural population. The strategy should aim to define the basic approaches to reach remote regions, poor communities, and farmers through targeted subsidies, vouchers, low-cost technologies, information intermediaries, community development, and capacity building.

The proposed strategy should also balance the current top-down, centrally driven approaches of rural informatization with bottom-up initiatives to promote local ownership, innovation, adaptation, and learning. It should emphasize the development of demand-driven services. It should ensure learning from the diverse models piloted so far and build on the most promising ones. And it should emphasize partnerships with local ICT industries, telecommunications operators, community organizations, agriculture extension services, cooperatives, professional associations, academic institutions, and the media.

The optimal level of integration with national programs is at the township level. The township level is where bottom-up efforts are linked to top-down programs, and where capacity building and monitoring and evaluation efforts can be built. This should become the locus for coordination, collaboration, local content development, and ICT integration with regional development strategies and programs.

Conclusion: Tapping Synergies and Managing Cross-Cutting Issues

China faces fundamental structural barriers that slow e-transformation, and many of these barriers cut across all elements of e-development and require mutually reinforcing measures. Informatization has been initiated while China is undergoing a more basic process of industrialization and as it attempts to move from a planned socialist economy to a socialist market economy. The information society requires new styles of leadership, information sharing, and market-based solutions. Similarly, overcoming the digital divide in rural areas requires acting on many fronts: affordable access, relevant content, e-literacy, and community awareness and mobilization.

Large-scale informatization projects, although necessary to establish shared infrastructures and common data bases, have often yielded limited immediate results. Investment returns have been uneven in some areas, and despite high investment in telecommunications infrastructure, demand for ICT applications overall has been relatively weak. Low Internet use and limited demand for applications that can serve China's economic and social development goals suggest underutilization of existing infrastructure and information resources. In addition, IT systems are often improperly managed and maintained after initial implementation. Public data and information resources are locked in silos within government agencies, seldom shared with citizens, private sector, or among agencies concerned with service delivery.

China's vast, diverse territory and large population increase the difficulty of equitably spreading ICT. Measures to narrow the digital divide need to be mutually reinforcing. China's digital divide may intensify the rising inequalities in income and opportunities that have come partly as the by-product of its transformation from an agricultural to an industrial economy. There are gaps in access to ICT infrastructure between rural and urban areas, as well as between poorer, more isolated western provinces and wealthier, more developed eastern ones. A number of groups remain underserved and have limited access to ICT. China's many minority groups – including rural farmers, the vast "floating" population, the elderly, and the learning disabled – have increasingly fewer opportunities to join the information society.

The issues surrounding informatization include not only economic strength and technological advancement, but also social equality and institutional capacity building. As its society becomes more mobile and information intensive, the Chinese government needs to improve regulations on information flows, overcome a general unwillingness to share information, and foster community development and mitigate social conflicts.

To address these challenges, China needs to take key cross-cutting and synergistic actions: develop e-leadership capabilities and institutions, develop human resources to support national ICT diffusion priorities, promote affordable and shared access to ICT, and orient the national innovation system and ICT industry development to support local adaptation and local users.

Establishing Multidisciplinary, High-Level E-Leadership

Most organizations in China, public and private, have not established ICT positions at a senior management levels, undermining the ability of these organizations to use information as a strategic tool and to adopt integrated e-strategies for their respective sectors and enterprises. One way of enhancing the visibility of ICT within an organization is by establishing a CIO as a senior position and elevating the CIO function to a higher level, with associated power, prestige, and pay. In business, CIOs need to be able to influence company decisions and understand the company strategies, customers, markets, and world trends that affect their firms. Appropriate management of ICT adoption requires leaders who can combine knowledge of business and technology. In government, CIOs should be made responsible for leading government informatization and spreading ICT for internal efficiency and external service delivery.

As the government's role in the economy shifts from micromanagement to macrocontrol, vision provider, and innovation promoter, the role of public leaders changes as well. Public CIOs and e-leaders then assume more critical roles as strategists, transformational leaders, and institutional change managers. The rapid pace of technological change and the general purpose nature of ICT indicate that these leaders must be educated about the potential and pitfalls of applying ICT in their respective sectors. The development of ICT as a sector, and the use of ICT in other sectors, will be felt throughout the economy, and decisions made by public leaders about ICT can be viewed as decisions on the course of the entire economy.

China aims to develop its leadership institutions to promote the national IT industry as a whole and in line with the government's aims to sustain the country's competitiveness through innovation. Currently, the IT industry is significantly influenced by intercity rivalries. It has not built the marketing sophistication required to withstand global competitors, particularly in the software, IT services and IT-enabled services. Business leadership is critical for the health of the IT industry and advancing China from being the "world's factory" to a technology leader and innovator, but it is equally critical for partnering with government leaders, CIOs, and other stakeholders. This is to tap synergies across all e-development components and promote ICT use throughout the economy. India's National Association of Software and Services Companies, NASSCOM, plays such a key role in trumpeting the world-class capabilities of its members to the world, lobbying for enabling laws for transforming India into a knowledge services economy, and advocating for reforms to facilitate IT diffusion in the economy.

Linking Human Resource Development Strategies to National ICT Priorities

An ICT human resources strategy should be defined in the context of industry development trends. In that respect, there needs to be a better understanding of the market for ICT skills, ongoing official forecasts of supply and demand, and regular monitoring of the situation to minimize gaps. Structural changes to government administrations and business enterprises are needed to incorporate ICT as a strategic function. China's governments, enterprises, and schools must work together to increase ICT knowledge and skills at all stages of people's lives to enable them to participate in an inclusive information society.

In the case of rural informatization, efforts to build capacity and raise awareness are expected to span many departments and levels of policymakers and administrators. These include the Ministry of Agriculture, Ministry of Culture; Ministry of Information Industry, provincial decision makers and administrators; managers, owners, and entrepreneurs of information centers; central and local content and service providers; leaders of rural communities and farmer groups; rural commercial and agricultural enterprises; farmer and professional cooperatives; and ICT technical staff and information intermediaries. The poorest and most remote areas may be targeted for specially tailored awareness campaigns and Internet literacy.

Internet access points and information center managers and entrepreneurs are at the heart of ensuring sustainability and impact by selecting and adapting appropriate services and content, developing viable business plans, mobilizing resources, analyzing markets, and building partnerships with various sources for content and support services. Telecenter networks and educational institutions around the world have been developing specially tailored programs for training such local pioneers. India has developed a consortium of partners, including the NASSCOM Foundation and WorldCorps, to develop common training modules for entrepreneurship, community development, grassroots marketing, services development, and infomediary skills.

Capacity building should also cover traditional and potential information intermediaries. In rural areas where literacy (including IT literacy) is low, the sophistication of ICT tools and Internet search methods may intimidate users. Increasingly, ICT intermediaries (or so-called agents of change) such as lead farmers, agriculture product associations, and nongovernmental organizations (NGOs) are actively involved in providing explanation and demonstration information to rural populations.

Promoting Affordable, Sustainable Public Access to ICT

Access is a key to the success of ICT literacy, e-government services, and a host of e-business and e-society applications. Public facilities with access to ICT are needed for people without access at home, school, or work. E-government can be promoted by increasing the number of Internet access centers in public buildings, enabling individuals to access local, national, and international information resources. China's government should consider a wide-scale program that would ensure access to e-government applications – including training and assistance – through a network of public facilities.

Providing public access points for information services is a particularly critical element for rural informatization. Although various government ministries have built up many public access points such as cultural stations, rural information service stations, and informatization "experience" centers through their own projects, most are heavily dependent on government subsidies and suffer from low sustainability. In addition, rural areas in China often lack the subscriber density to make ICT deployment economically viable for private investment. The key issue is how to ensure that rural ICT projects eventually generate reasonable returns to cover at least their operating costs (after one-off initial capital investments).

In a few developing countries, innovative business models have emerged involving PPPs. They use private sector contributions to provide basic public access for free or nearly free, generate and maintain relevant demand-driven content, adapt ICT to provide affordable and maintainable products, and provide training and capacity building for rural residents. These approaches, among others, ease the burden on government for fully financing such initiatives. They can be adapted to the Chinese context.

International experiences also suggest that engaging NGOs and local communities or targeted user groups (such as women or rural youth) can promote community learning and innovation in services and business models. Some NGOs have used the franchise model and been able to achieve scale. Some have engaged in community development and reached out to the poorest groups in rural areas and other vulnerable groups. Still others have partnered with the private sector, ICT multinationals, foundations, and aid agencies. China's national strategy should accommodate these diverse models and encourage local hybrids.

Many government projects in China have already been initiated with the goal of providing needed information and services for rural consumers. The Golden projects offer access to key government services (tax, registration, payments, and so on), coupled with ongoing distance education and initiatives providing agricultural information. These projects offer a variety of services relevant to rural users. Aggregating government information and services at one-stop shops can reduce transaction costs for farmers and rural enterprises. Such centers may also be able to provide cross-subsidies between the most profitable, high-demand services and new services that may require demand mobilization, market development, or capacity building for the poor. In China the development of such comprehensive public service platforms at the township or village level would be a step toward improving service offerings and government coordination.

Developing Intermediary Institutions and Networks

Intermediary or support institutions can help support individual service centers as well as groups of them to exploit economies of scale and scope. These networks, associations, and support institutions can offer common services and day-to-day support for business management, technical troubleshooting, and product and content development, among other services. A common thread is that these intermediary institutions work with the information service centers to make them more effective, sustainable, and valuable to the communities they serve. In China such horizontal and grassroots networks have not been encouraged because most initiatives have been vertical and supply-driven, and local centers have been looking upward – not locally or regionally – for direction and support.

These networks and support institutions can also provide training, mentoring, support, and coaching on management issues, and about services and techniques used in other centers. Peer learning and knowledge sharing should be a critical feature of the new strategy. These networks can also provide peer-support email lists, onsite maintenance, and monitoring and evaluation services. Finally, these networks can provide advocacy- and policy-related activities, and thus provide valuable feedback to provincial and central level policymakers.

Encouraging E-Business Through E-Government Initiatives

In a society and economy dominated by government, as in China, the government can set the example as an ICT leader and effective user. Government provision of online information and services can demonstrate the effects of ICT on businesses by spreading awareness of the potential for online delivery and interaction, and help build trust and security in online transactions. As model users, governments (central and local) can also act as standard-setters for ICT adoption by firms. To ensure access to public services and meet obligatory requirements for business purposes, firms would be encouraged to adopt ICT and adjust their choices of systems and software to maintain interoperability with existing online government services. Public e-procurement provides such an example. In addition, e-government efforts in fiscal and customs can have strong exemplary value.

Improving Links Between the ICT Industry, Innovation System, and Local Users

The Chinese government should work with local ICT firms to leverage its significant equipment industry to fulfill domestic needs. For example, it could provide incentives to local computer manufacturers to develop low-cost PCs to increase penetration among lower income households. This could have tremendous export potential as well, since many developing countries face the same challenge of being unable to afford ICT products. The large Chinese market means that producers can achieve significant economies of scale with consequent lower prices. The government should also move more quickly to remove obstacles to the rapid launch of new technological products and services into the Chinese market. This would allow leading-edge technologies to be implemented soon after standards approval, giving China a head start over other countries. Implementing these measures would produce substantial benefits, enhance sales, and establish China as a showcase for new technology.

Addressing barriers to innovation and to matching supply and demand of applications will require action across many elements of e-development. Structural barriers include an ivory-tower approach to engineering education, weak links between universities and industries, ineffective intellectual property protection, state-owned industries' domination of large markets, scarce venture capital funding, and lack of ICT-aware enterprises and e-leaders to articulate ICT needs in business terms and work with specialists on innovative applications. As the largest investor and lead user in ICT, the government can play a significant role in stimulating and matching ICT demand and supply.

The Chinese government can assess its incentives and support for R&D in application development, in support of local ICT adaptation for both business and government users. It can also assist firms by partnering with the private sector and supporting the development of complementary institutions and associations that provide advice on technology choice, identify and disseminate information on best practices, and assess e-commerce technologies and approaches.

Continuous R&D is also needed in technologies that enable network convergence. China's government, research institutes, operators, equipment manufacturers, and content and service providers need to collaborate and establish a comprehensive, multistakeholder process to determine key convergence goals to develop the needed hardware and supporting applications.

A big challenge for China is to entrust the private sector to participate in the next wave of important e-government initiatives and to create incentives for the country's application providers to develop the capability for supporting such complex tasks and innovating local solutions. Financial incentives could include outright funding support as well as tax holidays and interest subsidies for loans. Enforcing intellectual property rights more strictly could further support incentives for invention and local adaptation.

The same logic applies to seeking synergies across the supply and demand of e-development components in the software and information services. Building local capabilities in certain niches of software and in emerging areas like cloud computing could provide substantial capacity for China to adapt ICT for local government and small and medium-sized enterprises while building competitive advantage for exporting software and information services.

Promoting Learning, Monitoring, and Evaluation

As a large and diverse country, China presents a laboratory for innovation and learning about different business models, technologies, services, and partnerships. Substantial resources are being invested in informatization, yet evidence of the impact of these investments on growth, employment, and poverty reduction are lacking. Most initiatives are piloted and scaled up without the benefit of any common frameworks for monitoring and evaluation or institutional mechanisms to promote learning and experience sharing.

A learning, monitoring, and evaluation culture is critical to impact and sustainability. Thus, China's informatization strategy should invest in nurturing such a culture, and encourage the sharing of practical knowledge and experience. When designing ICT strategies and programs, governments and businesses have to bear in mind that informatization is not the ultimate goal, but an effective enabling tool for achieving economic transformation and poverty alleviation. Thus, it is important for governments and businesses to define the objectives that need to be achieved as well as the indicators and measures of progress. Otherwise there is a danger that ICT development programs could eventually be abandoned once initial expectations are not met and the original hype is over.

Acknowledgment The authors thank Kaoru Kimura for conducting excellent research analysis for this chapter.

References

BMI (Business Monitor International). 2008. "China Telecommunications Report Q2 2008." London.

BMI (Business Monitor International). 2010. "China Telecommunications Report Q4 2010." London.

CCID (China Center for Information Industry Development). 2005. "Relationship among E-government, E-commerce and E-community." Beijing.

China Dong Wu Ren Cai Hotline. 2005. "Ministry of Information Industry: Lack of Human Resources is an Obstacle for the IT Industry in China." Su-zhou. [http://www.dwrc.sz.js.cn/dwrc/Common/winopen.asp?ID=339&Type=1.].

China Netcom. 2005. http://www.china-netcom.com/english/inv/Corporate.htm.

China Telecom. 2005. http://www.chinatelecom-h.com/eng/corpinfo/structure.htm.

China TechNews, "Chinese Ministers Appointed for New MII." 26 March 2008.

CNNIC (China Internet Network Information Center). 2010. " Statistical Report on Internet Development in China (July 2010)".

—. 2008. "21st Statistical Survey Report on the Internet Development in China (January 2008). " CNNIC.

Gregory, Neil, Nollen, Stanley, and Tenev, Stoyan. 2009. *New Industries from New places.* Washington, DC: World Bank.

Hanna, Nagy K. 2008. "Why a Holistic e-Development Framework?" In *Information Technology and International Development Journal.* Mass: MIT Press Volume 4, Number 4, Fall/Winter 2008, pp 1–7.

—. 2009a. *e-Transformation: Enabling New Development Strategies.* New York: Springer.

—. 2009b. *Enabling Enterprise Transformation: Business and Grassroots Innovation for the Knowledge Economy.* New York: Springer.

—. Transforming Government and Building the Information Society: Challenges and Opportunities for the Developing World. New York: Springer.

Hanna, Nagy K. and Christine Zhenwei Qiang. 2009. "Trends in National E-Government Institutions" in *Information and Communications for Development 2009: Extending Reach and Increasing Impact.* Washington, D.C.: World Bank.

Horsley, Janie P. 2004. "Shanghai Advances the Cause of Open Government Information in China. " Yale Law School, China Law Center, New Haven, Connecticut. [http://chinalaw.law.yale.edu/shanghai_article.pdf].
Letner, R. L. 2005. "China's Electronic Signatures Law Goes into Effect." http://www.dwt.com/practc/sha_chi/bulletins/04-05_ElectronicSignatures.htm.
Ministry of Commerce. 2004. *China's E-commerce.* Beijing: Economic Science Press.
Ministry of Education. 2003. *National Statistics Yearbook of Graduate Student Enrollment, 1996–2002.* Beijing: Aviation University Press.
IDC (International Data Consulting)/BSA (Business Software Alliance). 2003. "Expanding Global Economics: The Benefits of Reducing Software Piracy." [http://www.bsa.org/resources/upload/IDC-White-Paper.pdf].
IMF (International Monetary Fund). 2010. International Financial Statistics and Balance of Payments databases.
ITU (International Telecommunication Union). 2010. World Telecommunication/ ICT database.
OECD (Organization for Economic Co-operation and Development). 2010. Information Technology Outlook 2010. Paris. OECD.
Perkinson, Ron. 2005. "Beyond Secondary Education: The Promise of ICT for Higher Education and Lifelong Learning." In Robert Schware, ed., *E-development: From Excitement to Effectiveness.* Washington, DC: World Bank.
Qiang, Christine Zhenwei. 2001. "Building the Information Infrastructure." In *Seizing the 21st Century: China Knowledge Economy.* Ed. C. J. Dahlman and J. Aubert, Washington , D.C.: World Bank.
Qiang, Christine Zhenwei. 2007. *China's Information Revolution.* Washington, D.C.: World Bank.
Qiang, Christine Zhenwei, Nagy K. Hanna, Asheeta Bhavnani, Kaoru Kimura, and Sudan, Randeep. 2009. *Rural Informatization in China.* Washington, D.C.: World Bank.
Qiang, Christine Zhenwei, George R. Clarke, and Naomi Halewood. 2006. "The Role of ICT in Doing Business. " In *Information and Communications for Development 2006: Global Trends and Policies.* Washington, DC: World Bank.
Qu, Weizhi. 2005. "Opening Remarks. " Presented at the workshop "Informatization Strategy and Economic Transformation: Trends, Experiences and Outlooks, " sponsored by the World Bank and the Department for Information Development (Dfid), Su-zhou, May 6.
UNCTAD (United Nations Conference on Trade and Development). 2007. "Foreign Direct Investment Statistics. " Geneva.
World Bank. 2009. *Information and Communications for Development 2009: Extending Reach and Increasing Impact.* Washington, D.C.: World Bank.
——. "Policies for the 11th Five-Year Plan." Mimeo. Washington, DC.
——. "China ICT Level and Investment Needs Assessment Survey." Washington, D.C.
Yong, James SL. 2005. *Enabling Public Service Innovation in the 21st Century: E-Government in Asia.* Singapore: Times Editions.
Yusuf, Shahid, and Simon J. Evenett. 2002. *Can East Asia Compete? Innovation for Global Markets.* New York: Oxford University Press.

Chapter 4
Toward a Community-Based E-Development in Canada

Garth Graham and Nagy K. Hanna

Canada's experience tells a story of e-development that started with great promise and a national vision of "Connected Canada," then got stuck in the snow. Canada became a highly connected nation early in the twenty-first century, thanks to citizens' enthusiastic experimentation with the Internet use, coupled with federally led initiatives to secure universal access and government online services. Since, Canada's ranking as information society has declined. This chapter explores the reasons for this decline. E-leadership capacity was not institutionalized. E-development was undermined by changes in the political leadership and an ideological commitment to reduce the role of government. Vested interests from primary telecom carriers, among others, took full advantage of the leadership vacuum to obstruct the structural reforms necessary for Canada's further transition to an information economy. Canada neglected to build on its earlier achievements and to learn from its earlier experiments.

This chapter examines the interplay between top-down policy directions and grassroots, community-level initiatives, and how this interplay and balance can evolve over time, reflecting the nature of a networked economy. The authors suggest that an Internet culture and the building of community-level capacity for e-development can compensate, at least in part, for limited e-leadership at the federal and provincial government levels. Community-driven e-development is a promising approach, if not an imperative, for countries such as Canada where significant levels of connectivity and e-literacy have been achieved.

It is hoped that Canada will not continue to spin its wheels in the snow, and instead, will build on its strengths for community collaboration and grassroots initiative to develop a community-level capacity for e-development. A renewed national vision and federal leadership commitment can complement and support these community-based efforts and further improve the structural conditions and accelerate the transition to an information society and digital economy.

The coverage of Canadian e-development initiatives in this chapter is selective. The aim is to illuminate the political economy and policy reform process

N.K. Hanna and P.T. Knight (eds.), *Seeking Transformation Through Information Technology*, Innovation, Technology, and Knowledge Management,
DOI 10.1007/978-1-4614-0353-1_4, © Springer Science+Business Media, LLC 2011

shaping e-development. This country case shows the influence of the political and cultural factors, and the Internet in particular, on the role of ICT in transforming existing structures and creating collaborative ecologies and innovative commons. It then examines the rationale for and potential of community-driven e-development. It ends with calls for action arising from growing concerns that Canada is slipping in its e-readiness and competitiveness rankings as well as a reversal in its progress to reduce the digital divide and use ICT for public good and social development.

Beginning a Discourse

Early in the 1990s, there was a discourse on e-development in Canada. But now it is silent. In deconstructing the silence, it would be untrue to state that Canada has abandoned its position as a "world leader" in the uses of the Internet for development. That would imply someone had thought about it. If the silence is a sin, it is one of omission. There is no longer a sustained commitment to a comprehensive national vision. The issues of e-development are not a concern of everyday politics. The reasons why are embedded in the general context of Canadian politics and public administration.

Success in Canadian political decision-making can be understood as a process of holding competing visions of Canada in balance. But the Canada of today has no means to examine its collective aspirations as a nation, never mind the particulars of its response to the complexities of an Internet Economy. Conscious of this absence, the Canadian electorate has just voted three times for minority governments.[1] They presumed correctly that national capacity for government can continue while the ability to govern should be limited.

This put Canadian politicians in a double bind. Partisan conflict has risen because of the tensions that have been produced by sharing power in minority governments. Canadians are not hard-nosed partisans. John Ralston Saul has listed the "strategic elements"[2] of Canadians:

- Obsession with egalitarianism.
- Desire to maintain a balance of individuals and groups.
- Delight in playing with a nonmonolithic idea of society – a delight in complexity.
- Tendency to run society as an ongoing negotiation, which must be related to our distaste for resolving complexities.

[1] Since June 2004 to the date of writing, Canada has had 5 years of minority government and current polls predict a continuation of the trend. When asked to choose, Canadians are consistently saying, "None of the above."

[2] Saul (2008) pp. 54–55.

- Preference for consensus – again an expression of society as a balance of complexity, a sort of equilibrium.
- Belief that behind the formal written and technical face of society lies something more important, which Canadians try to get at through complex relationships.
- Sense that the clear resolution of differences will lead to injustice and even violence.
- Preference for minimal impairment – the obligation of those in authority to do as little damage as possible to people and to rights when exercising that authority.

In the jargon of global Internet Governance debates, Canadians believe in the efficacy of "collaborative peer-to-peer relationships in open systems" in the resolution of complex problems. By causing an enormous shift in the autonomy of individuals, the Internet intensifies the significance of their local knowledge and practices. The Internet intensifies the self-determination of identity and redefines the nature of governance.[3]

The networks of an "Internet Economy" are made up of people, not technologies. Viewing the Internet as a symptom of a transformation already in being makes it possible to ask – what happens when a nation, acting as an organizational system that learns, begins to internalize that transformation?

This question is at the heart of e-development planning as a practice. As individuals, many Canadians would recognize the importance of modeling the Canadian society[4] as an organizational system that learns. But, at the national government level and in current Canadian politics, there is no obvious repository of intellectual curiosity about the nature of the socioeconomic and political shifts in the system's worldview and governance that the Internet's existence reveals. And yet, there is a rapidly growing political responsibility to apply what we now know about daily life online.

Canada is almost a fully wired country.[5] But the Government of Canada is resting on the assumption that the technology in itself is the job, and that the job is largely finished. Deregulation of the telecommunications industries in favor of a "market-based approach" has slowed down Internet-oriented infrastructure investment. As a consequence of policy drift, and because of growing bandwidth limitations and an absence of plans and policies to address them, growth in capacity for the effective use of ICTs in Canada has stalled.

Whatever the Canadian experience of addressing and then neglecting e-development shows, Canada is a nation with an advanced networked economy. Its economy is Internet based. Yet its capacity to formally recognize and address the significance of that fact is extremely limited.

---

[3] Although the roots of the shift appear in the arts and sciences in the early years of the twentieth century, the new voices for governance this amplifies have only begun to speak.

[4] As opposed to the "Government of Canada."

[5] OECD Broadband Portal – as at June 2008, Canada was tenth overall in broadband penetration per 100 people.

Canadian Experience with Federally Led E-Development

What was e-development in Canada, where did it come from, what does it do, and why does it do that? This section describes four examples of agencies and initiatives enabling Canada's initial capacity for e-development and provides brief histories of their current status in terms of the evolution of public policy. These are Government OnLine, Community Access Program (CAP), the Canadian Network for the Advancement of Research Industry and Education, and the Telecommunications Policy Review Panel (TPRP).

Under the heading of the "Connecting Canadians Agenda,"[6] many of the key federally initiated e-development activities were led by Industry Canada, the Department of the Government of Canada that oversees technical and industrial elements of telecommunications. Industry Canada's mandate is "to help make Canadians more productive and competitive in the knowledge-based economy, thus improving the standard of living and quality of life in Canada."[7]

A complete description of all such initiatives falls outside the scope of this chapter.[8] That description would review policy evolution related to many other programs including SchoolNet, Broadband for Regional and Northern Development (BRAND), the Smart Communities Program, convergence with Heritage Canada's Broadcast Act, e-Commerce Policy and Canada's role in the OECD, the relationship between the Information Technology Association of Canada (ITAC) and the Information Highway Advisory Councils, and Canada's international role in Internet Governance forums. But the picture of a disconnection between past experience and future needs provided by these four examples would remain unchanged.

Government On-Line[9]

In 1999, the Government of Canada committed to become "known around the world as the government most connected to its citizens, with Canadians able to access all government information and services on-line at the time and place of their choosing." Championed by the Treasury Board Secretariat Advisory Committee on Information Management Subcommittee, the Government On-line (GOL) Initiative

[6] First appearing in a platform statement prior to the 1993 election called, "Creating Opportunity: The Liberal Plan for Canada," and later incorporated into annual budgets. In Canada, Parliamentary Acts of Appropriation (budgets) are a form of law.

[7] Department Mandate Statement. Industry Canada Web site.

[8] For a deeper look into policy evolution, see: Bodnar et al. (2005). "This document constitutes a 'policy map' summary of activities relating to telecommunications and broadcasting in Canada, network access, e-commerce, e-learning, and various other informatics initiatives leading up to and through the development of what is now known as the Internet."

[9] Public Works and Government Services Canada. Web site.
Treasury Board of Canada Secretariat. Web site.

was officially launched on April 6, 2000. The program sunsetted in 2006 as intended and, as it concluded, its operational responsibilities for e-government services delivery transferred from oversight by Treasury Board to Public Works and Government Services Canada (PWGSC). What got lost in the transfer were its significant strengths in organizational transformation processes.

As a key component of the Government of Canada's service strategy, it was guided by two principles:

- Organizing services and information in a client-centered way, to meet the needs and expectations of citizens and business.
- A "whole of government" approach to provide access to the entire range of government services regardless of what channel is used (telephone, in-person, or Web) or which department, agency, or level of government is responsible for the service.

The GOL Initiative generated:

- A common look and feel for all government Websites
- Access to integrated information and services through Government of Canada Web portals
- On-line availability of the 130 most commonly used services, offering various levels of on-line functionality
- Secure transactions
- An electronic payment capability
- Introduction of an on-line authentication service known as epass

GOL included significant development of Organizational Transformation Readiness Assessment (OTRA) processes for measuring the current capacity of governmental agencies to utilize e-government for their own services improvement. The long-term goals of government service transformation were quite ambitious, involving:

- A significant improvement in the quality and the delivery of government services to Canadians
- Transforming the internal operations of government to achieve efficiencies and increased transparency
- Laying the foundation for the future, enabling the ongoing transformation of government services across all three levels of government in Canada
- As a "client-driven exercise," helping government employees put an end to the "silo syndrome," enabling them to see themselves as part of the broader enterprise

For three consecutive years, 2002–2004, the international consultancy firm Accenture singled out Canada as the world leader in e-government. In large measure, this rating was due to its progress in the "service transformation stage" of e-government.

> Once again, Canada's focus on self-examination and its relentless pursuit of user feedback have allowed it to continue to build what is clearly one of the world-leading customer-focused government online programs.[10]

[10] Government Executive Series (2004).

But Accenture also noted that, even in Canada, the GOL job was only a beginning.

> The agenda now is to move from driving development of e-Government for its own sake, to driving public-sector value through transformed service delivery. The government of the future must be ready for the customer of the future: the up-and-coming generation, with a familiarity and ease with multiple technologies and an assumption of always-on service, ready for them whenever they desire. These are not the people running governments today, nor are they by-and-large the populations governments currently serve. They soon will be, however, and governments need to be ready for them (p. 48). ... Canada needs to move more quickly to leverage its gains and achievements to date and accelerate the implementation of the next wave of seamless, multijurisdictional service offerings.[11]

The sunsetting of the GOL Initiative occurred as planned in the early days of the first conservative minority government. There has not been a successor program. The Treasury Board's Chief Information Officer Branch (CIOB)[12] includes a responsibility to coordinate information management and information technology strategies in "communities of practice" across the Government of Canada. But, the equivalent of the outwardly oriented GOL Advisory Panel, which featured largely in the "feedback" successes outlined in the Accenture critiques, is now absent from the CIOB.

Within the CIOB, the Organizational Readiness Office (ORO)[13] supports "government change initiatives that impact the IM and IT communities." Unlike the OTRA processes, their focus shifted to the internal information management and information technology "community," and away from departmental capacity to outwardly and openly orient services toward citizens.

Such introversion has consequences. A disconnect has emerged. For example, in 2001, a horizontal networked community of practice related to the use of open source software[14] emerged across departments in the Government of Canada. They actively sought to work "under the radar." Fully aware of the implications for organizational transformation, they feared that, if senior public servants understood their work, they would shut it down.

Technological changes continue to offer opportunities to transform government online services that could be captured by a more active and collaborative government. For example, Canada's public service provision could increasingly rely on citizens, communities, and NGOs as collaborators in providing citizen-centric services and bottom-up regulatory solutions. But this assumes that government leaders would assume the role of transformational leaders, to build an open and collaborative public sector culture, support change agents within the government, and commit to citizen-centric service.

Under the current administration, IT managers are unlikely to be made into change agents for the uses of e-government for socioeconomic development and political reform. The target for changed organizational behavior to address issues of

---

[11] The Government Executive Series 2005. (Accenture ceased making reports that ranked e-government progress in countries after 2006.)

[12] CIOB web site.

[13] Organizational Readiness Office web site.

[14] Largely a matter of networking software applications, not desk-tops.

e-governance needs to include socioeconomic development strategists, political decision-makers, change managers, and transformational leaders – not just IT operational managers. Skills development at an operational level is only one of several essential dimensions of capacity to use the Internet in the reform of governance.

The Community Access Program

The story of the CAP chronicles a drift in digital inclusion policies. At the "program" level, CAP was extremely successful in leveraging networked cooperation among thousands of community-based social service organizations across Canada. At the "policy" level, it was successful in causing autonomous network capacity to emerge. But that success revealed underlying tensions among the governors and the governed over functions and values in the local application of e-development. Canadian community networkers have been steadily learning collaborative practices in using the Internet for community development. The means of sharing that experience more broadly is available. Steadily and consistently, the voices telling that story have been ignored.

Beginning in 1995, CAP was initiated as a 10-year digital divide program under Connecting Canadians. Originally it was intended to sunset Mar 31, 2006. But, because of strong public pressure organized by participating regional CAP networking agencies,[15] it continues to exist. Because of its crosscutting impacts on social policy and its "community" emphasis, it has never really had a comfortable home in the department responsible for its design and operation, Industry Canada. In 2009, it is administered by the Department's Regional and Rural Development Initiatives. Its aim is "to provide Canadians with affordable public access to the Internet and the skills they need to use it effectively":

> With the combined efforts of the federal, provincial and territorial governments, community groups, social agencies, libraries, schools, volunteer groups, and the business community, CAP helps Canadians, wherever they live, take advantage of emerging opportunities in the new global knowledge-based economy. Under CAP, public locations such as schools, libraries, and community centers act as "on-ramps" to the Information Highway, and provide computer support and training. The program plays a crucial role in bridging the Digital Divide; contributing to the foundation for electronic access to government services; encouraging on-line learning and literacy; fostering the development of community-based infrastructure; and promoting Canadian e-commerce.[16]

CAP is complemented by the Community Access Program Youth Initiative (CAP YI), providing employment opportunities to young Canadians between the ages of 15 and 30 in various CAP sites across the country.

---

[15] For some of the history of that pressure see: CAP (b).

[16] CAP (a).

Just prior to the launch of CAP in 1995, a workshop was held at the Third Canadian Community Networking Conference and the First Annual General Meeting of Telecommunities Canada[17] in Victoria, BC, August 1995. Its title was "The SchoolNet and Community Access Programs; Bringing Rural Canada into the Information Age." It was hosted by Industry Canada and the consulting agency contracted to design those two programs.

Conflict arose at that Conference when community networkers noted that the program would only be successful if it converged with community networking practices for digital inclusion. The federal program representatives objected that CAP's role was far more narrowly limited to "access," particularly to the downloading of government information at publicly accessible "sites" once the Government of Canada went online. A break occurred between community networking as a practice and community access as a program that took a decade to heal. Oddly enough, the key model for the early stages of SchoolNet, and CAP in particular, was National Capitol FreeNet, a community-based grassroots initiative.

Beside CAP, Industry Canada's planning and implementation of many Connecting Canadians programs[18] did include participatory or advisory processes. But both participation and mandate for these processes were narrowly defined and carefully selected. Participants from outside government and industry often felt coopted, as if advice was a euphemism for the assessment of political threat. Every time community-based organizations formed independent coalitions to address the Internet's implications for positive social change, they recommended open national processes for public dialogue.[19] Every such recommendation has been ignored without comment.

Anticipating the sunsetting of the Program, representatives of a now extensive CAP "community" met at a community networking "Summit" in Vancouver in March of 2003. They agreed that a national CAP Association was needed. The gathering endorsed a proposal "From Access To Inclusion"[20] which called for an association and a reinvigorated CAP Program. At the summit one person from each province and territory was nominated to take the work forward. They requested that the Government of Canada:

- Establish a national policy and plan to lead delivery of connectivity and access strategies aimed to develop community socioeconomic opportunity, equity, inclusion, and well-being

[17] Telecommunities Canada (TC) is a national community of practice about the uses of online networks for community development. Together with like-minded groups, its goal is to connect theory, policy, and practice in ways that expand and improve the ability of communities to design their own future. TC has become a significant repository of, and network for, the local experience gained through public participation in the Community Access Program. TC advocates for control of open broadband networks as a local responsibility. http://www.tc.ca.

[18] IHAC, SchoolNet, CAP, Smart Communities, BRAND, etc.

[19] The most comprehensive example is: Key Elements of a National Access Strategy: A Public Interest Proposal. IPRP, Faculty of Information Studies, University of Toronto.

[20] National CAP Pictou–Vancouver Working Group 2004.

- Provide sufficient multiyear funding to enable effective community-based planning and delivery
- Establish, in concert with local Community Access partners, accountability criteria that enables community development and innovation
- Establish a National Community Access Steering Committee to liaise with provincial, regional, and local partners

When Industry Canada ignored the request for support of a National Community Access Steering Committee, they formed their working group into an association under the heading of CANCAP in March 2004. CANCAP's subsequent synthesis of "best practices" surfaced two new perspectives on national program needs in a society where everyone is online:

- That horizontal community-based control of socioeconomic development was an essential capacity for national success in an Internet Economy.
- That the view of a "digital divide" as a time-bound problem of technical access needed to be replaced by a view of "digital inclusion" as an on-going community-based process that helps provide all Canadians with the opportunity to succeed in an Internet Economy.

In 2005 and 2006, CANCAP successfully continued its lobbying efforts to have CAP extended, to the degree that current CAP site Contribution Agreements include a clause that states, "no part of a contribution will be paid towards the cost of lobbyist services."[21] In Feb 2005, they noted:

> CAP Program ends Mar 31, 2006 leaving an unused legacy of local, regional, and national cross-sectoral networks with significant technology infrastructure.
>
> Renewed CAP Program Strategy: We are unable to guess at how a community will use technology to enhance their local community sustainability. That decision needs to come from communities, and so we are proposing that a "site model" of service delivery be enhanced. It is through the sharing of strategies and best practices in communities that we will achieve our goal of enhancing the sustainability of local communities. Within the CAP movement the infrastructure of networks exists to support this work.[22]

It became clear to the CANCAP members that they needed to find a collaborative governance structure for themselves that represented a strong community perspective in terms of ICT use. Noting the "enormous support" they'd received from the board of Telecommunities Canada, they decided that the work of CANCAP could effectively continue under Telecommunities Canada's umbrella without the necessity of forming another national association:

Through Telecommunities Canada we can continue to:

- Develop our strategy to share best practices (Stories That Travel).
- Be a strong advocate and national voice for those who are working with and integrating technology at a community level.

---

[21] Applicant Declaration on Lobbying. CAP.

[22] CANCAP (2005).

- Weave together a strong network of regional access networks, individual organizations, and committed individuals and begin to share the wealth of knowledge and experience that is out there.

This bridged the gap that had occurred in 1995 between community networking and community access. Industry Canada has never acknowledged or reacted to this decision.

The effort continues to ensure that the voices[23] of community-based experience for action on digital inclusion are heard. In thinking about what could occur "beyond CAP,"[24] Telecommunities Canada has called for development of a National Strategy for Digital Inclusion, noting:

> What CAP proves is that, in a society that is online, people marginal to that society are going to be online. Their problem is not access to infrastructure. Its access to the means of using what the infrastructure enables. "Digital Inclusion" programs are designed to enhance their capacity to use the Internet for their own personal development. … Getting acceptance at all levels of government to a community-based approach for the support of digital inclusion will involve:
>
> 1. A need for open forums for discussion of the existing program's "lessons learned" and its future potential under an evolved program.
> 2. New public policy that endorses the role of digital inclusion in Canada's national strategies for the uses of information and communications technologies in socioeconomic development (and, yes, we know there are not any such strategies).
> 3. Support of a new federal-provincial "transitional" program, allowing for a staged transfer of primary operational responsibility to the provinces along with an annual federal funding in recognition of on-line delivery of federal services and programs. It is the provinces that have the most direct involvement with the community-based organizations and institutions that act as delivery points for digital inclusion services as essential infrastructure. It is that local control that will make the program relevant to community-based economic development.

Both CANCAP and Telecommunities Canada's efforts to facilitate pressure from community-based organizations receiving CAP contributions have been fairly successful in keeping CAP alive. In a letter,[25] Dec 30, 2008, to the Minister of Industry, Tony Clement, Telecommunities Canada noted:

> Our ability to compete in the global economy will depend on making our communities more resilient and less dependant on external supports. Over the last few years, broadband has become an essential part of local infrastructure. But we are still without a national strategy that supports and promotes the use of this new infrastructure for socio-economic development at the community level.

There is no reference to CAP, (in fact, no reference to its parent the Information Highway Applications Branch (IHAB) or, except for Computer for Schools, any of the programs it hosted under Connecting Canadians), in the 2009–2010 business

---

[23] Internet for Everyone Campaign.

[24] Graham (2010).

[25] Correspondence from Gareth Shearman, President, Telecommunities Canada.

plans of Industry Canada. And, although limited public funding continues, there are no obvious channels for public dialogue on CAP's future direction. While it still acknowledges that CAP contributes "to the foundation for electronic access to government services," the Government of Canada is slowly backing away from a significant example of a successful public–private partnership with civil society.

The Canadian Network for the Advancement of Research Industry and Education Partnership[26]

Based in Ottawa, the Canadian Network for the Advancement of Research Industry and Education Partnership (CANARIE) was created in 1993 by the private sector and academia under the leadership of the Government of Canada in order to accelerate the introduction of high-speed networks. CANARIE continues to be the coordinating authority for advanced research networks on the national Internet backbone. It serves universities, colleges, schools, government laboratories, research institutes, hospitals, and other organizations in a wide variety of fields in both the public and private sectors. It is supported by membership fees, with major funding of its programs and activities provided by the Government of Canada through Industry Canada.

> "By promoting and participating in strategic collaborations among key sectors, and by partnering with peer networks and organizations around the world, CANARIE Inc. stimulates and supports research, innovation and growth, bringing economic, social, and cultural benefits to Canadians"

It serves to facilitate the "flexible use of network resources and flexible use of distributed equipment and resources" in that context of research. But its formation also served to begin the move toward total privatization and deregulation of Canadian communications systems. Prior to the creation of CANARIE, the Internet "backbone" had been developed and maintained through a cooperative and largely open arrangement among governments, the private sector, and academia. Since the Government of Canada largely financed that arrangement, the Internet's governance and its transport layer "ownership" were essentially in the public domain.

As CANARIE became established, Industry Canada transferred ownership and responsibility for the transport layer to Bell Canada Enterprises. The "nuts and bolts" of the Internet backbone were gifted to Canada's ICT and telecommunications industries by the Government of Canada, forgetting that those agencies must act in a framework of broader strategic concepts in order to have any direct relevance to a conscious development direction. In spite of strenuous efforts by some participants in the original open arrangement, all attempts to debate the transfer of ownership as an issue of Internet governance in the public interest failed.

---

[26] CANARIE web site.

Some of CANARIE's successes in the development, demonstration, and implementation of next-generation technologies include:

- Under the original title of *CA*net*, CANARIE upgraded Canada's research and education Internet backbone by increasing the network's capacity over 400 times between 1993 and 1997.
- In April 1994, CANARIE established the *National Test Network* (NTN) to help industry, universities, hospitals, and government research institutions work together to explore new technologies, test hardware and software, and develop new services.
- In June 1997, CANARIE launched a new advanced networking initiative called the *CA*net 2*.
- The *Applications and Technology* program has involved over 500 companies and has created over 2,250 well paying, high-tech jobs since 1995.
- In October of 1997, CANARIE's *Pilot Project for Aboriginal Networking* awarded $1.25 million to further accelerate the development of network-based products and services by Canada's aboriginal communities.
- In 1998, CANARIE built the National Optical Network *CA*net 3*, the world's first nation-wide Internet built directly around wave-division multiplexing technology. Its design was then replicated by many other network operators, both in the research and education as well as commercial domains.
- Then exponential growth in network traffic, expected growth in new high bandwidth applications, and planned extreme high bandwidth grid projects required that a new network be built to support leading-edge research in Canada. To this end, the Government of Canada committed $110 million to CANARIE for the design, deployment, and operation of CA*net 4, completed in May 2003.

Provisioned at 10 Gbp speeds, CAnet 4 was intended to yield a total initial network capacity of between four and eight times that of CAnet 3. But its funding appropriation was actually a trade-off to block a budget request for $1 billion to complete Connecting Canadians made by Industry Minister Brian Tobin.

In looking forward, CANARIE has noted that, "Solving the so-called 'last mile' problem for broadband services is one of the grand challenges facing the networking world." In addressing the problem, they support the concepts of municipal fiber networks, and "Customer Empowered Networking" from the home to the ISP. But CANARIE remains a privileged walled garden. It has been given no incentive to scale its applications or to apply its practical experience outside the world of science.

Telecommunications Policy Review Panel

In April 2005, the Minister of Industry appointed a TPRP to examine the policy and regulatory frameworks surrounding telecommunications. It was to make recommendations to ensure that Canada has "a strong, internationally competitive telecommunications industry, with world-class services for the economic and social benefit of all Canadians." On Mar 22, 2006, the Panel proposed 127 legislative, institutional, and social recommendations intended to improve the effectiveness of the current regulatory framework.

In keeping with its mandate, the TPRP deliberately restricted its viewpoint to the "telecommunications and ICT sector" within Canada, rather than to anything as broad as a "vision" for e-development. It was intended as a return to something rather more pragmatic, and more "consistent with the government's smart regulation commitments," than as an extension of the Connecting Canadian Program. Reflecting a kind of technological determinism, it saw the technologies themselves as the primary agency of change:

> "The products and services of this new sector are fuelling productivity, economic growth and competition. They are changing the way Canadians communicate, create, learn, work, live and are entertained. They present the hope of better government, improved public services and a more inclusive society. They have the potential to strengthen communities and to help bridge the divides that exclude some Canadians from full participation in economic and social life."[27]

The liberal government of Paul Martin defined the mandate of TPRP. But it completed its mandate and delivered its report to the Conservative minority government of Stephen Harper. By that time, the Minister of Industry, David Emerson, had crossed the floor of the House of Commons and become the Conservative Minister for International Trade. In effect, with Emerson in the Cabinets of both governments, TPRP's recommendations articulate a two-party consensus by coincidence.

So, both the Liberals and the Conservatives believe that it was pragmatic to leave the future development of adequate broadband infrastructure to the primary telecommunications carriers. No one asked what would happen when there is a market failure in which the telecommunications industries do not deliver on broadband development. Any action in Canada to align the principles of an e-development policy agenda with the public good is going to require that a capacity for critical analysis emerge from somewhere. But no party and no effective national lobby group challenges the assertion that achieving market-based efficiency in the telecommunications sector is an adequate response to the changed structures of an Internet Economy.

However, TPRP made good policy recommendations, including:

- Separation of carriage and content
- Creation of a National ICT Advisory Council
- Establishing a new Department of ICTs as a unifying center[28]
- Formulation of a National ICT adoption strategy
- Ongoing evaluation of efforts to address primary issues

[27] Telecommunications Policy Review Panel (2006). Final Report.

[28] Or, to use the language of the e-development framework, TPRP did recommend a "cross-functional department to promote collaborative actions on policies and program implementation."

None of these recommendations were addressed. And, given three minority governments in a row and no real public pressure to address these concerns, it is unlikely that they will be.

Public interest groups sharing a commitment to community development online expressed common themes in their submissions to TPRP. The groups in question do have direct experience of what daily life in a fully connected Canada might feel like. Therefore, the nature of their themes is of particularly significant for the social action components of any national strategy for e-development. So the fact that they are almost entirely absent from the submissions made by industry and provincial governments is also significant. Themes listed as, "key policy issues for citizens of a knowledge society,"[29] included:

- Symmetrical peer-to-peer broadband as a basic service, because, online, everyone is a producer. But striving to achieve universal access to that service must maintain multiplicity and local involvement.
- Community-based open networks.
- A need for a technologically neutral definition of broadband oriented to use.
- A shift to a revenue/services model as central to an understanding of markets in a networked economy. This requires a clear separation of infrastructure providers (the physical layer) from services providers (the applications layer).
- A government role in defending Internet Protocol in the sense of a commons.
- A government role in leveraging procurement by specifying community-based open access in the purchase of network support.
- Continued Federal involvement in programs that support local engagement and choice in transition.
- Acknowledgement of the need for municipalities to address policies for ICT use.
- A vision of public policy grounded, not in the current conflicts over market ownership, but in the experience that Canadians now have of daily life online.
- Awareness that the price of universal access to technologies is not the primary social issue. Because Internet Protocol affects relationships, participation in and effective use of changed social institutions is now the primary social issue.

What the TPRP Report gave the Minister of Industry was exactly what he asked for – a blueprint of how to reform public policy and regulation to make the telecommunications industry, "more efficient and productive," at least in the short term. The minister asked an industry question and got an industry answer. What the minister did not get was a blueprint for how, in a knowledge-based society, the uses of information and communications technologies can be made to serve Canada's socioeconomic development.

In moving to deregulate telecommunications in favor of a market-based approach, the Government of Canada assumes that competition exists or can be made to exist in a given "market." But the prime carriers manipulate the market in the physical transportation or access layer in order to maximize the gain from their existing

[29] Graham (2005b). See also: Graham (2005a) and Graham (2006a).

infrastructure without change or transformation of business processes. The more that telecom providers are able to do this, the more that competition in the markets of the applications layer will be inhibited.

Following from TPRP and Industry Canada recommendations, the Cabinet issued a Policy Directive[30] to the Canadian Radio-television and Telecommunications Commission (CRTC) on Dec 14, 2006:

> The Policy Direction to the CRTC is an element of the Government's broader telecommunications policy agenda to decrease regulatory burden and make regulation more efficient and effective through increased reliance on market forces. ... In exercising its powers and performing its duties under the *Telecommunications Act*, CRTC shall implement the Canadian telecommunications policy objectives set out in section 7 of that Act, in accordance with the following:
>
> (a) The Commission should
>
> 1. Rely on market forces to the maximum extent feasible as the means of achieving the telecommunications policy objectives and
> 2. When relying on regulation, use measures that are efficient and proportionate to their purpose and that interfere with the operation of competitive market forces to the minimum extent necessary to meet the policy objectives

When relying on regulation, the CRTC was also instructed to use measures that satisfied very narrow criteria, excluding reference to any broad interpretation of the public good or Canada's socioeconomic benefit.

Speaking in terms of "gutting the Telecom Act,"[31] Philippa Lawson, Director of the Canadian Internet Policy and Public Interest Clinic, has noted that the TPRP proposals and the Cabinet Directive to the CRTC "reflect a much narrower view vision of the role and value of telecommunications in Canadian society than that held by many Canadians." She also noted that, "the proposed changes to Section 7 of the [Telecommunications] Act would significantly reduce the CRTC's flexibility to regulate for the benefit of Canada and Canadians." The effect of gutting the socioeconomic benefit objectives of the Telecommunications Act to support the recommendations for "reliance on market forces is to shift the onus for those calling for deregulation to those calling for regulation."

In other words, the burden of proof for the demonstration of harm shifts to those making the claim that harm has occurred. Clearly this offends John Ralston Saul's strategic element of "minimal impairment, the obligation of those in authority to do as little damage as possible to people and to rights when exercising that authority." Most Canadians are unaware that this change in policy direction has any implication for themselves. And, even if they were, there are no obvious institutional forums where they could speak to the issues. The phrase "deregulation of telecom policy through a market-based approach" completely bypasses an essential debate about what kind of a society Canadians might want in an Internet Economy.

---

[30] Telecommunications Act: Order Issuing a Direction to the CRTC on Implementing the Canadian Telecommunications Policy Objectives (2006).

[31] Lawson (2008).

A Need for a New Perspective on Internet Use Policy

These four capsule histories illustrate the texture of the public policy and program response of Canada's Federal Government as Canadians first encountered the Internet. The existence of all of these agencies shows a willingness to explore the transformation of institutions toward forms of structure that were more horizontal, networked, and interactive. The experience of these agencies revealed the necessity of making that shift. But, emerging as they did from an industrial society, they were based on the metaphorical assumption that the Internet and ICT could be understood as just a tool for making existing structures and markets more efficient, rather than as a potential enabler for transforming socioeconomic structures and markets, and for creating a collaborative ecology.

What if that assumption about the nature of technology is completely wrong? What if the technologies are not the cause of structural change but rather an inscription of changing practices in society? What if structural change has already occurred from within and has yet to be acknowledged? What happens then to the content of policy in the public interest? The key to a revised understanding can be found by taking a deeper look at the word "Protocol" in the phrase "Internet Protocol," and the implications it has for a change in our understanding of the nature and practices of governance.

What Is "Internet" About the Internet Economy?

Canada's failure to advance its embryonic institutional capacities for e-development to the next level ignores two key drivers of change. First, all countries, not just Canada, need to obtain a nuanced view of the complex realities for social change and governance implicit in the Internet's existence. The section following here describes elements of that view. The second factor is the current political context for Canadian public policy formulation. That factor is addressed in this section.

What motivated Canadian politicians and public servants to neglect their own experience of e-development? They believed it was prudent and pragmatic to reduce the role of government in the economy, ignoring that the economy is embedded in the society and not the reverse. Acting according to their belief, they accepted the familiar advice of the primary telecommunications carriers that communications could be privatized safely. They forgot that the act of communicating is an expression of culture, and that those who accept to govern have a responsibility to protect the broader public good as that culture defines it and no matter how rapidly it shifts.

In Canada, so far no one has asked – if we fully privatize our telecommunications infrastructure, will we still be Canadian? But they should. It matters not merely that Canadians communicate but how they communicate. We become who we are through the ways we talk among ourselves.

This is not, in any way, a matter of seeing culture as "content." It is a matter of culture as the way we see the world. In a Knowledge Society and Internet Economy, politicians and public servants have a responsibility to honor the cultural mindset that makes the Internet possible. In a society that only connects, finding the way forward requires honoring a major shift in the model of change on which those connections are based.

The Social Ecologies of Internet Culture: Open Systems of Self-Organization

The words governing a discourse matter. That "e" in e-development, e-government, e-governance, and e-transformation categorizes those processes as electronically mediated. That categorization runs the risk of shifting the discourse about those processes toward technological determinism.

> The Internet was first brought to the attention of government policy analysts though the lens of technological determinism. Viewed as technology policy, the Internet was understood as the province of engineers. We have been using spatial models (metaphors) to describe the feeling of daily life online – cyberspace, information highway, digital divide, desktop, etc. In reflecting categorically on the nature of our changing society itself, we've used classification models such as information society, knowledge society, knowledge-based economy, etc. We have only begun to use social orientation metaphors – interactive, connected, collaborative, etc. But they don't really resonate yet, except as abstractions or utopian desires.
>
> What is interesting, although still not satisfying, is the emergence of models that mix spatial and social orientation metaphors – network neutrality, commons-based peer production, community online, etc. This suggests that experience of "Internet Culture" is causing a shift to occur in our perceptions of what it is. We are moving away from seeing the Internet as a sort of built environment, and moving toward seeing it as a kind of mirror for a social ecology that grows through autonomous self-organization.[32]

First comes worldview. Then comes policy. Internet Protocol is the artifact that reveals the mindset of Internet Culture. Public policy has yet to flow from the worldview that Internet Protocol expresses.

The rule that governs the society we now live in is that things self-organize.[33] What we can know comes to us only through networks of relationship. Somehow the system makes itself. Natural selection only makes sense in a relational world, where structure arises through self-organization. Because it contradicts the notion of hierarchy as a principle of organization, there is strong resistance to this view of the origins of structure.

The Internet should be viewed as a symptom of change, not a cause of it. And the effective use of the Internet for development is also a symptom of the same change, not a cause of it. That shift in understanding of the relationship of cause to effect lets

---

[32] Ramirez et al. (2007).

[33] Smolin (2003).

us anticipate the future from the viewpoint of Internet Culture. The Internet can then be understood as a mirror that reflects an enormous cultural shift in both the autonomy of individuals and the significance of their local knowledge and practices.

Familiarity with the Internet as technology is not a guarantee of capacity to think about its socioeconomic impact. Nationally, the Government of Canada does not yet see Canada as making a transition to an Internet Economy. That view limits national capacity to think about the Internet's implications for a different understanding of organizational structure and productivity.

In order to adapt to this new worldview of self-organization, even democracy must evolve as it faces continually changing networks of relationship. It becomes necessarily pluralistic, experiential and experimental because, when everybody can connect to everybody, anybody can initiate something at any moment. And no one will be so unwise as to grant anyone the authority to "represent" them.

If we work backward from the desired future state – open and transparent governance in a society of open networks, a society where the functions of collaborative production and use are self-organized and distributed – it becomes very clear that the fundamental assumptions about how change is occurring need to be continuously reexamined. But, overall, Canada has no collective means of surfacing and evaluating whatever models of change are now in operation.

The correct model for growth of broadband infrastructure must be the Internet model itself. When it is, then the reasons why Internet Protocol must be protected and regulated as a commons, not as private property, become clear.

Internet Protocol as Social Contract Governing Use of a Commons[34]

The Internet, and in particular Internet Protocol, is the key symptom of change in the current communications context, not "telecommunications technologies." Much more than changes in processes, products, and services, Internet Protocol implements fundamental shifts in our understanding of the way that things get done.

Just as Alan Turing's original design for the computer was a mathematical concept that did not specify any devises for building it, Internet Protocol is a concept that is independent of the devices and software that can be invented to implement it. In essence, the Internet is the Internet Protocol, and is not the "physical layer" that transports you into the commons that Internet Protocol creates.

Internet Protocol is a set of rules for writing software that lets devices negotiate or self-organize for themselves the paths that packets of bits follow. All it does is state what should govern the movement of packets of bits across routers acting as

[34] Graham (2007).

reciprocating peers. At any one moment, the constituent bits that make up the Internet's flow are the result of millions of decisions to connect that occurs at its edges.

Internet Protocol is an agreement about the nature of a public good or a Commons. It defines a "place" where social interaction occurs. To the degree that it specifies the rules of a space of socialization, being "in" the place it defines mediates human relationship through its own fundamental structures of social organization, language and cognitive structures, material production, and ritual processes.[35] The Internet is the expression of a cultural point of view.

Vint Cerf, one of the creators of Internet Protocol, has said that agencies using ICTs for social change have an essential role in "communicating the meaning of the Internet's evolution in the context of a collaborative ecology."[36]

Internet Protocol challenges most of our assumptions about the structural nature of relationships. The programmers of Internet Protocol were assuming that the packets were heading toward individuals who would act socially in the same way as the routers do online. Out of the simplicity of that assumption arises something wondrous and new in the experience of social networks.

In an online society, each and every one of us are the URLs – the "Universal Resource Locators." It is self-defeating for businesses to block our capacity to decide what and where to place our live links among each other. For example, when a market is informed by peer-to-peer relationships then everyone in it is a member. In a networked economy, every market is a community that informs its decisions. There are no more passive customers. To imagine consumers as passive receptacles of products and services is to ignore the interactive roles we all now play as producers in networked systems of demand and supply.

> "By 'the Internet,' we ordinarily mean a network of net-works built upon a set of basic protocols called TCP/IP. Owners of physical equipment choose whether to run the protocols on their technology. Obviously, that choice should be unconstrained. ... Technically, this design creates an 'innovation commons.' Everyone has the freedom to innovate in this space without seeking the permission of anyone else." – Lawrence Lessig[37]

Lessig concludes, "If the freedom to deploy a technology depended upon permission from the network owner, then the uncertainty of securing such permission would weaken the incentive to innovate." In Lessig's terms then, in the current Canadian debate on telecom policy, by pushing for deregulation of telecommunications in favor of a "market-based approach," the major network owners or primary communications carriers are, in effect, asking government for a property right to block all innovations "that do not benefit network owners, even if they benefit network users."

The power of Internet Protocol comes from the capacity it gives us to spin webs of significance through the choices we make about links. To paraphrase Cifford

[35] Thornton (2008).

[36] Verbal comments during the ceremony to sign a Memorandum of Understanding between ICANN and the new North American Regional At Large Organization. June 2007.

[37] Lessig (2004)

Geertz, "We are animals suspended in webs of significance we have spun ourselves."[38] For new meanings and new perceptions to emerge and survive, it is essential that our decisions about connecting remain self-determined.

Identity in Open Systems

A conventional view of the role of technology in social change sees a society as the result of the technologies it obtains. To avoid making technology an end in itself, or technological determinism, that view needs to be turned completely upside down. The technologies, the way that things are done, are always the result of the emergent mind of the society that created them. Put differently, *how technology shapes society is a socio-political choice.*

Canada needs to build public capacity to understand what is happening to the society as the Internet penetrates all aspects of daily life. If the application of the e-development framework leads to the provision of feedback in relational terms, then it can supply that capacity. An open approach to developing a national strategy for the uses of the Internet for development would begin to address the absent and essential feedback loops that sustain a system's consciousness of what it is learning.

Governments need to think through a strategy for the uses of the Internet for development. Some national leaders seem to be increasingly aware of this.[39] Open systems learn, closed systems do not.

Heavy use of the Internet in daily life online is a massive change in a person's environment of relationship. Changes in your environment produce changes in your behavior. Since identity is a product of relationship, changes in relational behavior represent changes in the determinants of identity. The person online acculturates to a very different sense of self than does the person who is not. The failure to act in concert with the nature of this acculturation is the real "digital divide."

---

[38] Geertz (1973). "The concept of culture I espouse … is essentially a semiotic one. Believing, with Max Weber, that man is an animal suspended in webs of significance he himself has spun, I take culture to be those webs, and the analysis of it to be therefore not an experimental science in search of law but an interpretative one in search of meaning. It is explication I am after …"

[39] Speakers at the OECD Ministerial Meeting on the future of the Internet Economy, Seoul, Korea, June 16–18, 2008:

– Mr. José Mariano Gago, (Minister of Science, Technology and Higher Education, Portugal): "Governments are committed to creating the conditions for the Internet to grow – even though we don't know what they are. … the relation of amateurs to professionals is shaping the new organizational structure, and the Internet helps that movement to explode."

– Mr. Juhan Parts, (Minister of Economic Affairs and Communications, Estonia): "They forgot to mention that Skype is an Estonian company… There is an economy and an Internet Economy? No, they are very difficult to separate. We will see Internet everywhere in sectors and affairs. … "users" are not users any more. They produce content. The level of complexity is rising."

– Mr. David Cunliffe, (Minister for Communications and Information Technology, New Zealand): "States must use their power to offset the incumbents."

In the formation of an individual's identity, the Internet shifts the balance from other – determined to be self-determined. The Internet treats everyone as if they had a right to self-determination. Thus, the social contexts online that define individual identity are experientially configured to enhance ability to:

- Transcend locally imposed norms.
- Inhabit a range of cultural settings that are wildly diverse.
- Simulate or design new cultural contexts and social networks at will.
- Interact socially with autonomous agents that are, in fact, machines.

The Political Context Shaping Canadian Decision-Making

Canada was a good example of progressive e-government and ICT inclusion. Canada was also explicitly experimenting with and adapting its institutions over time to lead and coordinate its national ICT strategies. Canada did provide an example for the world of how "an integrated view of e-development can provide a powerful synergistic dynamic." That is no longer true.

Over time, Canada has moved from having an e-leadership institutional framework where policy coordination emerged among several agencies, largely as a consequence following from program initiatives taken by Industry Canada, to one where responsibilities for e-development program coordination and implementation is completely absent.

In any sector, Canada's regulatory capacity is often a model for the world. As a consequence of the confidence this instills in its regulators, their initial instinct was to merely encompass the Internet's existence within existing regulatory spaces. Only after Internet penetration approached universality did regulatory issues begin to be contested.

In Canada's particular climate of complex and continuous change, there is no feeling that anything needs to occur to frame the issues and their dynamics as a response to change. If you should ask – where now does reflective practice and critical thinking about e-development occur? – The answer is that it does not. But, with so much initial success, why then have not Canadians defended e-development policies that have, presumably, benefited them? What caused this shift in policy making?

There are several possible explanations. Perhaps there is a national indifference to the policy implications of listening only to the advice of primary telecommunications carriers. Or perhaps it reflects a lack of citizen engagement with political decision-making processes. On perhaps political decision-making processes are increasingly out of step with citizen understanding of distributed and collaborative systems of interaction in online networks.

In 2008, Canada saw the second election won by the Conservative Party, and the third minority government in a row. For the most part, Canadians are unaware of the degree to which minority government has turned their worldview inward.

Political Agendas and the Policy Context

Parliaments formed during Canada's Internet Era

Election date	Type of government	Prime Minister
Oct 14, 2008	Conservative Minority	Stephen Harper
Jan 23, 2006	Conservative Minority	Stephen Harper
June 28, 2004	Liberal Minority	Paul Martin
Nov 27, 2000	Liberal Majority	Paul Martin from Dec 11, 2003 Jean Chretien
June 2, 1997	Liberal Majority	Jean Chretien
Oct 25, 1993	Liberal Majority	Jean Chretien

Connecting Canadians was first a Liberal Party election platform plank, stated in the "Red Book"[40] of 1993. Then it became a funded program in the governments of Jean Chretien, Prime Minister for 10 years from November 1993 to December 2003. By the time of the 1997 Speech from the Throne, the "pillars" of the Connecting Canadians initiative were supported primarily by Industry Canada activities and programs, and included: Canada Online; Smart Communities; Canadian Content Online; Electronic Commerce; Canadian Governments Online; and Connecting Canada to the World.

Chretien passed his role as Prime Minister to Paul Martin.[41] Martin's intended reforms[42] to the role of government were remarkably similar to the Conservative governments that followed him. This new role of government was primarily to facilitate business by abandoning large portions of the commons:

> "We need to redesign the role of the government in the economy to fit the size of our pocketbook and the priorities of our people. What is that role? It is to provide a framework for the private sector to create jobs through responsible policies ... The government is committed to privatizing and commercializing government operations wherever that is feasible and appropriate."

But signs that the Liberal Party was abandoning "Connecting Canadians" occur much earlier. During Chretien's last term as Prime Minister, an announced plan by Industry Minister, Brian Tobin, to complete the building of the "Information Highway" that Connecting Canadians had started did not make it into a budget tabled in Parliament, December 2001, by Paul Martin:

> Industry Minister Brian Tobin's pet project to create a multibillion broadband Internet project linking rural areas of the country received neither a direct mention nor anywhere near the

[40] "Creating Opportunity: The Liberal Plan for Canada," set out the platform of the Liberal Party of Canada in the 1993 federal election.

[41] Martin inherited the role of Prime Minister from Jean Chretien in December 2003. He won an election, in June 2004, but with a minority, and then was defeated by the Conservative Party of Canada under Stephen Harper in January 2006.

[42] Dobbin (2003).

> $1-billion Mr. Tobin had sought. Instead, Mr. Martin went to great lengths to explain that Canada already boasts 100% satellite coverage and one of the fastest Internet backbones .... In the last Liberal Red Book, the government said it would "open up new opportunities for Canadians" by building a high-speed Internet network which would extend to rural parts of the country. At the time, the Liberals said: "Broad access to the Internet will enable Canadian citizens to engage in the democratic process by having an electronic pipeline to government and to their representatives in Parliament."[43]

It is likely that the Liberal Party viewed the shift of priorities toward fiscal restraint, and toward diminished the role for government so as to favor market-based approaches, as merely pragmatic, rather than ideological. It was in that context that Martin's Liberal Government, working through the Minister of Industry, established the TPRP in April 2005 and stated its Terms of Reference.

For both Canada and USA, the roots of efforts to fix problems perceived in regulatory design by governments go back to Osborne and Gaebler's "Reinventing Government."[44] Paul Martin, during the later years of Chretien's governments, when he was Minister of Finance and in his own short minority government, paid significant attention to the concept of "smart regulation"[45] emerging out of the environmental movement. In particular, he was influenced directly by the work of Davis Boyd,[46] environmental activist and lawyer, who accepted an appointment as a policy analyst in the Privy Council Office.

In working with government, the "what is in it for us?" for environmental activists was the opportunity to change perspectives in public policy debates toward "whole system" views. But, in a climate of fiscal restraint and of outsourcing the role of government, it is unlikely that politicians overlooked the opportunities that smart regulation presented for diminishing the "burden" of government on business. Smart regulation reinforced the Government of Canada's increased preference for working to regulate through hands-off approaches:

> "In particular, the public can potentially play a large role in controlling the actions of self-regulating bodies. The public can act as consumers, either through directly consuming (or not consuming) the service provided by the industry (such as in the case of Green Consumerism) or through punishing those who use low quality services (such as in the case of investors not investing in companies using low quality auditors). The public, if harmed by the decisions of the self-regulating body, may be able to use the courts to either alter decisions or obtain damages for harm. Finally, the public can participate in the decision-making process of the self-regulating industry – providing the industry with information about issues or monitoring the exercise of self-regulatory powers."[47]

---

[43] Tournemille (2001).

[44] Osborne and Gaebler (1992).

[45] Smart regulation, see:

— Priest (1997).

— Gunningham and Grabosky (1998).

[46] Boyd (2003, 2004).

[47] Green and Hrab (2003).

The environmentalists helped the government to see that behavior change could best be influenced through pricing goods and services correctly – transferring responsibility for environmental impacts from government to consumers, and thus privatizing the policy dialogue and further reducing the need for government intervention.

> "... regulatory reform must take place in an environment of shrinking regulatory resources, making it necessary in some contexts to design strategies capable of achieving results even in the absence of a credible enforcement regime (as when dealing with small and medium-sized enterprises), and in almost all circumstances to extract the 'biggest bang' from a much diminished 'regulatory buck' ... This will involve the design of a 'second phase' of regulation: one that still involves government intervention, but selectively and in combination with a range of market and nonmarket solutions, and of public and private regulatory orderings. ... In essence, achieving efficient and effective regulation and encouraging innovation is a far more complex activity than mainstream neo-classical economists believe(d) it to be, requiring a much broader range of strategies, tailored to a much broader range of motivations and harnessing a much wider range of social actors."[48]

In practice, in the follow-up to deregulation, there was rarely any significant capacity for administration and oversight. The reduction in the scale of regulation was usually accompanied by a reduction in the volume of the regulators. So, as the markets failed to deliver on the underlying commitment to resolve issues of the public interest over all, governments have failed to step back in and honor the part of their role that remained as a consequence of the bargains they made with businesses.[49]

The current conservative minority government intends to seize every chance it gets to refocus the role of the Federal Government in a way that shifts major responsibilities for governance to the Provinces. It intends to achieve a restructuring of powers between the national and regional governments in order to minimize the federal presence in local affairs. What this means for e-development policy is that their attention span for adding new forms of responsibility for any national policies and programs is limited.

Access to broadband has never been a critical issue of national election debate. But, there is a difference in attitudes between rural and urban voters toward the development of broadband infrastructure that could be used to create a distraction. Both the Conservatives and the Liberals are appealing directly to that perception of difference, while the New Democratic Party's position locates broadband as an urban issue.

Late in the election of October 2008, the Conservative Party of Canada did issue a press release[50] on rural broadband:

> Prime Minister Stephen Harper today announced that a reelected Conservative Government will partner with the private sector to work toward completing Canada's broadband network.

---

[48] Gunningham (2007).

[49] Webster and Cathro (2007). "The Canadian Environmental Protection Act (CEPA) ... stands as a shining example of smart regulation principles built on promises of strict enforcement. But [Margo] Priest says CEPA has been weakly enforced, and she should know: as the chief review officer hearing appeals of Environmental Protection Compliance Orders issues under CEPA, she laments 'I do nothing'."

[50] Ensuring a modern economy throughout rural and remote Canada: investing in rural and remote broadband access. Conservative Press Releases, Oct 11, 2008.

> "Broadband technology is a gateway to educational, economic, cultural and health care opportunities for individual Canadians, families and businesses," said the Prime Minister. "A reelected Conservative Government will work to ensure more Canadians have access to this all-important resource."
>
> As it currently stands, one in ten Canadians does not have access to broadband. A reelected Conservative Government will invest $100 million per year over a 5-year period toward completion of the country's broadband network.

The problem with the plan's potential impact on e-development and digital inclusion strategies is that it talks in terms of "completion of the country's broadband network," as if it were an engineering project. They fail to recognize that national capacity for effective Internet use in development is an ongoing process, not merely a one-time creation of technological infrastructure. Holding that view makes it unlikely they will move forward to enable the design and implementation of e-development and digital inclusion.

In the New Democratic Party platform section on, "Supporting Culture, the Arts and Our Canadian Cultural Identity"[51] there were three "Internet" references scattered throughout:

> To invest in our shared cultural heritage, Jack Layton and his team of New Democrats will:
>
> … Invest in a pan-Canadian broadband strategy to bring high-speed Internet to more communities in Canada.
>
> … Implement "net neutrality" to protect everyday Canadians' right to freely access the Internet content of their choice at a flat rate and with clear and transparent rules. We will end price gouging and "net throttling," preventing a two-tiered Internet in Canada.
>
> … Develop a digital on-line culture service to give ordinary Canadians expanded access to Canadian content.

In the Liberal platform, Sect. 4. "Strong rural and northern Canada,"[52] it said:

> We will focus much of our infrastructure effort on rural Canada. That doesn't just mean roads and bridges – it's also about communications. That's why a Liberal government will: … complete the job of making broadband Internet service available to rural communities; …

In the October 2008 election, none of the political parties treated the absence of any national strategy for the uses of the Internet for development as an issue. None of the parties situated the issue in the broader context of socioeconomic development planning in an Internet Economy. The NDP placed it in a "culture" context, and the Liberals and Conservatives limited the scope to rural development.

All of those party platform statements severely circumscribe the breadth of the original vision in "Connecting Canadians." One measure of the drift is that the current Conservative Government has removed the fullest articulation of that vision, the "Information Highway Advisory Council Reports," from the Industry Canada Web site.

---

[51] New Democratic Party of Canada (NDP) Web site.

[52] The Platform statement was removed from the Party web site after the election, but the origin of the policy was from Findley (2007). "Broadband, connecting Canadians," is a significant issue all across the country in what are still underserved rural areas.

On taking office in their second minority government, the Conservative Party's "Speech from the Throne" made reference to a "Building Canada Plan." The Speech does not mention broadband, but the Plan[53] itself included details:

> In particular, the $8.8-billion Building Canada Fund will help provinces, territories and municipalities to address urgent public infrastructure priorities. ... To build a more competitive and prosperous economy, Building Canada will invest in: ...
>
> Connectivity and Broadband: funding in this category will be directed toward projects designed :
>
> - To improve the delivery of public services, such as government services, education, and health
> - To improve quality of life, social development, reduce travel requirements, and increase the potential for innovation and economic development by connecting Canadians – particularly in rural and remote communities
> - In order to promote competitiveness, funding criteria will require that the project proponents conduct a commercially and technologically neutral Request for Proposals. In addition, the projects will be required to provide for third-party open access

What is missed in the Conservative's approach to reducing the role of government through renunciation of central power is that the "local" to which they intend to devolve that power is not the same in an Internet Economy as it was in an Industrial Economy. If, by making that attempt, they intend to "go back" to community-based values, in fact they would be leaping far forward into an unexamined future. Since the local is, at the same time, global in an Internet Economy, the autonomy that they would be granting to self-determine the direction of local socioeconomic development is infinitely greater than they imagine.

Simply put, there is no political party in Canada who is looking to the future of the Internet as a factor in public policy. Even as the Internet transforms Canadian society from within, nobody is imagining what daily life online in an Internet Economy might mean. There is a growing awareness among Canadians about the number of nations around the world where a coherent narrative about the nature of that transformation is beginning to emerge.[54] This inattention in Canada is unsustainable in the longer term. What will prompt a discourse that can shape a new Canadian Idea?

Business, As Usual

In addition to the swamp of federal-regional tensions, there is another negative thread in Canadian capacity for policy formulation – the dominant insiders' role played by Canadian corporations. The approach to the deregulation of everything, including telecommunications, is corporate driven. Canadian politicians do require a radical shift in thinking about the wisdom of receiving their advice primarily from

[53] Infrastructure Canada Web Site.

[54] Preparing Europe's digital future: i2010 Mid-Term Review. European Communities, 2008.

telecommunications companies whose business plans are threatened by the Internet Economy's structural implications.

> Changes in telecom policy mirror the same challenge that is occurring in agricultural policy: how to sustain the public domain in trust for everyone in the face of efforts to privatize it. The communications system is being industrialized in parallel to the industrialization of the food system. Just as agro-business essentially seeks to place farmers in a dependency relationship, the primary communications carriers seek to complete the movement of individual Internet users from a peer-to-peer relationship to that of a client.[55]

There is a need for new perspectives on business–government alliances in an Internet Economy.[56] There is a need to find a different balance for the role that prime communications carriers now play in the evolution of Canadian capacity for e-development policy.

The definition of e-development assumes, correctly, that the use of technology in society is a development policy question, not a technology policy question. That is a shift in policy perspective that has yet to occur in Canada. Because Federal Government departments have always operated in silos, there has never been a time when the elements of Canada's e-development strategy could be characterized as the product of an overarching design. This means that limiting the view of telecommunications policy as regulating only an industrial sector allows for it to be explicitly uncoupled from responsibility for its socioeconomic development implications, and nobody will notice.

The Information Highway Advisory Council (IHAC) established in early 1994 by John Manley, Minister of Industry, did recommend an overarching design. This was a council that met behind closed doors, and the model of change made explicit in its reports was one of technological determinism. Inherently, "building" Canada's "information infrastructure" was seen as the engineered construction of a "highway" for information. For example, IHAC 2 said the knowledge society "remains a vision floating out of the potential for good in the information and communications *technologies now transforming the world*."[57] Those metaphorical assumptions have never been revisited.

However, unlike TPRP, the IHACs did recognize that it was "Canada" that was to be developed through Internet use, not just the telecommunications sector. The IHACs called for a "monitoring" capacity to track the progress of that transformation. That call has been ignored. TPRP called for a "monitoring" capacity. That call was also ignored.

So … in a world where indigenous knowledge informs process and productivity, under rules of self-organization governed by Internet Protocol, is the government of Canada leaving the uses of the Internet for development to the private sector?

---

[55] Ramirez et al. (2007), p. 10.

[56] For example, Canada has no coherent energy or environmental strategies either. The reason for those absences is simply that they get in the way of business as usual.

[57] Information Highway Advisory Council (1997).

The Internet must evolve but the goals of that evolution must remain in the public domain. The capacity of an organization acting as a self-organizing system is its ability to do a good job of letting individuals create value for one another.[58]

Recent actions of the Government of Canada have focused attention on the profit of telecommunications companies, as opposed to economic growth via online networks for society overall. The dynamic of corporate influence plays a significant role. In every forum for thinking about Canada as an Information Society, it has been the primary telecommunications carriers that played the largest role in agenda setting. The IHACs were dominated by the primary telecommunications carriers, particularly Bell Canada Enterprises (BCE) and key large corporations in the ICT industries coordinated through their primary lobbying organization, the ITAC. It is not too strong to state that Canada's capacity to think its way forward by leveraging the Internet's existence to its advantage has been deliberately constrained by its primary telecommunications carriers.

In the guise of competition, the primary carriers actually seek to contain the impact of Internet Protocol on existing business practices. If they gain protection from competition in the market for carriage and connection, they will inhibit competition in the market for content and trade on the Internet. For society overall, the critical value is not the network itself so much as what you can do once you have it.

During 1993–1994, evidence emerged from an explosion of self-organized community networking associations that Canadians were about to embrace the Internet. This came as news to the country's primary telecommunications carriers. They only reacted after a corresponding explosion of small ISPs also emerged in response to that evidence of a new demand:

- They bought up the ISPs or drove them out of business
- With the help of Industry Canada, they replaced the cooperative arrangements with universities and major user organizations that had governed the backbone with CANARIE
- They dominated policy setting agendas via their role in the IHACs, including the adoption of the phrase "Information Highway" as the hook for public relations spin

Telecommunications as an industry is no different than any other. It seeks to maximize profits with a minimum of government interference, unless, of course, that interference involves subsidies. So, maintaining a healthy suspicion of its substantial lobbying activities and the content of its public relations is an essential responsibility of informed citizenship. The Internet has created competition to their current and intended business practices and they are trying hard to kill that competition.

The Government of Canada also assumes that business will build broadband infrastructure in respond to market demand. Two articles[59] from the Globe and Mail newspaper, August 2008, provide evidence that the two largest telecommunications carriers in Canada have no intention of bringing real broadband anywhere near the home on any kind of discernable timetable. They also show every intention of

[58] Shirky (2009).

[59] See, for example, Avery (2008a, b).

throttling all peer-to-peer distributed applications that take advantage of the Internet's neutrality, thus killing the very qualities of Internet use that lead to innovation, social experimentation, and economic growth.

The primary carriers claim that controlling the Internet as a managed resource, not as a Commons, will allow them to ensure quality of service while earning enough to invest in the growth of broadband networks. To do this, they intend to actively monitor and control every packet and to know and act on what it contains. They intend to run every Internet transaction through a tollbooth. They seek to complete the process of turning as much of the Internet as they can from a public bazaar, where anyone can set up shop, to a private mall with rents. In the name of those "benefits," they are gaining ever more control of the desktops of everyone. They say they are doing this because Canadians want it.[60]

Allowing the market to control the impact of Internet Protocol on socioeconomic development means that innovation from the grassroots or "from the edges" will stall in Canada. For example, trying to figure out how to sell Canadians Internet Protocol TV without them realizing that peer-to-peer lets them sell IPTV too, would be a deliberate attempt to contain the impact of innovation on current business practices. This is a corruption of regulation to benefit the existing incumbents against new innovations that erode their existing business models.

What can reduce the role that the primary communications carriers now play in the evolution of capacity for e-development policy? In any new forums for dialogue on e-development, what could possibly counter-balance the weight of the primary communications carriers. We will know real change has begun when decision makers in politics and policy stop saying things like:

> "The goal of this strategy is to have broadband service available in every community in Canada within 5 years,"

... and they begin to say:

> "The goal of this strategy is to ensure that every Canadian controls sufficient broadband to allow them to become effective participants in daily life online."

In the short term, it is difficult to shift the discourse. The telecommunications industry is acting effectively in a political vacuum to preserve their advantage. Perhaps the best means available to affect the lock that the primary telecommunications carriers have on Federal policy is to act at the municipal and provincial level,[61] to advocate for community-based approaches to the uses of the Internet for socioeconomic development.

---

[60] McTaggart (2008).

[61] Here are two examples:

(a) Digitalontario. The Government of the Province of Ontario does have a strategy for the uses of the Internet in development, "Strengthening Digital Infrastructure Capacity." It contrasts starkly with the total absence of anything comparable at the Federal level.

(b) Coquitlam Optical Network Corporation (Qnet). At the municipal level, "QNet delivers superior, carrier grade fibreoptic network access within the City of Coquitlam, providing residents and businesses with the most competitive telecommunication choices of any municipality in Canada."

A renewed national vision of e-development could support and complement community-based initiatives. Understanding Internet Protocol as a public good allows us to focus on what the beneficial results of using Internet Protocol's power might be for society overall.

Some cities in other countries[62] have held intense dialogues over the best routes to social change in a digital age. Their citizens are learning that it is hard work to negotiate the transition from vertical institutions to horizontal networked relationships. What they have learned should be shared.

The nature of governance itself is changing. And there are, of course, elaborate and legitimized channels of discourse. But they only serve to reinforce the comfort of familiar opinions. Those channels are not established for the encouragement of new thinking. The political necessity of reacting or evolving in the face of that change toward self-organization is not apparent, because a constituency to state the need does not yet exist and may not be officially enabled.

Politicians and public servants, who do understand that the existence of Internet Protocol, speak to a new form of commons.[63] They do understand that Internet policy is socioeconomic development, not a technology issue. But in Canada, that class of politicians and public servants[64] simply want to offload responsibility for regulating the consequences of those shifts. Canadians' indifference, allows this policy failure to continue.

The Silence of the Governed

Why does government take the corporate side in an uneven struggle with its own citizens? The politicians are listening to the primary carriers because there are no countervailing voices. Is this a debate that can be opened up for public view? Yes, because silence from the governed on the need for an e-development strategy does not signify consent.

National decision makers in politics and policy clearly stated their intentions to deregulate and modernize telecommunications through the use of a market-based approach. They believed they could use that means to reduce the role of government while, at the same time, to benefit productivity in the telecommunications industries. Nothing in their experience to date has altered that belief.

---

[62] Partnership For A Digital Chicago: The city that net/works: transforming society and economy through digital excellence. Also, Stockholm Declaration on Open (broadband) Networks.

[63] For example, Ms. Viviane Reding, Commissioner for Information Society and Media, Commission of the European Community, speaking at the OECD (2008a), said: "Internet, like sea, space, the air, is shared by mankind. Net neutrality is a political question to be answered by people. The Internet is theirs. Do NOT weaken its openness as a public space. ... The notion of Internet as a public utility must continue to be the primary guiding principle, backed by a stable notion of Internet Governance."

[64] Graham (2006b).

Canada's story is about early federally led initiatives that assisted citizens' enthusiasm with the Internet and built an electronically connected nation, followed by political and ideological changes that have marginalized the role of government in further evolution toward an inclusive information society.

When the idea of the Internet first surfaced in the mind of Canadians in a way that was practical enough to let them take hold of it, they embraced it. For a time, the formal institutions of politics and government in Canada appeared to assist their citizens' enthusiastic experimentation. The apparent marriage of will and ideas served to make Canada a "world leader" in a socially enlightened use of the Internet for development.

Those early successes were produced by a handful of individuals who were able to act rapidly, largely in a vacuum of indifference, and prior to the realization of the primary telecommunications carriers that the Internet was a massive threat to their business plans. Now, Canada's universal access programs are sunsetting without obvious replacement. In the face of changes in national political attention, the will to evolve those policies and programs has diminished.

Where Will Canada's Future Growth Come from?

Canada has a vast geography, with only 33 million people, 80% urban and 20% rural, and with 90% of the Canadian population located within 100 miles of the US border. With a relatively small population, policy formulation is limited to a small number of actors that the key players know each other personally. This means that the dynamics of informal and negotiated accommodation largely governs policy formulation. The primary weakness of this process is that those communities of practice are ordinarily closed to outsiders. The operating model for political interaction remains closed-door management of citizen expectations. However, the Internet has opened up new spaces for participation.

Various indicators suggest that Canada's relative position in the global transition to an Internet Economy is likely to continue to decline:

> Canada is woefully positioned for future Internet usage and the quality of current broadband networks is barely enough to cope with current traffic because of a lack of investment by providers, according to a new study … While Japan was the only country to meet the study's standards for future readiness, broadband networks in countries such as Latvia, Romania and Bulgaria scored better than Canada, which ranked 27th out of the 42 nations covered.[65]

Canadians are technophiles governed by technocrats. When they first saw the Internet, they embraced it as rapidly as anyone. That easy acceptance of Internet access in Canadian society caused a perception that Canadians understood the technology's uses and impacts only as consumers. But Canadian experience with the impact of fully converged Internet Protocol-based communications devices in

---

[65] Nowak (2008). The study Nowak refers to is Oxford Said Business School and Universidad de Oviedo. Broadband Quality Score: a global study of broadband quality.

the context of open and real broadband is limited only to people who have access to corporate and university-based research networks. Canadians have accepted the labeling of themselves as merely "consumers" of online services, but not as producers of e-services in an Internet economy. And it is Canadians' perception of themselves as producers that will cause then to ask for access to open broadband networks adequate to that role.

> Over the past 25 years, the creative class (the growing number of workers who are paid to think) has grown from 24% of the work force to 34%; the service class has been steady at 41%. In the mean time, the working-class percentage has fallen from 29% to 22%. Only 3% of workers are in the remaining class of farming, fishing and forestry occupations. ... the percentage of employment in our manufacturing industries has also been falling.[66]

Citizens are becoming producers in an Internet-based economy. Here are some of the factors that are altering the nature of productivity:

- There is a subtle shift going on in business culture. That shift is in the definition of ICTs from a passive to interactive voice ... to ICTs defined as "Information and *Collaboration* Technologies."[67]
- In highly networked markets, the real market is for the uses, the applications or services that the network makes possible.
- Communities have begun to realize they will never be able to create and leverage an open network as a public good that serves their own socioeconomic development until they own a significant chunk of the backbone themselves.
- Some provincial governments are using procurement to leverage open networks to disaggregate development to the local level, thereby simplifying and diminishing the risks inherent in infrastructure investment by distributing them widely. They are trusting communities and businesses in communities to get it right.
- WEB2's "cloud" of application services makes it possible for very small groups of people to self-organize extremely large structures of production and distribution, especially if they can leverage what the economist Yochai Benkler has called "commons-based peer production."

While telework is conventionally considered to be "the workforce trend of the twenty-first century," the idea does not go far enough to anticipate the changing nature of work. It is based on the assumption that work will continue to occur in the context of large-scale managed organizations. That is not a very good assumption for seeing the future of work clearly.

The Discipline of Thinking It Through

The current Canadian public policy process that is typical of federated governance does not think about the long-term future. It defaults to regional myopia and to

[66] Florida and Milway (2008).

[67] Zara (2008).

interregional competition in the context of narrow provincial views. Specific to telecommunications policy, no one is asking, "In an Internet Economy, what kind of society do we want?" If Canada does not develop a capacity to think about this question, its global competitiveness will decline in relation to nations that do.

Politicians and policy makers believe it is important to reduce Canadian expectations of what governments should do. They inhabit a culture of political decision-making that favors modest over significant intervention. They believe the attention span of the Canadian electorate for contemplating the impact of an Internet Economy is even more limited than their own.

Heavy Internet use in a society is a symptom of an open or opening society. An open society, and its attendant cooperative interactions, depends on trust. What is the basis of democracy if there is no faith in even the possibility of an informed electorate? Interaction with an informed electorate that views society as networked systems cannot be based on staying "on message" through the manipulation of public opinion and the application of marketing solutions to meeting the needs of "consumers" of government services.

The current Conservative Government appears to wear a shell of distrust against open processes of public dialogue. It is not clear how it intends to publicly explore the best way forward, except in political forums of intense partisan competition. For those who seek to represent a public interest but are outsiders to the Party in power, this desire to tightly control the public policy agenda appears to represent a disavowal of fresh ideas.

In facing the changes in society, economy and governance revealed by the Internet's existence, the time for experimentation is only beginning. Both Canada's politicians and institutions are acting as if it was over. But Canadians as individuals are not.[68]

Canadians are learning through experience to relate in a different way. But there is still no strategy for enhancing awareness of the competencies they acquire as they act to structure their social networks in terms of relational systems. In moving forward in the context of a Knowledge Society and Internet Economy, no one is asking which new behaviors are the ones that best fit the needs. The core of an effective policy capacity in response would be a willingness to learn from experience.

Economic life online in an Internet Economy requires a radical shift in thinking about the implications of network dynamics for structures of production, distribution, and consumption. The essential development conversations that follow will need to be inclusive of all stakeholders. But Canadian capacity for dialogue on public policy contains two structural flaws:

1. The systems of public policy formulation are closed, vertically oriented by sector, and not collaborative.
2. There is a disconnection at all levels of government between the planners and those who are the presumed beneficiaries of planning's results.

---

[68] Veenhof et al. (2008).

Politicians have sought to disconnect an essential relationship between the public service and the electorate it serves. There are many capable people in Canadian public service. But they face disincentives that inhibit them from sharing what they learn through public interaction. The Liberals have sought to reduce the role of government as a means of reducing a deficit. The Conservatives have sought to reduce the role of government as a matter of ideology. In both cases, political decision makers have viewed the public service as a threat and have muzzled the public service's capacity to facilitate any open public discussion that could test the validity of what they intended to do.

Are We Back on the Road?

It is unrealistic to predict what equilibrium will emerge following an abrupt transformation in governance. But it is both realistic and essential to anticipate what the nature of beneficial outcomes might be.

> "We are in the midst of a technological, economic and organizational transformation that allows us to renegotiate the terms of freedom, justice and productivity in the information society. How we shall live in this new environment will in some significant measure depend on policy choices we make over the next decade or so. To be able to understand these choices, to be able to make them well, we must recognize that they are part of what is fundamentally a social and political choice – a choice about how to be free, equal, productive human beings under a new set of technological and economic conditions. As economic policy, allowing yesterday's winners to dictate the terms of tomorrow's economic competition would be disastrous. As social policy, missing an opportunity to enrich democracy, freedom and justice in our society while maintaining or even enhancing our productivity would be unforgivable."[69]

While it is okay for Yochai Benkler to challenge us to reach for an opportunity, what action must we take to ensure that the outcomes are beneficial? If capacity and behavior are the same, what behaviors need to change and how will that change occur?

Since the Internet Economy is already here, it is not just a question of anticipating and planning for some future state. It is also a question of authentic involvement in the present moment. The task is not only to define what kind of future we want. It is to find a way to enable a sustainable presence in the world as it is. In a relational world, it is individual Canadians acting in the context of community that will do this, not "Canada." In a democracy that is moving beyond the representative to the interactive, it is not just politicians who get to evolve the role of the state.

It is essential to acknowledge and enhance the capacity of the individual to make that choice to connect. The task is not to ensure that the technologies can work. It is not just to enable the use of the Internet for development in Canada as an impersonal abstraction. The task is to ensure that the individual, with the technology in hand, has a sustainable presence in the world.

---

[69] Benkler (2006).

Capacity for E-Development Policy

Is there anything that can be done to increase awareness of the need for a national capacity to anticipate what is required for effective action by individual Canadians in an Internet Economy? What could evoke deep change in existing patterns of public policy behavior?

While Canada's broadband penetration remains relatively high on global scales, other OECD and ITU measures of Canadian relative position in Internet use are slipping.[70] Are the declines in economic productivity or social response to change, caused by the absence of e-development capacity, being felt? Is there a problem if neither the governors nor the governed perceive one? Is there anything that would cause the Government of Canada to alter its current direction:

- On its own introverted behavior?
- On telecom policy?
- On its unhealthy and unbalancing reliance on the advise of major corporations?
- On its resistance to thinking about the implications of community-based self-organization in relational networks that the Internet makes possible?

Political ideology drives the style of leadership, and that leadership does not want to hear about increases in the effectiveness of national government. When a public service is confronted by an ideological commitment to the reduction of the role of government, the result is likely to be bureaucratic stagnation. And the silos of bureaucracy are actively defending what turf they have left.[71]

> With major changes in technology that cause deep structural adjustments, the policy structure always becomes seriously maladjusted to the requirements of the new technology. Old policies need to be altered or scrapped, and until this is done, existing policies inhibit needed changes. New policies need to be established. All of this takes place in yet another conflict-ridden situation; those with vested interests in old laws, rules, and regulations resist change, while others press for it.[72]

Because they intend to reduce the impact of government on business, Canada's national leaders are highly sensitized to resist calls for processes of structural change and institutional transformation. They are more amenable to accommodate political elites behind closed doors than to accommodate special interests through community-based discourse.

---

[70] OECD (2008b). According to the OECD, in 5 years Canada has dropped from second "most connected" to tenth.

[71] Lenihan et al. (2007). "...... the reality is that governments are very ambivalent about using community approaches on a large scale. There are at least two reasons for this. One is organizational. Governments still operate very much from within the old paradigm – the self-contained, hierarchical silos. As a result, even when they want to collaborate, the system makes it difficult, if not impossible. The other is more legal and constitutional. In many ways, our system of government was actually designed to discourage collaboration."

[72] Lipsey (1996). The maladjustment is over beliefs underlying the technologies more than the technologies themselves.

The existence of the Internet as a structural institution points toward a very different form of governance – the governance of evolving systems that self-organize. No one can anticipate what people will actually do when they settle into something new. And people are settling into daily life online in unanticipated and all-embracing ways. Eventually, public policy will mirror that experience. But, for now, the political judgment that the question of e-development does not exist as an "issue" in public policy is correct.

Waiting with a Prepared Mind

There is no apparent sense of a crisis painful enough to break the hold of vested interests on government policy makers. But there are pressures or demands outside the Federal Government that could serve to influence a decision to institute a capacity for e-development policy. There are spontaneous processes in motion that may serve as nucleuses for the formation of coalitions working to effect change in the socio-political system's self-perceptions. Here are examples of spaces where new forms of thinking may emerge:

- There could be a tipping point where citizens become aware of their need to defend their potential as online producers, forcing primary carriers to rethink plans to invest in broadband infrastructure.
- Canada's youth may ultimately begin to exert their influence on e-development policies. Canada's youth are well connected, nonideological, and repelled by conventional political processes.[73] Not perceiving a problem for themselves, they are unlikely to notice the absence of a national capacity for thinking about e-development policy. But they are very sophisticated in the politics of distributed social organization in networked communities.
- Relatively slow productivity growth compared to countries (particularly Canada's neighbor, USA) with high levels of ICT investment and use could be viewed as a crisis, causing greater reflection on the role of the Internet as a driver of increased productivity.[74]
- Programs that address a transition to green infrastructure[75] such as smart energy grids have an inherent capacity to heighten understanding of Internet Protocol's significance and the significance of local ownership of open fiber networks as a public utility and citizen ownership of the last mile.
- Canada has yet to have its first Internet election. When it does, a better understanding of e-governance could emerge, first at the local political level, where a shift to cooperative actions that use the Internet to bridge special interests gets you elected.

---

[73] Tapscott (2008).

[74] Research on comparative statistics relating broadband to national productivity is in its early stages. For examples, see Gillett et al. (2006), Katz (2008), Roberts (2007), and Welsum (2008).

[75] Creech et al. (2009).

- Growing municipal concern for ownership of open networks as public utilities may influence the provinces to request greater support for broadband as essential infrastructure. That could shift the policy focus from national communications sector's demands, toward citizens' needs.
- Given the Province of Quebec's greater comfort with discussion of social policy issues, the role of digital inclusion in Quebec politics is likely to grow. The experience gained through actions on public policy that occur as a consequence of that debate may translate to the national level. The Quebec "manifesto" for a digital framework calls for developing national and provincial digital strategies and for participatory development of a digital economy.[76]
- The emergence of Web2 or "cloud-based" approaches to collaboration on program and social services delivery among community-based nongovernment organizations.

The sum of the impact of all of these factors can be significant. That state of denial may not continue for long.

The collective mind of Canadians goes right on changing its opinion about the nature of reality in accordance with its experience. Self-organizing networked interactions in the context of online communities of practice may be hollowing out Canadian organizational structure from within. As conventional understanding of what works in the "management" of organizations is displaced by commons-based peer production, doing nothing to facilitate beneficial change may be an option. Vertical organizational structure may go horizontal, even if that outcome is not planned.

Young Canadians know they have gained more autonomy to define themselves precisely because they are connected in online social networks. They understand that the freedom of this independence is a function of those commitments. Young people recognize that the Internet is a symptom of a new mode of social practice that can make us more fully accessible to one another when we choose to use it that way.

Ideally, policy leadership at the national level can complement and accelerate bottom-up initiatives and self-organizing networks. Under prevailing political conditions, neither government nor corporations are likely to act to bring Canadians the kind of broadband infrastructure that will support their engagement with the Internet economy. But Canadians can and should do this for themselves.[77]

---

[76] Communautique (2010).

[77] For example see: First Nations Technology Council (FNTC). British Columbia. Pathways to Technology Project. "... a First Nations-led initiative to provide all 203 First Nations in BC with high-speed Internet services. The project is being implemented and managed by First Nations organizations although many other organizations are being engaged in various capacities and are making important contributions."

Evolving by Doing, Not Planning

The functional capacity to plan (i.e., the sum of communities of practice among planners) can be a closed system of technocratic expertise that undervalues indigenous knowledge. With that attitude, planned interventions into the community could disrupt the community's capacity to self-organize.

Governance everywhere works, not through rigid planning, but through pragmatic political accommodation, most usually of elites. Politicians will ignore all supposedly rational processes that fail to take political accommodation into account. And development practitioners should take political accommodation into account.

Effective planning aims to expand the range of possible actions. But effective politics, on the other hand, decides which of those actions can be lived with. In a Digital Age, the range of possible actions has changed and vastly expanded.

As a federation, Canada has no center and the political economy of Canada is not centrally planned. It evolves through a series of situated and negotiated compromises.[78] And, therefore, any story about e-development policy in Canada is unlikely to be based on assuming that Canadian governments will primarily rely on a planned approach to e-development.

Canadian governments are suspicious of anticipatory and planned approaches to change, yet comfortable with approaching change through pragmatic and negotiated approaches. But neither instinct is useful when faced with the transformative change from authority to authenticity that the Internet enables. What "Canadians" are busy learning about e-development, particularly with respect to the institutional transformation of the means to their own productivity, Canada's governments may be missing.

The missing component is not knowledge or experience of effective practices. Given the high degree of basic connectivity in Canada, the know-how in business, government, and civil society is very high. For example, CA*Net 4's collaboration of business, government, and research agencies brings together a substantial body of experience in the implementation and use of advanced networks that could be leveraged. It is the feedback loops connecting and aggregating community actions, the capacity to synthesize and express that experience in terms of structural change and institutional transformation that are missing. While it is not necessary to manage all key interdependencies, it is quite useful to understand, anticipate, and leverage them as social experience and learning evolves over time.

The planner's idea of development is only relevant to the degree that the social system being planned incorporates that particular way of doing things into its own way of doing things. A social system's utilization of the technology of planning to alter its behaviors has to be learned and integrated into its process of self-organization.

[78] Lenihan (2007). As a constitutional federation, the balance of national and local issues among the Federal Government and the Provinces and Territories has been the subject of continuous negotiation since 1867. But, as Don Lenihan says, "Now, with almost a century and a half of experience behind us, a clear lesson has emerged about our federation. The distinction between local and national roles is a relative one. Whether something is local or national often depends on how we look at it."

Relating E-Development to Community-Based Development

The current lack of institutional mechanisms to promote coordination and collaborative synergy in e-development does have consequences. It represents blindness to the structural conditions for productivity. It is also a waste of human resources in terms of already transformed skills that exist which are not being fully utilized. It stalls broadband growth while the efforts of the primary telecommunications carriers have shifted to benefit from 3G mobile phone networks. And it ensures that the question of what kind of society Canadians want now that they are in an Internet Economy never gets publicly debated.

Societies can find value in having a national capacity to use ICTs in transformation of behavior, process, and organization in relation to a coherent vision of how to achieve a knowledge-based economy within an Information Society.[79] Creating an Information Society "can be accelerated by providing direction from a national ICT-enabled development strategy." But that assumes that the value of arriving in a knowledge-based economy within an information society can occur without addressing what the nature of that society might be.

The e-development framework suggests that having a comprehensive view of ICT for development:

> ... allows designers and implementers to prioritize, select, and sequence the most critical interdependencies in view of the whole and of the overall availability resources and capabilities. It helps anticipate, recognize, and manage the key interdependencies over time.

E-development strategy is a holistic approach that can be created and implemented at all levels of governance – national, regional, municipal, and community levels. Accordingly, it contributes to an increased understanding among stakeholders about the nature of an emergent holistic approach. An e-development capacity can seek to increase consciousness of the systemic elements of national development. E-development's promise is that integration of the elements of development capacity through a coordination of the stakeholders will render a county's response to transformation imperatives most effectively. But coordination does not have to be done exclusively from above, at the national level. In a highly connected society, much of e-development capacity and learning can be created at the local government and community levels.

The assumption of this chapter is that a consensus emerges from within those members of a society who have acculturated to daily life online, and that the capacity for public policy evolves in reaction to that experience. Canada's connectedness continues to grow, in significant part due to early policy initiatives and subsequent community appropriation of the assets created from the federally led e-development programs (as discussed in Sect. 2). And, as connectedness grows, Canadians' awareness of complex interdependencies continues to grow in parallel.[80]

---

[79] Hanna (2007).

[80] Lenihan (2007). "These technologies have an extraordinary ability to connect people and institutions in new ways. While we can still make many choices about the form our new levels of connectedness will take, that they will profoundly deepen interdependence – at all levels – is hardly open to question. It is simply a consequence of living in the information age."

Nagy Hanna has noted some broad trends in evolving e-leadership Institutions:

> At the outset of the ICT revolution, or when national awareness was nascent, governments convened special task forces, commissions, and panels to advise them on the new directions to take. Typically these ad-hoc bodies made their recommendations to relevant ministers or heads of state. At that stage, the central message was to raise attention to the enabling role of ICT across the bureaucracy and society. Ad-hoc processes were often used to reach out to key leaders and constituencies beyond government and to identify potential e-leaders and stakeholders for the subsequent institutions. Over time, these temporary bodies and ad-hoc processes were transformed into permanent institutions and formal coordination mechanisms.[81]
>
> These institutions are complemented by leaders: "Through their compelling visions, leaders provide meaning and direction in a chaotic world. They bridge boundaries, model risk taking, and show others the future."[82]

By those terms, Canada may have ceased to develop its capacity to build coordinating institutions and informed leadership for a meaningful future-oriented direction. Some may even doubt that the Government will be able to anticipate the future direction of transformation sufficiently enough to create decision-making processes congruent with their anticipation, that is, to ask: Transformation to what? What are the qualities that will be present after the shift to realize the assumed benefits? If the connections among diverse stakeholders in an Internet economy are emergent, relational and self-organizing, can these connections be "shaped" or "coordinated" by a central agency?

When local problems are immediate, and the government is thousands of kilometers away, self-reliance becomes essential. The functions of governance in an Internet economy are relational, combining horizontal as well as top-down and bottom-up interactions. The networks of an Internet economy internalize and distribute control functions at all levels, and can be grounded in demand-driven uses that reflect "community-directed interaction."

Given the degree to which local patterns of response govern productivity in Canada's highly variable geographic regions, the form of social organization that most closely mirrors the rules of self-organized and distributed systems (an ecology of networks) is the community. The very existence of an online community of practice or interest over time means that a shared framework of interpretation and meaning about context is being sustained through its interactions.

In an Internet economy, achieving full benefit from globalization depends on the localization of knowledge. In effect, all real knowledge is localized, internalized, and tailored knowledge. Speaking on, "The epistemological foundations of development,"[83] Joseph Stiglitz said:

> "I see a role far more subtle than just the technology-driven visions of downloading" global knowledge – as useful as that may be. I want to argue three main theses:
>
> 1. The overwhelming variety and complexity of human societies requires the localization of knowledge

[81] Hanna (2007), pp. 92–93.

[82] Hanna (2007), p. 97.

[83] Stiglitz (1999).

2. Practical know-how is largely tacit knowledge that needs to be learned by horizontal methods of twinning, apprenticeship, and seconding and
3. Each society, through its knowledge institutions, should take the active role ("in the driver's seat") in the local learning process

That is, one size of "clothing" does not fit all societies or all communities. Communities making up the fabric of a society learn to be "tailors" by apprenticeship. And each community should be its own tailor to find the best fit.

A Community E-Development Perspective

In line with the arguments presented above, an e-development perspective can be adopted at the community level. In Chap. 1 of this book, Nagy Hanna proposed an "e-development framework"[84] in which he articulated the need for a coherent approach to e-development at the national level. A Community e-Development framework would view the uses of information and communications technologies for development from the "bottom-up." It would emphasize capacity development and governance at the community level as a primary driver for building an information society. This perspective should complement e-development at the national and provincial levels. In this section, we elaborate on the elements of capacity for community e-development (Fig. 4.1).

Vision (Self-definition): We can ask ourselves – what kind of a community do we want in order to live our lives more meaningfully and productively? To govern our way forward, what must we look like to ourselves? The more inclusive the process of asking this question, the better the answer. The direction we then decide to achieve will become much more probable and sustainable.

Learning processes: This is about building learning processes and capacity to question, "the way things are done around here," in order to identify and address the unexamined assumptions that are blocking improvement of basic systems. The objective is to attain a form of community that is self-conscious, and providing individuals and "communities of practice" with new means to connect, collaborate and coordinate local responses. The aim of investing in communities of practice is to empower them, rationalize the use of resources, and increase productivity in the design and operation of local systems.

Organizational and institutional adaptation: Online and networked, local business and organizations must acquire capacity to interact more thoughtfully and flexibly. We may have entered an era when the imperative is for both governments and businesses to become more "community-like." That will lead to distributed collaboration in community online becoming a significant factor in local control of socioeconomic development.

---

[84] Hanna (2007).

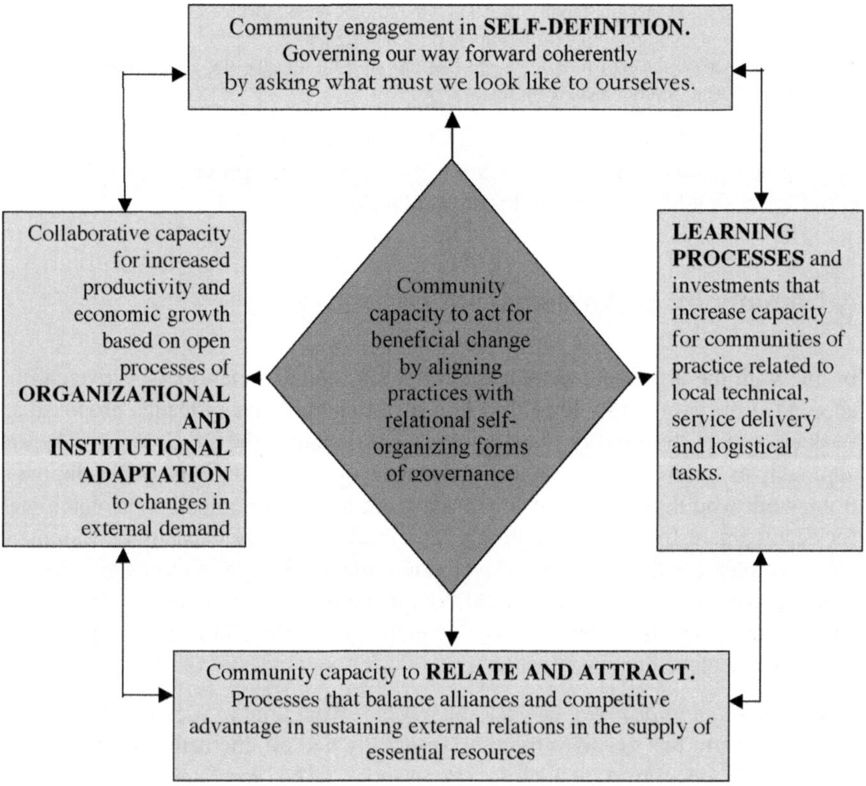

Fig. 4.1 Elements of capacity for community e-development

Relate and attract: This is about community capacity to relate, build alliances, and attract external suppliers of resources.

Community governance: The e-development framework is not limited to the national level, and for highly networked societies such as Canada, it may be most relevant to apply this framework at the community level. Given the self-reliance demanded by Canada's immense geography, the average Canadian's approach to nationhood is actually "the product of a long history of arrangements that were generated locally."[85] This approach parallels the Internet's capacity to reinforce the resilience of local action. And it resonates with Canadians' instincts to disintermediate whatever institutions that attempt to act as gatekeepers.

At the community level, e-development may rely on more distributed and relational leadership than may be possible at the national level. Local politics can accommodate complex horizontal issues where it seems that national politics

[85] Saul (2008), p. 30.

cannot. The Internet allows for the emergent principles of self-organization particular to the resolution of any local issue, before it can be scaled across a broader range of jurisdictions.

A community-driven e-development calls for a new conception of governance and a new role for national leaders. Elected officials at all levels have to act as facilitators of public deliberations of e-development, and as supporters of local attempts to institutionalize horizontal collaboration.[86] The primary tasks for e-development may remain with local communities who would engage in context-revising transformation.[87] Hard times should reinforce the drive leverage the Internet for e-transformation at the community level.

> Hard times can destroy the fabric of community. Or, they can be the stimulus for creative destruction, enabling community to transform. To be effective in hard times, all the players have to work together ... Only a few Canadian cities have formed community-wide coalitions whose goals are to deal with the root causes of economic decline.[88]

Adequate Internet is "infrastructure" that enables that capacity "to work together" as a "natural ecosystem." Whether the "community" is urban, rural, remote, or municipal, the principle is the same.

As a matter of survival, communities do see the need to break down vertically organized "silos" of service delivery. In defending their boundaries, those silos make integrated approaches to solving complex problems of local socioeconomic development impossible to address. The inclusiveness of this discourse is shaping a new idea of Canada.

Ensuring that community-based discourse becomes a national conversation should be the essential function of a Canadian e-development strategy. E-development can become collaborative development. In Canada, communities are poised to recognize the power of the Internet to mirror and support the horizontal and collaborative relationships and changed behaviors they are seeking. When Canada does attempt a national strategy for the uses of the Internet for socioeconomic development, the need to ground it in community-based and local processes should become clearer. An e-development strategy must free local economies to self-organize their responses in line with local resources and challenges. This will render them more resilient and flexible in their ability to adapt. A digital inclusion strategy would support people whose capacity to "self-organize" is in some fashion diminished.

In the longer term, it is not the only contribution of the telecommunications industry to Canada's "productivity agenda" that will lead to global success. It will be because all Canadians paid attention to the interactive capacity of every one to think, to know, to inform, and to collaborate. It will be because Canadians have begun to understand and to apply more effectively Internet's strengths.

---

[86] Lenihan (2007). "So our point is that a new emphasis on community engagement of the sort we are advancing would greatly enhance the role of elected officials by creating a new opportunity for them to act as facilitators in these processes."

[87] The concept of context preservation and transformation comes from: Roberto (1984).

[88] Maxwell (2008).

Conclusion

Through a variety of federal initiatives, Canada built initial leadership capacity for e-development, but due to relatively recent political factors, this capacity was not sustained. Going forward, e-development must engage Canadians at all levels, with increasing reliance on local levels of leadership and governance.

Canada's case suggests that central policy and program leadership were influential and perhaps optimal in the early phases of e-development, but with a political shift, e-development at the federal level moved off center stage, and had to rely primarily on community-level initiatives. While Canadians cannot give up on national e-leadership and centrally managed policy directions and incentives for e-development, they certainly can no longer depend on them alone. Given the early achievements of connectivity, e-government, and e-literacy, and political culture of openness and participation, bottom-up initiatives and community-led e-development may now provide a better fit for the political and social culture of the country.

Technological changes such as social networks and mobile devices provide new and powerful platforms for self-organizing, dialogue and continual improvement, supporting collective action, building community-based and participatory regulation, and strengthening governance from the ground up.[89] E-transformation promises to become more driven bottom-up, where informed and empowered citizens would make smart personal choices, create content and community services, personalize public services, participate in policy making, and strengthen social and ecological accountability.

E-development proposes systemic integration and "leverage" of a number of functional capacities as a prescription for effective national response to the transformative implications of the ICT revolution. It stresses the synergies and interdependencies of those capacities to support the uses of ICT for development. E-development assumes that synergies among its components are substantial and beneficial and that national and local institutions that are independent and competitive can move toward cooperative interdependence to exploit these synergies and network effects. But there is no discourse either among the governors or the governed in Canada about these assumptions and possibilities.

There are some promising signs of mounting demands and pressures from outside the federal government that could serve in building capacity for e-development policy and strategy at all levels of governance. At the national level, calls for action and proactive government are coming from chambers of commerce, academia, and professional and private sector associations.[90] They are calling on the government to take a leading role, together with private sector and other social forces to help prepare an advanced digital infrastructure for twenty-first century, attend to

[89] Tapscott and Williams (2010).

[90] See, for example, Canadian Chamber of Commerce, and Information Technology Association of Canada.

the soft infrastructure, develop ICT talents at all levels of education and learning, help ICT adoption by small and medium enterprises, promote ICT-based innovation in public and private sectors, and set programs to support ICT in priority sectors such as e-health and energy (smart grid).

At the local levels, various communities, municipalities, and provincial governments are also calling for action at all levels, based on engagement and dialogue with a broad cross-section of Canadian citizens and organizations. They are calling for broadening public understanding of the Internet and information society, developing holistic approaches to Internet policy and governance, addressing the digital divide, promoting universal access to broadband, and exploring how Internet-based innovation can be encouraged for inclusive and sustainable development.[91] Some view the best course for communities to learn their own way forward would be to gain control of the local portion of the Internet backbone and to operate it as an open public utility. For some community leaders, it appears impossible to imagine a scenario where national political debate in Canada would step outside the free-market paradigm that dominates current discourse to see the wisdom of community-based economic development through broadband network ownership.

We have hypothesized the measurement of transformation by reference to an "Internet Culture," where complex realities for social change and governance are implicit in the Internet's existence. In the Internet world, the capacity of individuals and communities to shape context for themselves has increased. An appropriate response to that transformation, reflecting Canadian culture and values, should support the individual and community in the development of a passionate and authentic relationship with the present moment. And that takes us back to John Ralston Saul's "strategic elements" of the Canadian identity – egalitarian, able to balance relations of individuals to groups, delight in relational complexity, capable of negotiating consensus and compromise, acceptance of differences, and emphasizing obligation over authority.

Those outside demands should coalesce and scale up to push the federal and provincial governments into action to capture lost ground, to partner with civil society and a broader number of stakeholders, to pursue holistic and balanced approaches to the digital economy, and to harness and build on the substantial resources and energies of community organizations.

References

Applicant Declaration on Lobbying. CAP. http://www.ic.gc.ca/eic/site/cap-pac.nsf/vwapj/declaration_on_lobbying.pdf/$FILE/declaration_on_lobbying.pdf, accessed 13 March 2009.
Avery, Simon. 2008. BCE moves into the future – slowly. Globe and Mail, August 25, 2008.
Avery, Simon. 2008. Why Telus is keeping its TV plans under wrap. Globe and Mail, August 13, 2008.
Benkler, Yochai. 2006. The wealth of networks. Yale University Press.

[91] Communautique (2010); Chebucto Community Net (Halifax); K-Net; First Nations Technology Council; Wiring the social Network; Vetter et al. (2009).

Benkler, Yochai and Nissenbaum, Helen. 2006. Commons-based Peer Production and Virtue. The Journal of Political Philosophy: Volume 14, Number 4, pp. 394–419. http://www.nyu.edu/projects/nissenbaum/papers/jopp_235.pdf, accessed 17 March 2009.

Bodnar, Christopher, Moll, Marita and Shade, Leslie Regan. 2005. Information and Communications Technology (ICT) Road Map. Canadian Research Alliance For Community Innovation And Networking, July 2005. http://www3.fis.utoronto.ca/research/iprp/cracin/policy/e-policy_map.html, accessed 13 March 2009.

Boyd, David R. 2003. Unnatural law: rethinking Canadian environmental law and policy. Vancouver, UBC Press.

Boyd, David R. 2004. Sustainability within a generation: a new vision for Canada, Vancouver, The David Suzuki Foundation.

Canada's Community Access Program (CAP) (a). Industry Canada web site. http://www.ic.gc.ca/eic/site/cap-pac.nsf/eng/home, accessed 12 March 2009.

Canada's Community Access Program (CAP) (b). Telecommunities Canada web site. http://www.tc.ca/cap/ accessed: March 13, 2009.

Canadian Chamber of Commerce, July 13, 2010. Submission on a Digital Economy for Canada: Capitalizing on the Digital Economy.

CANARIE web site, accessed 15 March 2009. About: http://www.canarie.ca/about/about.html. Advanced networks: http://www.canarie.ca/advnet/index.html Gigabit Internet to the home: http://www.canarie.ca/advnet/gitts.html

CANCAP. 2005. The Future of CAP: Proposed Recommendations to Industry Canada for feedback from the CAP Community. February 2005. http://cap.vcn.bc.ca/uploads/1336/CAP3.pdf, accessed 13 March 2009.

Chebucto Community Net (Halifax). 2010 Internet Town Hall Meeting Series on possible digital divide solutions for Nova Scotia. http://www.chebucto.ns.ca/townhall/index.shtml Accessed December 2010.

CIOB web site. http://www.tbs-sct.gc.ca/cio-dpi/index-eng.asp, accessed 15 March 2009.

Communautique. (2010) "Manifesto. A Digital Framework for Quebec." http://www.communautique.qc.ca/reflexion-et-enjeux/internet-citoyen/manifesto-digital-framework.html. accessed 20 December 2010.

Correspondence from Gareth Shearman, President, Telecommunities Canada, to Hon. Tony Clement, Minister of Industry, December 30, 2008., archived to: http://vancouvercommunity.net/lists/arc/cracin-canada/2009-01/, accessed 15 March 2009.

Coquitlam Optical Network Corporation (Qnet). http://www.qnetbc.net/default.htm, accessed 18 March 2009.

Creating Opportunity: The Liberal Plan for Canada. (a.k.a. "The Red Book") By the Platform Committee. (Co–chairs: Haviva Hosek and Paul Martin). Ottawa: Liberal Party of Canada, 1993.

Creech H, Andjelkovic M, Vetter T, MacLean D, Rothman D, Vergragt PJ. 2009. Mapping the Future of the Internet onto Global Scenarios: A preliminary view. International Institute for Sustainable Development (IISD), January 2009. http://www.iisd.org/pdf/2008/internet_global_scenarios.pdf, accessed 21 March 2009.

Department Mandate Statement. Industry Canada Web site. http://www.ic.gc.ca/eic/site/ic1.nsf/eng/h_00018.html, accessed 2 February 2009.

Digitalontario Web Site. http://www.digitalontario.mgs.gov.on.ca/, accessed 18 March 2009.

Dobbin, Murray. 2003. Liberal or Neoliberal? What can we expect from P.M. Martin? Read his budget speeches. *(This article is an excerpt from his book, Paul Martin: CEO for Canada?).* Ottawa, The Canadian Centre for Policy Alternatives, December 2003. http://www.policyalternatives.ca/monitorissues/2003/12/monitorissue840/?pa=ddc3f905, accessed 17 March 2009.

Ensuring a modern economy throughout rural and remote Canada: investing in rural and remote broadband access. Conservative Press Releases, October 11, 2008. http://www.conservative.ca/EN/1091/107195, accessed 18 March 2009.

Findley, Martha Hall. 2007. Platform Outreach 2007 Report. P.6. http://www.liberal.ca/pdf/docs/platformreport_e.pdf, accessed 18 March 2009.

First Nations Technology Council (FNTC). British Columbia. Pathways to Technology Project. http://www.pathwaystotechnology.ca/home Accessed December 2010.

Florida, Richard and Milway, James. 2008. Creative class the most recession proof. Globe and Mail, November 24, 2008, B2.

Geertz, Clifford. 1973. Emphasizing Interpretation. *The Interpretation of Cultures*, pp. 4-5.

Gillett SE, Lehr WH, Osorio CA, Sirbu MA. 2006. Measuring Broadband's Economic Impact. Final Report Prepared for the U.S. Department of Commerce, Economic Development Administration National Technical Assistance, Training, Research, and Evaluation Project #99-07-13829. MITÐs Communications Futures Program, February 28, 2006. http://www.eda.gov/ImageCache/EDAPublic/documents/pdfdocs2006/mitcmubbimpactreport_2epdf/v1/mitc-mubbimpactreport.pdf, accessed 18 March 2009.

Graham, Garth. 2005. Community online and public policy: Telecommunities Canada's submission to the Telecommunications Policy Review. Victoria, BC, Telecommunities Canada, August15, 2005. http://www.tc.ca/telecompolicyreviewed.pdf, accessed 15 March 2009.

Graham, Garth. 2005. Home Truths For Citizens Online: Telecommunities Canada's Second Round Submission To The Telecommunications Policy Review, September 15, 2005. http://www.tc.ca/home_truths.pdf, accessed 15 March 2009.

Graham, Garth. 2006. Canadians online – creators not consumers: A critique from a community networking perspective of the Telecommunications Policy Review Panel's Report. Victoria, BC, Telecommunities Canada, June 21, 2006. http://www.tc.ca/TC_on_TPRP2.pdf, accessed 18 March 2009.

Graham, Garth. 2006. Internet policy as socio-economic development: Market forces alone are not the answer! Panel. Telecommunications and the public good: Alternative Telecommunications Policy Forum, October 20/06. http://www3.fis.utoronto.ca/research/iprp/cracin/alttelecomcontent/Graham%20alternate%20view.pdf, accessed 17 March 2009.

Graham, Garth. 2007. IP rules! Internet Protocol as Commons and social contract. April 23, 2007. (Appendix A of Ricardo Ramirez, Garth Graham, Fred G. Bigham, and Dan Pellerin. Broadband for what? Policy implications of an essential public utility. April 30, 2007. pp 34-41). http://kmdi.utoronto.ca/broadband/publications/Files/ramirez_paper.pdf, accessed 15 March 2009.

Graham, Garth. 2010. Towards a National Strategy for Digital Inclusion: a discussion document adopted by Telecommunities Canada to support participation in public forums on the role of broadband in social change. January 19, 2010. http://tc.ca/digital_inc4.pdf

Green, Andrew and Hrab, Roy. 2003. Self-regulation and the protection of the public interest. Paper Prepared for the Panel on the Role of Government. June 2003. p.82. http://www.law-lib.utoronto.ca/investing/reports/rp26.pdf, accessed 17 March 2009.

Government Executive Series. 2004. eGovernment Leadership: High Performance, Maximum Value. Accenture, May 2004, P11. http://www.accenture.com/NR/rdonlyres/D7206199-C3D4-4CB4-A7D8-846C94287890/0/gove_egov_value.pdf, accessed 15 March 2009.

Government Executive Series. 2005. Leadership in Customer Service: New Expectations, New Experiences. Accenture, April 2005. (P.61). http://www.accenture.com/NR/rdonlyres/F45CE4C8-9330-4450-BB4A-AF4E265C88D4/0/leadership_cust.pdf, accessed 15 March 2009.

Gunningham, Neil. 2007. Reconfiguring Environmental Regulation: Next Generation Policy Instruments. Chapter 8 of Industrial innovation and environmental regulation: developing workable solutions. Edited by Saeed Parto and Brent Herbert-Copley. UNU Press/IDRC.

Gunningham, Neil and Grabosky, Peter. 1998. Smart regulation; designing environmental policy. Clarendon Press.

Hanna, Nagy. 2007. e-Leadership Institutions for the Knowledge Economy. Washington, D.C., The International Bank for Reconstruction and Development/The World Bank. http://siteresources.worldbank.org/EXTEDEVELOPMENT/Resources/Nagy_Hanna_ELeadershipInstitutionsFinal.pdf?resourceurlname=Nagy_Hanna_ELeadershipInstitutionsFinal.pdf, accessed 18 March 2009.

Information Highway Advisory Council. 1997. Preparing Canada for a digital world: final report of the Information Highway Advisory Council. Ottawa, Industry Canada, September 1997. P. 124.

Information Technology Association of Canada. 2009. Upping our Game" A National ICT Strategy for Canada.

Infrastructure Canada Web Site: http://www.buildingcanada-chantierscanada.gc.ca/plandocs/bg-di/bg-di-info5-eng.html#eco5, accessed 18 March 2009.

Internet for Everyone Campaign. http://www.internetforeveryone.ca/en.html, accessed 15 March 2009.

Katz, Raul L. 2008. The economic and social impact of telecommunications output: empirical evidence in the US and Europe. ETNO Regulatory Economics Task ForceBrussels, April 30, 2008. http://www4.gsb.columbia.edu/null/download?&exclusive=filemgr.download&file_id=133716, accessed 20 March 2009.

Key Elements of a National Access Strategy: A Public Interest Proposal. Universal Access Project of the Information Policy Research Program [IPRP], Faculty of Information Studies, University of Toronto, August 5, 1998. http://www3.fis.utoronto.ca/research/iprp/ua/nacstrat.htm, accessed 13 March 2009.

K-Net, located in Northwestern Ontario, applies a social enterprise model for governing broadband development in remote Aboriginal communities in high cost serving areas. K-Net operates under the not-for -profit stewardship of the Keewaytinook Okimanak (KO) Tribal Council. http://knet.ca/ Accessed December 2010.

Lawson, Philippa. 2008. Gutting the Telecom Act. In: For sale to the highest bidder; telcom policy in Canada, edited by Marita Moll and Leslie Regan Shade, Ottawa, Canadian Centre for Policy Alternatives, pp. 17–26.

Lenihan D, Milloy J, Fox G, Barber T. 2007. Progressive Governance for Canadians: What You Need to Know. Crossing Boundaries Governance Program, Public Policy Forum, March 2007. Pp65-66. http://www.ppforum.ca/common/assets/publications/en/book-progressive%20governance%20for%20canadians.pdf, accessed 18 March 2009.

Lessig, Lawrence. 2004. Coase's First Question: When should there not be property rights? Cato Institute. Regulation, Vol.27, No. 3, Fall 2004. http://www.cato.org/pubs/regulation/regv27n3/v27n3-4.pdf, accessed 17 March 2009.

Lipsey, Richard G. 1996. Economic Growth, Technological Change, and Canadian Economic Policy. C.D. Howe Institute Benefactors Lecture, Vancouver, November 6, 1996. p28. http://www.cdhowe.org/pdf/lipsey.pdf, accessed 18 March 2009.

McTaggart, Craig. 2008. Net neutrality and Canada's Telecommunications Act. Prepared for the Fourteenth Biennial National Conference on New Developments in Communications Law and Policy, Law Society of Upper Canada, Ottawa, 25-26 April 2008. http://papers.ssrn.com/sol3/papers.cfm?abstract_id=1127203, accessed 24 March 2009.

Maxwell, Judith. 2008. Communities must mobilize to find local solutions to a global crisis. Globe and Mail., November 17, 2008, B2.

National CAP Pictou–Vancouver Working Group. 2004. From Access to Inclusion: A future vision for CAP. March 16, 2004.

New Democratic Party of Canada (NDP) web site: http://www.ndp.ca/platform/otherpriorities/supportingculture, accessed 18 March 2009.

Nowak, Peter. 2008. Canada's broadband networks not ready for future: report. CBC News, September 15, 2008. http://www.cbc.ca/technology/story/2008/09/15/tech-broadband.html, accessed 18 March 2009.

OECD. 2008. Ministerial Meeting on the future of the Internet Economy, Seoul, Korea, June 16-18, 2008. www.oecd.org/FutureInternet, accessed 17 March 2009.

OECD. 2008. Broadband subscribers per 100 inhabitants. June 2008. http://www.oecd.org/dataoecd/21/35/39574709.xls, accessed 18 March 2009.

OECD Broadband Portal. http://www.oecd.org/sti/ict/broadband, accessed 18 March 2009.

Organizational Readiness Office web site. http://www.tbs-sct.gc.ca/oro-bgc/index-eng.asp, accessed 15 March 2009.

Osborne, David and Gaebler, Ted. 1992. Reinventing Government: how the entrepreneurial spirit is transforming the public sector. Addison-Wesley Publishing.

Oxford Said Business School and Universidad de Oviedo. 2008. Broadband Quality Score: A global study of broadband quality. Sponsored by Cisco, September 2008 p8. http://www.sbs.ox.ac.uk/downloads/Broadband_Quality_Study_press_presentation.pdf, accessed 18 March 2009.

Partnership For A Digital Chicago: The city that net/works: transforming society and economy through digital excellence. Report of the Mayor's Advisory Council on closing the digital divide. Chicago, May 2007. http://egov.cityofchicago.org:80/webportal/COCWebPortal/COC_EDITORIAL/DigitalDivide.pdf, accessed 18 March 2009.

Preparing Europe's digital future: i2010 Mid-Term Review. European Communities, 2008. http://ec.europa.eu/information_society/eeurope/i2010/docs/annual_report/2008/i2010_mid-term_review_en.pdf, accessed 18 March 2009.

Public Works and Government Services Canada. Web site: http://www.tpsgc-pwgsc.gc.ca/apropos-about/fi-fs/ged-gol-eng.html, accessed 15 March 2009.

Priest, Margot. 1997. The Privatization of Regulation: Five Models of Self-Regulation. Ottawa Law Review, 1997: 29: 233 (1997-98).

Ramirez, Ricardo, Graham, Garth. Bigham, Fred G, and Pellerin, Dan. 2007. Broadband for what? Policy implications of an essential public utility. The Ontario Ministry of Government and Consumer Services. Toward a Broadband Research Agenda for Ontario. Working Papers. April 30, 2007. http://kmdi.utoronto.ca/broadband/publications/Files/ramirez_paper.pdf, accessed 15 March 2009.

Roberts, Sheridan. 2007. Measuring the impacts of ICT using official statistics. Directorate for Science, Technology and Industry, Committee for Information, Computer and Communications Policy, Working Party on Indicators for the Information Society, DSTI/ICCP/IIS(2007)1/FINAL. OECD/OCDE, October 2007. http://www.oecd.org/dataoecd/43/25/39869939.pdf, accessed 18 March 2009.

Saul, John Ralston. 2008. A fair country: telling truths about Canada. Toronto, Viking Canada.

Shirky, Clay. 2009. Ontology is overrated: categories, links, and tags. http://www.shirky.com/writings/ontology_overrated.html, accessed 18 March 2009.

Smolin, Lee. 2003. How science is like democracy. Technology, Entertainment, Design (TED), Filmed Feb 2003; Posted Nov 2008. http://www.ted.com/index.php/talks/lee_smolin_on_science_and_democracy.html, accessed 15 March 2009.

Stiglitz, Joseph. Chief Economist, World Bank. 1999. Scan Globally, Reinvent Locally: Knowledge Infrastructure and the Localization of Knowledge. Keynote Address, First Global Development Network Conference, Bonn, Germany. December 1999. http://www.inwent.org/E+Z/zeitschr/de400-3.htm, accessed 17 March 2009.

Stockholm Declaration on Open (broadband) Networks. http://www.1st-mile.com/resources/ospn-references/stockholm_declaration, accessed 18 March 2009.

Tapscott, Don. 2008. Grown Up Digital:How the Net Generation is Changing Your World. McGraw-Hill. http://www.grownupdigital.com/, accessed 18 March 2009.

Tapscott, Don and Williams, Anthony D. September 2010. Macrowikinomics: Rebooting Business and the World. Portfolio.

Telecommunications Act: Order Issuing a Direction to the CRTC on Implementing the Canadian Telecommunications Policy Objectives. P.C. 2006-1534 December 14, 2006. Canada Gazette, Vol. 140, No. 26, December 27, 2006. http://canadagazette.gc.ca/partII/2006/20061227/html/sor355-e.html, accessed 15 March 2009.

Telecommunications Policy Review Panel. 2006. Final Report 2006. Ottawa, Industry Canada. Chapter 1- p.32. http://www.telecomreview.ca/epic/site/tprp-gecrt.nsf/en/h_rx00054e.html, accessed 15 March 2009.

Thornton, Thomas F. 2008. Being and Place among the Tlingit. University of Washington Press.

Tournemille, Dale. 2001. Red Book: No new health, rural Internet spending. CTVnews.com Staff, Monday, December 10, 2001. http://www.theglobeandmail.com/budget2001, accessed 17 March 2009.

Treasury Board of Canada Secretariat. Web site. http://www.tbs-sct.gc.ca/media/nr-cp/2003/0616-eng.asp, accessed 15 March 2009.

Unger, Roberto. 1984. Passion; an essay on personality, London, Collier Macmillan. http://www.law.harvard.edu/faculty/unger/english/passion.php, accessed 18 March 2009.

Veenhof B, Wellman B, Quell C, Hogan B. 2008. How Canadians' use of the Internet affects social life and civic participation. Research Paper; Connectedness Series Statistics Canada, December

2008. http://www.statcan.gc.ca/pub/56f0004m/56f0004m2008016-eng.pdf, accessed 18 March 2009.

Vetter, Tony; MacLean, Don; and Creech, Heather. June 2009. Projecting the Evolution of the Internet, its Technologies, Communities and Management: Canadian stakeholders' understandings and perceptions of the issues. Report on a pilot workshop held in Vancouver, British Columbia, March 26–27, 2009. Winnipeg, International Institute for Sustainable Development (IISD), http://www.iisd.org/pdf/2009/projecting_internet_evolution.pdf Accessed December 2010.

Webster, Paul and Cathro, John. 2007. Hands off: is smart regulation dumb for Canada's wilderness areas? The Walrus, November 2007, p.41.

Welsum, Desirée van. 2008. Broadband and the Economy. Ministerial Background Report, DSTI/ICCP/IE(2007)3/FINAL. OECD Ministerial Meeting on the future of the Internet Economy, Seoul, Korea, 17-18 June 2008. OECD Working Party on the Information Economy, May 2007. http://www.oecd.org/dataoecd/62/7/40781696.pdf, accessed 18 March 2009.

Wiring the social Network (a growing conversation in Vancouver, British Columbia) <http://wiringthesocialeconomy.wordpress.com/> Accessed December 2010.

Zara, Olivier. 2008. Managing Collective Intelligence: Toward a New Corporate Governance. M21 Editions. http://www.axiopole.com/pdf/Managing_collective_intelligence.pdf, accessed 18 March 2009.

Chapter 5
E-Sri Lanka as a Deliberate and Emergent Strategy Process

Nagy K. Hanna

Introduction

This case study demonstrates that much of the success (or failure) of e-development programs can depend on continuous adaptation and learning during implementation, that is, on integrating deliberate and emergent strategies. It starts with analyzing the deliberate e-development strategy taken and the factors that shaped that design. It points out that this deliberate e-development strategy was not perfectly designed upfront, or guaranteed successful implementation. The design phase had to take account of political conditions, unknowns and uncertainties. The outcomes were expected to depend on many contextual factors that are beyond the control of the designers. Most critically, the outcomes were expected to depend on untested local capacity to adapt and learn during implementation so as to enable emergent strategies to reshape the original and deliberate strategy. Accordingly, strategy formulation assigned much attention to institution building and local capacity to learn, adapt, and innovate.

This case study gives an overview of the experience of e-Sri Lanka, moving from a vision of e-development to a full-fledged program design and then to implementation. It analyzes the process that motivated the design of e-Sri Lanka and came to guide its continuing evolution. It examines the dynamics of the donor–country relationship, the efforts to bridge the gap between local aspirations and capabilities, and the iterative process of moving from initial entry points to a holistic vision and integrated program of ICT-enabled development. It opens up the design process and the influence of stakeholders to examination and reflection so as to search for lessons – lessons in building e-leadership institutions, designing e-government programs, and promoting innovation in ICT use for reducing poverty and empowering communities. It sheds light on the dynamic

N.K. Hanna and P.T. Knight (eds.), *Seeking Transformation Through Information Technology*, Innovation, Technology, and Knowledge Management,
DOI 10.1007/978-1-4614-0353-1_5,

nature of partnership between the aid agency and client country and how this partnership has been shaped by incentives facing individuals and institutions. Finally, it examines briefly the challenges, adaptations, and outcomes of implementation over the last 5 years.[1]

E-Sri Lanka as a Case Study

Several challenges facing e-Sri Lanka give it broad relevance as a case study of e-development in action. First, the program was developed despite difficult initial conditions and political uncertainties. Sri Lanka is a poor country (with gross national income per capita (about US $1,000 at the start of the program, in 2004), and it shares with many other countries the challenges of a weak democracy undergoing conflict and social turmoil. That a coherent ICT-enabled strategy could be forged for Sri Lanka, and a national consensus reached on that strategy, raises hope that similar achievements are possible even in the most difficult environments.

Second, Sri Lanka lacked a focal point or ministry to lead e-development and partner with international aid agencies. The existing body for national ICT policy was politicized, dysfunctional, and marginal. It had to be dismantled, and new coordinating institutions created. This work had to be done in the context of a bloated civil service with limited access to ICT and little awareness of its potential as an enabler of development – common challenges among developing countries.

Third, with its small population (20 million), Sri Lanka presents a case relevant not only for countries of similar size, but also for poor states within large countries facing digital divides as well as digital opportunities. Advances in ICT in large countries, such as Brazil, China, India, and Russia, have attracted attention, but the highly aggregated e-readiness and knowledge assessments for these countries conceal the diversity among their regions.[2]

One key asset that Sri Lanka had at the start of this journey was its high literacy rate (around 90%), particularly for its level of income. This was in general literacy, not ICT literacy. But this base was still a critical platform on which to build e-literacy and broadbased e-development.

[1] The program has been subjected to several reviews by the World Bank and others, indicating overall satisfactory outcomes. But final and formal evaluation will have to await the completion of investments projects still underway (as of August 2010).

[2] The e-Sri Lanka model and experience are having much influence on other World Bank–assisted programs, including e-Bharat (in India), e-Ghana, e-Pakistan, and e-Rwanda. And the e-Sri Lanka framework is influencing programs in large countries. One example is e-Brasil [see Knight et al. (2007)].

Synopsis of the E-Sri Lanka Program

E-Sri Lanka is an integrated program and the first of its kind to be funded by the World Bank. This case study does not focus on the detailed design of the emerging strategy, but on the process of strategy formulation.[3] The process of designing the e-Sri Lanka program was as critical as the product, the aid-financed e-Sri Lanka project. The process not only produced a relatively coherent national e-development strategy, but also generated local understanding, political commitment, broad ownership, and initial implementation capacity for the first time in Sri Lanka.

The e-Sri Lanka program takes a holistic approach to ICT for development, making it a comprehensive national e-development project. Conceived as a multidonor-funded program, this national development initiative aims at using ICT to reduce poverty, promote growth, and foster social integration. The initiative cuts across government, the private sector, civil society, and communities at large.

The e-Sri Lanka program consists of six basic component programs:

- *ICT policy, leadership, and institutional development* – a policy development and capacity-building program to create an enabling environment for the knowledge economy and develop the local institutional capacity to lead and implement an ambitious ICT program
- *ICT human resource development and industry promotion* – an innovation fund to build ICT human resource capacity and create jobs through a dynamic ICT sector, foreign and local investment in the sector, and diffusion of ICT among small and medium-size enterprises
- *Regional telecommunications network development* – a smart, least-cost subsidy scheme to extend the information infrastructure and connectivity to serve poor communities and rural areas
- *Telecenter development* – smart subsidy and entrepreneurial development schemes to develop affordable access to ICT tools, ICT literacy, local content, e-government services, and e-commerce applications – utilizing the new information infrastructure, e-government applications, and grassroots-oriented innovation fund
- *Reengineering government* – a coherent investment program in ICT applications, information sharing, knowledge management, process reengineering, service innovation, and human resources to deliver faster, more efficient, and more transparent government services to all citizens and businesses
- *E-society* – an innovation fund to mobilize local knowledge, digitize and share local content, and use ICT for social development and grassroots participation, with the aim of promoting ICT-enabled rural development, social capital, mutual understanding, equitable access to knowledge, and empowerment of the poor

[3] A two-volume book (Hanna 2007a, b) captures in more detail the rich knowledge generated in designing a holistic e-development program and building knowledge partnerships with client countries.

The design of the e-Sri Lanka program aimed to capture key synergies among these components. A newly created national e-leadership institution, the ICT Agency, was designed, authorized, and equipped to realize these synergies and to partner with other stakeholders to create an ecosystem for capturing potential synergies and leveraging ICT for development. And monitoring and evaluation systems were designed to promote coordination across the entire program, maximizing learning and adaptation throughout its implementation.

The e-Sri Lanka program is still under implementation, and no one can claim final success or sustainable impact yet. What success may be claimed so far has been initiating a program from difficult initial conditions within the country and constraints within the World Bank, creating a new model of a national ICT agency, initiating many pilots and actions on the ground, and getting the buy-in of stakeholders on critical decisions. The process has already transformed initial perceptions and conditions, including producing greater awareness of the need to integrate ICT into development, substantial local learning and capacity building within the country, and greater acceptance within the World Bank of its role in supporting strategic and integrated approaches to ICT for development. In fact, since its approval to finance this program, the Bank has replicated this model in several other countries.

Origins of E-Sri Lanka

The initiative of e-Sri Lanka originated in the private sector, primarily in the National Chamber of Commerce and among local software industry leaders. The chamber prepared an early version of a national ICT road map, but focused mainly on developing the software industry. In parallel, local software associations worked with the US Agency for International Development (USAID) to promote the ICT cluster – inspired by the success of the Indian software export industry.

Sri Lanka's minister of science and technology took the proposal to the president of the World Bank, who in turn asked the Bank's chief information officer (CIO) to respond. These were unusual steps, prompted by widespread skepticism and the lack of a central contact point within the Bank to mainstream integrated e-development lending operations. The client country was unsure about where to seek assistance for such an unusual, cross-sectoral project within the Bank's complex bureaucracy. The global unit responsible for providing operational assistance to client countries in information and communication technology was then focusing on telecommunications and skeptical about venturing beyond its traditional strengths and mandate.[4] Yet, the CIO's office lacked the experience to move into operational

[4] The World Bank had just issued Information and Communications Technologies: A World Bank Group Strategy (World Bank 2002). This strategy focused on policies and investments to increase access to the information infrastructure (telecommunications); it left out the challenges of investing in the human resources and applications to integrate the infrastructure into other sectors. Meeting these challenges was delegated to the regional units of the Bank.

assistance and lending and had no precedent or mandate for doing so. In a sense, the country's request presented a challenge to the organizational structure of the Bank, and the low level of mainstreaming of ICT in development.

A First Mission to Sri Lanka

Informally testing the proposal on the Bank's stakeholders, the CIO found much skepticism about the role of ICT in development and about Sri Lanka's aspiration to emulate India's export drive in software. Given Sri Lanka's development challenges, the proposal was deemed unrealistic and perhaps irrelevant.

The CIO turned to an internal ICT champion to take up the challenge, acknowledging that earlier attempts to develop comprehensive ICT strategies had been stymied. Such strategies were viewed as a high-risk venture in an area, where the Bank had no precedent or demonstrated competencies. The ICT sector was viewed by mainstream economists and most country managers as irrelevant to poor countries and poverty reduction. The Bank's regional management agreed to a first reconnaissance visit (mission) to Sri Lanka but with the proviso that further assistance would be unlikely. The regional management viewed the mission as a one-shot advisory service in response to a high-level request.

A team was quickly formed to visit the country. The recruiting put a premium on having diverse perspectives and core skills. Some in this initial team came from Silicon Valley (for software industry expertise) and the Indian state of Andhra Pradesh (for e-government expertise). The team was expected to carry professional credibility with the client, but with the exception of the team leader (the author) most team members knew little about battling the Bank's bureaucratic constraints.

In Sri Lanka, the mission came under intense pressure from key political and private sector leaders to promise visible and immediate actions and extensive funding for an ambitious but still undefined program. The private sector, having driven the original proposal, lobbied for a large share of funding. Within the government, however, the sense of ownership seemed thin among senior civil servants. A few chief executive officers (CEOs) were engaged, including those of the Chamber of Commerce, the Software Export Association, and a major telecommunications company. The original ICT road map and the early engagement of these stakeholders were consistent with the then political leadership's vision of private sector-led, services-based growth.

The mission's return with findings and recommendations opened a debate on e-development within the Bank and provided the first opportunity to form a position on a client's request for funding for this purpose. The initial reaction was consistent with the risk aversion and skepticism then prevailing in the Bank about the relevance of ICT to development. Some raised valid questions about whether it was appropriate for government to support a business-driven sector like ICT. Some claimed that the team was advocating a "discredited" industrial policy approach of intervening selectively and picking winners. Others felt that e-government should be pursued sector by sector or ministry by ministry, thus fitting in with the Bank's sector-based lending.[5] Some saw a free-standing lending operation in the new field of ICT as competing with their already-established, sectorally allocated budgets. Some questioned the Bank's comparative advantage and competency in dealing with a new and fast-moving field. Many questioned the feasibility of a comprehensive strategy for ICT in view of Sri Lanka's weak record in implementing projects; they suggested starting (if at all) with a small pilot.

Generally, launching the mission in quick response to a government request – without first going through the elaborate process of including the project in the Bank's assistance strategy and lending program and conducting sector reviews, analyses, or even research – was seen as imprudent.[6] Entering such a new field of assistance called for substantial sector analyses. The initiative might reflect client priorities and international best practices, but how did it fit with the disciplined, conventional, sector-based reviews? How could management apply the traditional quality control reviews to such a high-profile project outside the Bank's traditional competencies?

This initial response was not unusual. ICT had not yet been mainstreamed into development cooperation.[7] Other aid agencies working in established sectors – including the two major funding agencies in the region, the Asian Development Bank and the Japan Bank for International Cooperation – had similar responses. USAID viewed its role solely as promoting the ICT industry cluster and its private sector associations. Other bilateral donors could not see the connection between ICT and achieving the Millennium Development Goals. A few aid agencies, while sympathetic to Sri Lanka's aspirations, were skeptical of its ability to implement the program. A narrow definition of ICT's role in development and a rigid division of labor among donors in Sri Lanka did not help making the case.

Gaining Traction, Changing Minds

Forging an alliance with the Bank's country management for Sri Lanka proved critical. New management, arriving in Colombo in July 2002, soon after the first mission, sensed an unusually strong interest at the highest levels of government and business

[5] This is a key issue: which aspects of ICT should be integrated into sectoral programs like education or rural development, and which treated as a coherent and independent program to build an ICT governance framework, shared applications and infrastructure, and a common platform for enabling all sectors of the economy?

[6] A few years later, the Quality Assurance Group of the Bank reviewed the informal economic and sector work done in support of program design and judged it to be of the highest quality, in terms of impact and responsiveness to client needs, even though it did not follow the Bank's established procedure.

[7] As of mid-2010, the Bank has launched a corporate-level effort to mainstream ICT across sectors. This initiative is in part a reflection of a change in senior management attitude (including a new President), the growing visibility of the Internet in all aspects of business and our lives, and the barriers broken by the e-Sri Lanka project.

in seeking Bank assistance for this new and untested area. On its recommendation, the Bank's regional management allowed the project team a chance to visit Sri Lanka again – as long as it came back with a simpler and much smaller program, perhaps even a pilot for a first phase and as long as it addressed many of the constraints on ICT mainstreaming and practice in the Bank. The internal audience remained highly skeptical. Rivalry among the CIO group, the Global ICT unit, and other sectoral units in the South Asia region did not help.

These challenges motivated the team leader to build a strong team, this time with staff drawn from across the Bank – which proved critical in building ownership and alliances within the institution – as well as consultants spanning different areas of expertise. The overall vision, the strong client interest, the initial resistance within the Bank – all this helped cement bonds among the new team members. It also helped motivate and focus the team's efforts in mobilizing counterparts in Sri Lanka's private sector, the country's political leadership, and leading authorities in the emerging field of ICT. Despite diverse backgrounds and disciplines, the local Sri Lankan team too was then shaped into a highly motivated group, both by the challenges it faced and by the window of opportunity then created by the start of a peace process and political interest in a new theme for unifying the country.

E-Sri Lanka also offered a rare opportunity to move Bank assistance in this area to a higher plane and to integrate best practices in leveraging ICT to accelerate national development, boost competitiveness, and alleviate information poverty.[8] Evidence of the high payoffs from adopting national strategies to build competencies in ICT production and use has been accumulating, particularly in East Asia.[9] A strategic role for governments, in partnership with the private sector, has been increasingly acknowledged and practiced in these strategies. Even the most advanced OECD countries are supporting national programs to promote innovation in and diffusion of ICT among their small and medium-size enterprises.[10]

Yet the opportunities came with tough options. The e-Sri Lanka program was tentatively estimated at US $500 million, with US $300 million to come from the private sector and, it was hoped, US $100 million from the Bank. Despite the apparent funding constraint, the client ruled out the option of starting with a pilot and only later moving to a full-blown program. That led to some tough decisions on priorities: What should be the minimal core elements of the program? What critical elements and interdependencies should be covered in an initial phase? Which areas might interest other aid agencies for cofinancing and export credit? What should be piloted first and/or phased in over time? How should the claims of different stakeholders be balanced in the critical initial phases?

---

[8] An early attempt in 1993 to help Sri Lanka harness ICT for national development was rejected by Bank management. Similar attempts to broaden the role of ICT in development for India in 1991–1992 were also thwarted. See Hanna (1994). For an early publication on how ICT can increase competitiveness and alleviate information poverty, see Hanna (1991).

[9] See Hanna (1996). For earlier studies, see Wade (1990). For more recent studies, see Yusuf (2003).

[10] See Hanna et al. (1995).

A key decision at this point was to focus on connectivity and e-government programs, which can require lumpy investments for critical infrastructure, platforms, and systems. For connectivity, having a regional focus within Sri Lanka (as with regional telecommunications and telecenter networks) was deemed necessary. This would have the dual advantage of accommodating funding constraints and deepening the focus on poorer regions of the country. Similarly, for e-government, focusing on shared platforms (like the country portal and government intranet) would help both to meet funding constraints and to avoid premature involvement in large ICT applications in specific sectors. Another critical decision was to focus on the human resources and training considered essential to implement the first phase of the program, leaving the vast area of ICT in education (and education in ICT) primarily to the Ministry of Education.[11]

As the project gained traction, the ICT champions spent more time communicating with colleagues in other sectors, feedback from the client reinforced the team's findings, and the program design gained credibility, it became easier for a new regional management to lend its support. The turnaround in the Bank was neither instant nor dramatic, however. Typically, it takes time to persuade people to adopt new ideas and for these ideas to filter down through a bureaucracy – particularly in large aid bureaucracies, where errors of commission count far more than errors of omission. And when leadership is still uncertain about a new initiative, the pioneers often attract more rivals and enemies than collaborators and supporters.

Building Local Capacity and Ownership

The next phase was to build an initial local capacity and to quickly manage political pressures and changing expectations. The Bank's team lacked full-time counterparts in Sri Lanka. Nor was there an established ministry or agency to follow up on mission findings and recommendations. Thus, the first priority was to look at the options for developing local capacity and organizational arrangements. When relying on an existing body or authority proved unpromising, the challenge became to establish an ICT agency and its governance mechanism as soon as possible.

The low level of ICT awareness and literacy among parliamentarians made gaining parliamentary approval for creating a new agency a challenge, but the effort eventually succeeded (Moragoda 2002). Once the Parliament passed the ICT law in 2003, recruiting the CEO and key program managers for the new ICT Agency was the next pressing step. Creating and staffing the ICT Agency became the key to localizing project preparation and building a true partnership between local stakeholders and international funding agencies.

[11] The Ministry of Education and public universities were judged to be slow to change, the minister was from a rival party, and major aid agencies worked with the ministry rather independently. Because of this, keeping its programs out of e-Sri Lanka was judged to conserve on coordination efforts as well.

The newly created ICT Agency faced daunting challenges. Its staff had no experience with preparing a program of this size or with meeting Bank requirements for project preparation. The CEO came from the private sector, and that was an asset because he brought a business culture to a new public agency. But it also meant that he lacked knowledge of the rest of the government and of aid agencies. He had to acquire this knowledge fast, even while recruiting and building up his team, piloting quick-impact projects, and preparing the e-Sri Lanka program for Bank financing.

The Bank's team had developed a project management tool laying out the many steps needed to prepare the program, to share the Bank's rigorous requirements for financing and to overcome skepticism among local partners and aid agencies. Luckily, many of the new staff were familiar with project management methodology, and they quickly appropriated the tools, adapting and improving on them.

The next big turning point occurred in the months surrounding the 2004 national election in Sri Lanka, which the opposition unexpectedly called for and won. In the months before the election the e-Sri Lanka program and the ICT Agency, the lead implementing agency, were subjected to relentless rumors and attacks.[12] But discreet efforts before the election to reach out to the opposition and address both misunderstandings and legitimate concerns paid off when the opposition won the election. Moreover, strategic pilots carried out during early preparation, targeting the ICT needs of the Parliament, President, and Cabinet, helped raise awareness and promote ownership of e-Sri Lanka among some key political officials, including some in the opposition parties.

Experience during this period showed how important demonstration projects, coalition building, and strategic communications are in building the "authorizing environment" – the mandate of an organization and its political and legal support (Moore 1997). It also suggested that the authorizing environment demands continuous attention and maintenance, particularly in a turbulent political environment like Sri Lanka's.

Once the new government was in place, a bureaucratic fight ensued over where the ICT Agency should be sited within the administration. The Bank did not have any definitive view from its own research at that time; it could only keep its ears to the ground.[13] It continued to emphasize the fundamentals: ensure autonomy and authority for the ICT Agency, maintain the integrity of the program, and provide it the flexibility to address the new government's priorities of rural development and poverty reduction.

[12] Some of the rumors were that the telecenters were to serve only members of certain religious groups. Some attacks focused on the lack of immediate results on the ground, even though Bank funding for the program had not yet been approved. Others focused on perceptions that e-Sri Lanka catered to the concerns of the private sector rather than poverty reduction. Questions were raised about the composition of the agency staff (education, class, ethnicity, and religious affiliations) and about whether staffing and salaries suggested an elitist organization, inconsistent with the ideology of the main opposition party at the time.

[13] Since, a comparative study of e-leadership institutions has been carried out and published by the Bank (Hanna 2007b).

By then, the ICT Agency had become agile enough to respond to a fluid and fast changing political environment, and competent enough to reprioritize and devise new initiatives to influence the outcome. As the newly elected government saw more of its political priorities integrated into the program, it attached increasing significance to e-Sri Lanka, holding negotiations with the Bank for the first time in the Prime Minister's office. The new government then positioned the ICT Agency to report to the Prime Minister's office, and later to the President's, reflecting a growing understanding of the program's cross-cutting nature.

Thus, the design of the e-Sri Lanka program survived a major political shift, with its core objectives relatively intact.

Growing Ownership in the World Bank

At the Bank, having the new lending operation led from outside the South Asia regional unit presented its own difficulties. Free-standing lending operations are seldom led from outside the Bank's regional units, where most of the expertise in traditional sectors is located. (Telecommunications has been the exception, viewed as a highly specialized technical area that needs little coordination or integration with other sectors within the Bank's regional structure.) With no regional or central home in the Bank, this new type of assistance had to be processed from the CIO's office, though this office was not positioned to do so.

The innovation represented by the e-Sri Lanka program was unlikely to sprout from within the regional structure, given the prevailing skill mix and the substantial up-front investment required in research and development in a new practice or business line like e-development. But it could not survive and grow in the long run without a home in that structure. This is a common dilemma in managing innovation or a new business practice in large and silo-based aid bureaucracies like the Bank.

As negotiations between the Bank and the Sri Lankan government proceeded and the project's presentation to the Bank's Board of Executive Directors for approval approached, changes were afoot to absorb the ICT "sector" into the South Asia regional structure. The senior regional management for South Asia declared its support for ICT as key infrastructure for Asia's economies. This commitment was confirmed after other South Asian client countries requested Bank assistance similar to that requested for e-Sri Lanka. Several other aid agencies expressed greater interest in collaboration as the e-Sri Lanka program began to provide a common framework for investment and technical assistance in ICT. All this helped reinforce ownership of the e-Sri Lanka program by the Bank's South Asia regional management. The central department responsible for telecommunications (and more broadly for ICT) also began to propose similar approaches for holistic e-development.

When e-Sri Lanka was presented to the Bank's Board members, in September 2004, members endorsed the program despite concerns about its ambitious scope and untested implementing agency. Indeed, they asked that a similar approach be adopted for the countries they represented, advanced and poor alike. James Wolfensohn, the World Bank's President at the time, stated at the Board meeting that he has been awaiting a project like that for a decade (most of his tenure at the Bank).[14] The regional management team committed itself to provide a home and the staffing to mainstream this innovation and to respond to growing demand from clients. Initial opposition and skepticism were weakened, but not eliminated. Some clients were encouraged to seek similar Bank assistance, such as Rwanda, Ghana, Armenia, and Vietnam.

Guiding Principles

The strategy design team strived to adhere to some key principles to guide the process of preparing the e-Sri Lanka program. These principles draw on lessons of development assistance, and the growing literature of "new development economics."[15]

Taking a holistic, long-term, and development-driven view – to ensure that national ICT strategy is driven by the overall national development strategy and development outcomes, not ICT investments, and to tap complementarities with other development programs as well as synergies within the e-development program.

Securing broad local ownership among key stakeholders – to create and implement a sustainable, cross-cutting program.

Adopting a knowledge-based partnership – to ensure ownership, knowledge transfer, capacity building, local innovation, sustainable institutional change, and a good fit with local conditions.

Ensuring programmatic flexibility – to accommodate limited up-front information, an uncertain political environment, untested capabilities, and adaptation during implementation.

Promoting bottom-up initiatives – to accommodate complexity and diversity, to stimulate innovation, to build local partnerships for social learning, and to complement top-down strategic directions.

Funding quick-results pilots – to nurture political commitment and social learning.

Building multiple feedback mechanisms – to support just-in-time learning and local innovation as well as institutionalize monitoring and evaluation.

---

[14] This was a notable opening remark from the President that suggests his commitment to ICT role in development, and the crucial role he played as an e-leadership in enabling e-Sri Lanka to be financed by the Bank. But it also indicates his frustrations that such e-strategies did not emerge earlier and the deep seated risk aversion, skepticism, and resistance to innovation down the line of the organization.

[15] Most broadly, these lessons of experience suggest the importance of holistic approaches and long-term visions and of broad local ownership and country–donor partnerships (Stiglitz 1998; Stiglitz et al. 2000). They also show a need to understand development as a process of structural change and institutional transformation (Fukuyama 2004; Rodrik 2000), joint human resource and technological capacity building (Lall 1999; Perez 2001; Wade 1990), learning and innovation (Rodrik 2004), and of unpredictability and uncertainty demanding extensive feedback and experimentation (Adelman 2000; Rodrik 2004; Scott 1998).

Taking a Holistic, Long-Term, and Development-Driven View

Political leaders in the governing coalition at the time viewed ICT as a potential source for a compelling and unifying vision that could help overcome a sense of missed opportunities, including two decades of development lost through civil war. They were well aware of the threats of globalization – including the stiff competition facing the local textile industry from China – as well as the opportunities – such as the prospect of Sri Lanka emerging as a modern trading nation and a regional logistics and services center. And as the government then pursued peace with the rebels, it saw e-Sri Lanka as a theme that would help energize and unify the country, particularly if the initiative produced dividends for social inclusion and for the poorest regions of the North and South.

This political view fit well with the pervasive roles ICT can play in development.[16] But to create a unifying force, it was critical to shift from a vision driven by the ICT industry to one centered on leveraging the ICT revolution to transform the entire economy – a vision in which the national development strategy would define the e-strategy.

An analysis of the recently established national development strategy, outlining how ICT could aid in achieving this strategy, helped build adequate consensus on a national vision of ICT-enabled development. The analysis sought to identify the competitive advantages of Sri Lanka that ICT could best leverage and the development programs that ICT could best complement. It also aimed to link Sri Lanka's aspirations as a regional services hub with what ICT might offer as an enabler. The emerging outline of a development-driven ICT vision was then adopted by the political leadership, as it resonated with deeply felt aspirations: national unity, dynamic growth, and poverty reduction.[17]

This demand-driven, development-focused view broadened ownership of the e-Sri Lanka program. Presenting the program as an enabler of established sectors and ministries, not a competitor, helped in increasing support within the country and the Bank. At the Bank, presentations emphasized how the project would complement Bank-assisted sectoral projects – for example, providing telecenter networks as delivery channels for agricultural, education, and health services.[18]

The holistic vision shaping the e-Sri Lanka program stresses the synergy among key elements of e-development: an enabling policy and institutional environment, a competitive and affordable information infrastructure, a dynamic and competitive

---

[16] For a comprehensive view of the role of ICT in development, see for example Hanna (2004), UNDP (2001) and ILO (2001).

[17] The e-Sri Lanka initiative was intended to "take the dividends of ICT to every village, to every citizen, to every business and to transform the way Government works … to develop Sri Lanka's economy, alleviate poverty, and improve the quality of life and the opportunities of all our people" (Sri Lanka, Ministry of Science and Technology 2002).

[18] The broad vision had an unexpected payoff: it signaled the government's commitment to donors and international investors, creating the brand name of "e-Sri Lanka" that helped attract investments from ICT multinationals and initiate business process outsourcing in Sri Lanka.

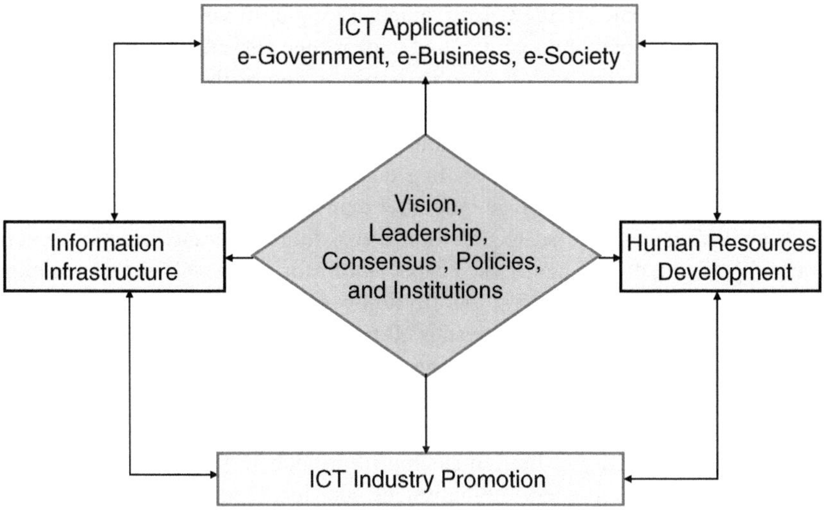

Fig. 5.1 Synergies among key elements of e-development

ICT industry, broad ICT literacy and education, a coherent investment program to apply ICT to modernizing the public sector, and incentives to promote the use of ICT in developing the private sector and empowering civil society (Fig. 5.1).[19] Creating opportunities to tap these synergy would accelerate and maximize the development impact of ICT investments and help realize the network externalities that occur only after a critical mass of ICT users has been reached.

Keeping this holistic view in mind, potential synergies were discovered along the way. For example, e-government services could not have much impact on the common man and small business without adequate connectivity, delivery channels, and shared and affordable access to ICT through telecenters. Conversely, telecenters were unlikely to be financially sustainable without local content and income from delivery of highly demanded e-government services.

Pursuing a holistic approach is demanding. It demands building strategic partnerships across sectors and disciplines. Establishing synergies requires creating and retaining a cross-sectoral team that can address all the elements of e-development simultaneously. In the Bank, this meant creating a virtual team that comprises specialists in different aspects of ICT and development disciplines from across several units, then protecting the team from turf battles. The new ICT Agency faced similar challenges of partnership and team building. It had to struggle to build bridges across agencies and constituencies whose turfs were long established and interests narrowly defined.

[19] This does not mean that a comprehensive e-development project is always the best way to bundle ICT investments and capture the synergies involved. But it provides a powerful lens for understanding potential synergies.

Achieving a holistic strategy also requires a long-term vision to keep the focus on the development outcomes of ICT and to phase the steps needed to realize these outcomes over time. The vision of e-Sri Lanka is one of the transforming public services, user industries, rural communities, and even the structure of the economy. Transformation is an energizing vision, but it cannot be achieved in the short term. E-government programs in leading countries, for example, are expected to reach a real transformational stage only after many years, possibly decades. This is no different from any large-scale structural and institutional transformation. But the hype and potential of ICT have raised expectations for instant ICT-driven solutions. Moreover, political uncertainties, the election cycle, the project cycle, and incentives in the civil service and aid agencies all favor a short-term orientation.

Thus, establishing and communicating a long-term perspective was deemed critical to maintaining a holistic vision while still allowing disciplined phasing and progressive integration of an otherwise unmanageably complex program. This long-term view was necessary to the sequencing of projects to keep complexity in line with e-readiness, stakeholders' commitment, and local capacity for coordination and integration. It was also critical that the first phase, the donor-assisted 5-year program, lay the foundation for many future activities. Building the capacity of the ICT Agency, establishing its track record, and developing national ICT governance and architecture were all expected to prepare the way for future scaled-up e-government programs.

A long-term vision also must encompass human resources, critical to an information society. But the Ministries of Education and Higher Education were unprepared to coordinate with the e-Sri Lanka program. A division of labor among donors, with the Asian Development Bank the lead agency for education, also made coordination difficult. Moreover, at the time, Sri Lanka lacked locally proven approaches to reforming the education sector with the help of ICT.

Adding a comprehensive component on ICT as an enabler of education reform to the e-Sri Lanka program would have introduced premature complexity to the national e-development strategy. Yet ignoring human resources would have put binding constraints on other parts of the program. The adopted tradeoff was to address immediate constraints in capabilities tied to specific steps in implementation and to establish a fund for demand-driven education pilots that could lay the foundation for full-scale programs for human resource development and ICT in education.

Securing Broad Local Ownership

To secure broad ownership, the ICT Agency invited focus groups of key stakeholders to work with it in shaping the design of each component of the e-Sri Lanka program. Engaging stakeholders was also necessary to enable the new agency to function and to contain its size and its dependence on expensive international consultants. Stakeholders participated voluntarily, often because of their interest and ability to contribute rather than just their position. While the Bank and ICT Agency teams worked out the overall design and analyses, the focus groups made many refinements, at times challenging and revising even the fundamental assumptions.

In addition, several "town hall" meetings were organized to hear views from the general public. The agency led these presentations from early on. That helped build confidence and ownership by emphasizing that e-Sri Lanka is not a donor-driven program but a framework for partnership for all.

Securing broad ownership of a national program is always a challenge, but particularly so in a conflict-ridden society under a coalition government. Some stakeholders held strong and uncompromising views about how to realize the vision. Some insisted that only the public sector should own and operate the telecenters that were to provide shared, affordable access to ICT – while others insisted that only the private sector should do so. Representatives of the ICT industry at times felt that the program's design had neglected their original vision or had tilted too much toward the needs of the public sector. And NGOs representing the rural areas at times felt that it was favoring urban elites. Balancing the program in response to different stakeholders and securing broad ownership was a continual challenge.

The need to keep key constituencies engaged as partners in shaping and implementing the program influenced the final scope of e-Sri Lanka and the balance among its components. There was growing pressure, for example, to drop funding for promotion of the ICT industry so as to simplify the donor-financed project and increase funding for the under-resourced e-government program. But these changes were resisted because they risked losing the ICT industry and the broader private sector as well as the potential to mobilize the resources of the Sri Lankan diaspora and ICT multinationals. Similar balancing was attempted between already-connected urban centers and rural and underserved areas.

Local ownership was sometimes threatened by the internal demands of the World Bank, including its project cycle, its Board schedule, and its budgetary limitations. Speed often compromises ownership, particularly when programs involve many stakeholders and the pace is imposed from outside (see Hanna and Picciotto 2002, p. 290). The problem can be worse for innovative and contentious lending operations, which fit poorly with the internal dynamics and rigorous schedules of large funding organizations.

Tension between securing ownership within the Bank and securing it within Sri Lanka arose in several cases. First, pilots to provide political payoffs and demonstration effects mattered more to the government than preparing the large program for funding by the Bank and other aid agencies. These pilots appeared essential to ensure the ICT Agency's legitimacy and immediate survival. But they also diverted its resources and attention away from meeting the aid agencies' timelines and appraisal requirements.

Second, building a new agency to lead the e-Sri Lanka program was necessary to secure local ownership, develop homegrown solutions, and continually adapt the program. Institution building is an espoused core objective of aid agencies. But it is also an intangible and long-term one. The incentives and accountabilities facing the Bank's team centered primarily on meeting internal deadlines for project appraisal and Board approval. Just as with the pilots, institution building competed for resources and attention at a time that the team had to meet the Bank's deadlines for preparation and Board presentation. The risks were high; delays could have discredited the team and undermined the legitimacy of a new type of operation.

Finally, the unexpected call for a national election made it tempting to advance project negotiations before the election to avoid the risk of a new government revising the program's design and the consequent delays in the Bank's Board approval. But securing ownership of e-Sri Lanka by the new government was judged more important than meeting the Bank's schedule. That decision proved to be beneficial. It led not only to ownership by the new coalition government, but also to the refinement of several components of the program to reinforce its rural development focus, in line with the new government's constituency. It remained essential that the e-Sri Lanka program be perceived as a homegrown initiative. The pace of processing and approval by the external financiers and partners could not be allowed to undermine this perception.

Adopting a Knowledge-Based Partnership

Program design was guided by the principle of a knowledge-based partnership between the Bank and the client – a partnership that emphasizes sharing knowledge in a way that adds value to the client's decisionmaking and capabilities.[20] The Bank was providing professional services for which the mode of delivery would be as critical to development outcomes as the final design of the program.[21] Moreover, the Bank lacked any "recipe" or standard model to follow in this new area. Advisory services had not been codified or "commoditized" by the consulting industry. A "black box" approach would not have worked, since both the expertise and its delivery required codesign and collaborative solutions.

A knowledge-based partnership would bring together the unique capabilities of aid professionals and local counterparts – and combine global and local knowledge. Moreover, such a relationship was increasingly demanded given the client institution's growing sophistication, the political visibility of the program, and the highly motivated counterpart staff.

Knowledge-based partnerships have their own dynamics, depending on the strength of each partner and the maturity of the relationship. In the early stages, when the ICT Agency was still being established, the Bank team had no choice but to take the lead in developing the overall conceptual design of e-Sri Lanka, in line with the aspirations of key stakeholders. But the agency caught up, progressively integrating, detailing, and advancing the program design to fit local experiences and stakeholder preferences.[22]

[20] For an excellent treatment of such partnerships in professional services, see Dawson (2005).

[21] See Hanna and Picciotto (2002), pp. 135–158.

[22] Except for the overall conceptual design of the e-government strategy, contracted out to a Singapore consulting firm (NCS), almost all aspects of the program were developed by the ICT Agency in collaboration with the focus groups.

Knowledge-based partnerships are not easy to build and are seldom used except by the best professional services organizations (Dawson 2005). The budgetary process and pressures of the project cycle in aid agencies do not always encourage or account for the time or resources needed for sharing information, building knowledge tools, developing communities of practice, and nurturing professional dialog. Moreover, playing the roles of coach, adviser, and facilitator does not permit aid agency staff to take credit for client actions or even to justify lending to a project. For the Bank's e-Sri Lanka team, empowering the local team to appropriate new tools and frameworks and giving it credit for the hard work and nascent program was a challenge – especially as both teams felt embattled and had to demonstrate the value they added to the joint design process.

The ICT Agency's lack of experience in preparing programs for external financing also tested the partnership. Once staffed, the agency moved quickly to propose more than 100 small but diverse projects, exceeding any possible donor financing and implementation capacity. These local initiatives, striving to exceed donor expectations, led to tensions and debates. But they also led to new ideas that were later disciplined by and integrated into the program strategy. Similarly, the agency was impatient with what it perceived as the Bank's slow and cumbersome procurement processes. It wanted shortcuts so that it could keep up with fast-moving technology cycles and respond to political pressures to produce results. That too led to creative tensions and at times to adaptations in Bank procedures.

As program preparation advanced, a stronger professional partnership grew. Both the need for new local solutions and the risks to individuals on both sides further cemented the partnership. That in turn inspired more local innovation and spurred the search for emerging international best practices that could be adapted locally, leading to a better fit of the strategy to local conditions. However, this partnership depended more on individuals than institutions.[23] Knowledge-based partnership proved particularly difficult to sustain in the face of budgetary constraints for implementation assistance and staff changes within the Bank.

Ensuring Programmatic Flexibility

At the time of project design, there were many uncertainties and no precedents to guide the design team. The Bank was used to funding specific ICT project components, applications, or systems defined according to a blueprint. But programmatic or sectorwide approaches, though increasingly used in established sectors, such as roads and education, had yet to be used in the ICT field.[24] During program

[23] Later in program implementation, knowledge partnership was at times strained by changes in team composition with the Bank and the ICT Agency, and by broader changes in government and the Bank.

[24] Programmatic aid is aid for broad public expenditure programs rather than specific projects. See Hanna and Picciotto (2002, Chaps. 8 and 9) for a discussion of programmatic approaches.

preparation, however, it became clear that a rigid, top-down investment plan would be infeasible and perhaps counterproductive.

Given the skepticism about the Bank's entry into this new area of assistance, it seemed impossible to get management approval without greater precision about the design, costs, and funding for such elements as e-government systems and telecenters. Yet these were exactly the programs that demanded continuous flexibility and adaptation during implementation, since community receptivity, institutional response, political commitment, and local capabilities had yet to be tested. Moreover, independent evaluations of integrated and comprehensive projects suggest that those that relied on blueprints, discrete investments, and Bank-controlled project implementation units – rather than building flexibility, local capacity, and incentives for coordination – often failed.[25]

Getting the broad directions right seemed more important than defining the detailed design, which would inevitably change or evolve during implementation. The design team faced many pressures to reduce uncertainties prior to the Bank's Board approval. These pressures typically lead to detailed rigid plans. The team tried to strike a balance between up-front commitment to clear priorities and accountabilities, and openness to change and learning during implementation. Emphasis was put on securing programmatic flexibility and building local capacity to adapt the program through implementation and learning.[26]

This approach paid off when unexpected changes occurred in the program environment, such as the change in government in April 2004 and the tsunami of December 2004. After the tsunami, programmatic flexibility and the institutional agility of the ICT Agency made it possible, for example, to place computers in refugee camps for children with no schools but ample time to learn. Similarly, the e-government program established priorities, pilots, and sequenced actions, but when ministries changed leadership or failed to live up to key accountabilities, the program resequenced their applications or dropped them altogether. And when donor funding became available for specific components, the flexible design permitted and even encouraged redeployment of funds within and across programs – as long as this did not jeopardize the fundamental strategy and development objectives.

Promoting Bottom-Up Initiatives

As initial program preparation unfolded, different stakeholders demanded resources to meet *their* urgent need for ICT investments or to promote *their* segment of the ICT industry. Proposals were springing up from the private sector, civil society, and academic and training institutions. The government lacked a mechanism for

[25] Hanna and Picciotto (2002), pp. 295–298.

[26] No amount of central planning or international consulting would suffice, nor could it substitute for able and empowered local leaders, adaptive organizations, and social learning.

aggregating and prioritizing these demands and for engaging as a partner in the many local initiatives, let alone for facilitating learning from them. The ICT Agency had to focus on large, complex, strategic investments and overall program management; it could not dissipate its limited capacity on appraising and promoting many small grassroots initiatives.

A search for appropriate mechanisms to aggregate and prioritize these demands, simplify program design and management, and maximize learning all at the same time led to the idea of creating two national funds. One, the ICT industry promotion and capacity building fund, would promote innovations to meet the ICT industry's human resource development needs, develop the domestic market, and to promote the country as an ICT-enabled service exporter. The other, the e-society fund, would promote grassroots innovation and community capacity to use ICT for poverty reduction and social development.[27]

Mechanisms like these to support bottom-up initiatives also aim to promote innovative partnerships across the public–private divide and institutions at large. Thus, the two funds have also been established to enable otherwise separate public, business, academic, and civil society sectors to partner in promoting innovative ways to upgrade ICT skills and to use ICT for poverty reduction and community development. Such cross-sectoral partnerships are also deemed critical to promote policy reforms, social learning, and sustainable institutional change (see Wilson 2004).

Funding Quick-Results Pilots

Proceeding with pilots even as the e-Sri Lanka program was being designed was an unusual aspect of program preparation. The bias for action was imperative. The client, particularly the program's political champions, perceived the Bank's requirements for rigorous design and appraisal as too slow and onerous. And the skepticism within the Bank meant that the design team could not afford to proceed with internal Bank reviews and approval without a relatively developed program design. The tension between the short- and long-term imperatives was palpable. Pilots were therefore critical – both to support the legitimacy of the program by producing rapid results and demonstration effects and to help refine program design for sustainability and scaling up.

Pilots also provided a learning opportunity for the ICT Agency, allowing it to test its capabilities and moderate its ambitions (the pilots were not intended for basic research or intensive data gathering). The agency set ambitious targets for itself, inviting proposals for pilots that exceeded its funding resources and initial

[27] The design of these funds drew on the experience of infoDev, a global grant-making program for pilots in ICT for development, and on that of the Bank's education sector in establishing competitive funds to promote proposals for upgrading educational institutions.

supervision and learning capabilities. The competitive process enriched the set of proposed pilots, though it also raised expectations and led inevitably to disappointment when worthwhile proposals failed to win resources.

But proceeding with the pilots during program preparation posed a challenge for the ICT Agency: balancing the immediate pressures of implementing pilots with attention to the long-term, strategic activity of preparing the overall program for the Bank and other aid agencies. Sometimes, a tradeoff was made in favor of the short-term, politically visible pilots. At times, the balancing act became difficult for the leadership of the ICT Agency, and the Bank's team had to try to mediate with political leaders to rebalance the pressures. Even so, the pilots created an exciting learning environment for the ICT Agency, helped shape the overall program, and prepared the new agency for the hard task of partnering with others for implementation.

Building Multiple Feedback Mechanisms

Aid agencies normally expect clients to undertake a rigorous process of preparing a strategy and detailed program design – through research, surveys, prior pilots, exhaustive evaluations, and sector studies. For the e-Sri Lanka program, doubts about this new area of development assistance and the cross-cutting approach being adopted reinforced the need for an up-front blueprint. But political pressure to launch the program was strong.

What could be done to reconcile these conflicting demands for speed and rigorous analysis during strategy formulation and program preparation? Invest in a credible, empowered, learning-oriented organization. The ICT Act creating the ICT Agency empowered it to implement a nationally driven e-Sri Lanka strategy. Thus, the agency is not a mere project implementation unit like those often created to implement a specific donor-funded program while following the donor's rules of accountability. The ICT Agency is built to be an agile, innovative, e-leadership institution. That was the fundamental rationale for spending a lot of energy and up-front attention on building an agile ICT Agency during program preparation for donor funding.

The ICT Agency had to develop knowledge management and evaluation systems to compensate for limited information and program preparation. But building formal knowledge management and rigorous monitoring and evaluation systems would take time and external technical assistance. While these systems were being put into place, the agency had to rely on informal, just-in-time feedback mechanisms – such as learning partnerships with NGOs and participatory evaluations through focus groups and pilots.

Multiple feedback mechanisms were also incorporated into the design of the two funds created to finance innovation proposals. These feedback mechanisms include testing demand for innovation through cost sharing arrangements and a competitive proposal process, engaging stakeholders through focus groups and fund committees, and creating results-based monitoring and evaluation processes. The aim was to develop credible local institutions to continually create and manage programs well beyond donor approval of funding – rather than designing and appraising such programs up-front.

This approach emphasizing institutional and technological learning is consistent with the new development economics literature (see, for example, Jomo and Fine 2006). For example, the early development (and neoclassical) literature assumed that information relating to the use of a technology is readily available to all potential users in the form of a "blueprint." Assimilating new technologies in developing countries was assumed to be easy and relatively risk free, with the cost limited to the purchase of the technology. Empirical evidence suggests otherwise: blueprints transfer little of the tacit knowledge needed to adapt and effectively use new technologies, and technological change in developing countries involves incremental innovation, costly learning, and investment in the necessary skills and capabilities. Deliberate active learning is an essential ingredient in competitiveness and technological dynamism.

Similar literature that has emerged in institution building and strategic planning confirms that the premium should be put on building learning organizations and adaptive planning processes – forgoing the comfort of buying comprehensive blueprints and one-shot solutions [see, for example, Scott (1998), Jomo and Fine (2006), and Hanna and Picciotto (2002)].

Underlying all the above guiding principles is perhaps the most basic one: the fundamental need to understand the local situation, the stakeholders, the political economy, and the broader context of development. For example, securing local ownership and developing a coalition of stakeholders require knowing who the stakeholders are. There is never a clear or static "list" of stakeholders. It often changes as the program develops – and in response to that development. Similarly, developing a knowledge-based partnership requires appreciation of local sources of knowledge and of think tanks with which to partner. Funding quick-results pilots requires initial knowledge of local capabilities and learning, and appreciation of which pilots are most likely to influence key stakeholders.

Prior sector and situational analysis and knowledge of country institutions matter. Even more important is getting close to the client and ultimate beneficiaries and developing ways to capture knowledge as it emerges from interactions with different actors, political dynamics, early pilots, and from multiple feedback mechanisms.

Lessons Learned

Aid agency engagement with client countries provides important learning experiences and tacit understandings. Such engagements typically are not documented in the final appraisal, blueprint design, and legal documents of the funding agencies.[28] Yet narratives describing how unusual situations have been handled can convey substantial knowledge and expertise (Denning 2005) for future engagements. Some of the lessons learned during the design of the e-Sri Lanka program are embedded in the development experience and principles discussed in the previous section. Five more key lessons are summarized here. Some of these principles and lessons are not unique to ICT-enabled development, some are contrary to conventional wisdom and some should be subjected to in-depth examination in diverse contexts and to the test of time.

Capturing, then moving beyond entry points. Flexibility is necessary to allow the design process to start with the most accessible entry points, then move toward and test the feasibility of a comprehensive e-development approach within which interdependencies and tradeoffs can be selected.

Securing effective local leadership and institutions. Leaders and institutions are needed throughout the process to integrate ICT into development strategies, to manage process and skill transformations, and to exploit the potential synergies among the pillars of e-development.

Integrating pilots into strategies. Pilots should be an integral part of program design, strategically selected and managed to foster political support and maximize early learning.

Learning from regional examples. Successful neighbors exert a more powerful influence on developing countries than abstract international best practices, particularly in fields where knowledge is not yet codified.

Integrating innovation and ICT into development assistance. Innovations involve risks and learning costs for both individuals and institutions. Integrating ICT into development assistance and strategies poses organizational challenges as much for aid agencies as for countries, and both sides should learn to assess and manage the risks and uncertainties.

Capturing, Then Moving Beyond Entry Points

An e-development program is unlikely to be comprehensive and well integrated from inception, despite the strong interdependence among elements of such programs. Proposals for initiatives are likely to come from isolated constituencies representing one pillar or another of e-development (see Fig. 5.1). National ICT ministries are typically created out of former ministries of telecommunications and thus tend to focus on infrastructure or connectivity. Many other interdependent

[28] Some of the leading management consulting firms like McKinsey & Company have learned to capture the lessons of these engagements in their knowledge management systems. But such systems often fail to capture the richness of such engagements and their context. They are no substitute for in-depth case studies.

elements of e-development are the domain of several ministries, fragmented business associations, or NGOs. Meanwhile, the ICT-user sectors such as education are typically represented by large, long-established ministries, and these ministries are unlikely to work with other players like the ICT industry to develop complementary actions for integrating ICT into education or improving the local software industry.

Countries usually lack coordinating agencies or mechanisms to bring all these perspectives into a coherent strategy. Further reinforcing the tendency toward partial and segmented approaches are the established sectoral structures of aid agencies.

So while it is often better to start with a comprehensive analysis, then strategically select the most critical entry points, it is rare that a full program is ready-made and merely in need of external funding. For e-Sri Lanka, the original proposal initiated by the software industry could have been dismissed as too narrow and too irrelevant to concerns about poverty reduction (indeed, that was the initial reaction of many aid agencies' reviewers). But it was important to be opportunistic and to go through the door that was open.

Once key Sri Lankan policymakers and stakeholders were engaged with the World Bank team to generate an inspiring vision of ICT-enabled development, it was possible to bring in other constituencies to shape the big picture. They began to see the payoffs from complementary investments in policies, institutions, business processes, change management, and human resources as well as ICT applications and information infrastructure. The vision and the underlying holistic framework allowed selective interventions and strategic choices to be made and investments phased – without losing sight of key interdependencies.

Entry points are critical to open dialog and initiate partnerships; comprehensive or integrated approaches to ICT for development cannot be imposed from outside. An "open learning model" of development assistance starts from where the client is: "helpers" have to design their assistance based on the starting point of the "doers," not on an imaginary clean slate.[29] In Sri Lanka, this was good practice for reasons not only of psychology and pedagogy, but also of political economy, since the probusiness government in office at the time would naturally be responsive to the concerns of the software industry.

All this does not mean that helpers and doers should be locked into bureaucratic silos, sectoral boundaries, or the perspectives of a single constituency. Instead, it means that entry points should be the start of a journey to explore, develop a vision, engage other key constituencies, and to learn from past experience and best practices.

The design of the e-Sri Lanka program was far more comprehensive than the original proposal of the software industry. Yet it did not encompass all possible elements of a holistic, full-scale e-development program. We learned that this 5-year donor-assisted program would have to be a first phase in a rather long journey.

[29] Ellerman et al. (2001), pp. 105–133.

How comprehensive should the program have attempted to be? The answer may come only in retrospect, as implementation continues to unfold. Pursuing comprehensiveness to capture synergies and interdependencies can lead to excessive complexity, beyond local capacity for implementation and coordination.[30] Yet narrowing the scope to isolated interventions has often reinforced bureaucratic silos, neglected prerequisites and critical bottlenecks, and led to investments in unsustainable components. Striking the right balance continues to be a key strategic decision in development assistance, one that should be guided by the local context and a clear vision of the development goals.

The scope and complexity of the e-Sri Lanka program would ultimately be determined during implementation, based on the aspirations of the client, key interdependencies, and desired development outcomes – and the client's commitment, political economy, learning curve, and implementation capacity. To reduce the risks from comprehensive coverage and management of multiple interdependencies, e-Sri Lanka program design took a flexible programmatic approach, focused on a coherent set of subprograms, developed clear governance frameworks, built on the ICT Agency's capabilities as facilitator and partnership shaper, and encouraged maximum outsourcing to the private sector and NGOs.

Did the preparation team strike the right balance? In hindsight, it may have underestimated the challenge of designing and implementing such a variety of novel and interdependent programs in a country with weak implementation capacity. It should have spent more time on securing robust governance mechanisms for the newly created ICT Agency. It should have invested more in building bridges with the Ministry of Education and its primary aid partner, the Asian Development Bank.[31] It should have sought more dialog and knowledge-based partnership with the Sri Lankan Telecommunications Ministry and Regulatory Commission. The balance chosen, however, reflected the team's need to strategically allocate its attention – balancing the demands of competing stakeholders on its scarce time and resources.

The e-Sri Lanka program itself can serve as an entry point for even more comprehensive ICT-enabled development, and aid agencies are expected to complement local efforts to build on the program. Early in program preparation the Bank team perhaps did not fully appreciate the opportunity to leverage the ICT infrastructure and telecenters as delivery channels for information and services for all sectors. Later, the team explored how the telecenters program could complement efforts in community development and livelihood improvement, how the e-government program could complement civil service reform, and so on. Opportunities for such complementarities became clearer as the program took shape and learning accumulated.

---

[30] Several attempts by the World Bank to design and implement knowledge economy projects may have suffered from an indiscriminate imposition of a framework encompassing all pillars of the knowledge economy.

[31] With changes in government (in 2006), the ICT Agency began to collaborate with the Ministry of Education to facilitate the mainstreaming of ICT skills training and infuse ICT into learning in other subject areas. The sectoral division of labor among donors, however, remains a challenge for building such cross-sectoral collaboration.

Starting with key entry points, then striving for synergies with aid agencies' ongoing and planned projects can help limit a single project's scope to manageable complexity, build alliances with other sector teams, and fully exploit the new information and communication platform for the entire economy. Capturing the complementarities requires leadership within aid agencies and the country and a holistic vision of ICT in development.

Securing Effective Local Leadership and Institutions

At least as important as preparing plans for an e-development strategy is building local capacity to learn and act strategically and to manage risk and uncertainty. In Sri Lanka, the public sector's lack of a focal point to lead or partner with the private sector and other stakeholders provided an opportunity to search for new institutional options. It was tempting to assume that general ownership of the e-Sri Lanka program by a few top political leaders, combined with rigorous technical preparation by the Bank's team or international consultants, would be an adequate substitute. Moreover, given the fragile political environment, there were strong local pressures to deliver visible results without having to nurture new institutions or broad local ownership. But investing the time and resources needed to create an autonomous ICT Agency turned out to be critical in supporting an integrated e-development strategy.

Later events – including the frequent changes in government and in the Bank's team and the inevitable decline in the Bank's support for implementation once the project was approved – confirmed the importance of the early investments in institution building. As of date of this writing, August 2010, the ICT Agency has proved to be adaptable and resilient to changes in the authorizing environment. It was able to adjust the program design to new opportunities and challenges and to convince the Bank of the need for such changes. But the short existence of the agency neither leaves room for complacency nor assurance of its survival.[32]

The leadership such an agency provides is the key to translating an e-development vision into reality. Experience suggests that leadership is just as essential to integrating ICT into national development strategies as it has proved to be to integrating ICT into business strategies.[33] Leaders must integrate ICT investments into broader

[32] New institutions are fragile. Moreover, political patronage is a double-edged sword: the new agency could have been politicized, leading to a progressive loss of its accountability to its many stakeholders. The Bank's role in coaching and advising the agency – even while allowing it to grow and to rely on local know-how and accountability – continued to be critical.

[33] See Broadbent and Kitzis (2005). Many recent books address this topic, but only for the business sector. In a June 2005 global forum on e-leadership for the public sector, cosponsored by the University of Maryland and the World Bank, participants from about 20 countries reached a consensus that a critical gap in e-leadership is emerging and that, if not addressed, this gap could lead to a strategic misalignment of national ICT strategies with development strategies and to continuing high levels of failure of e-government and e-development projects.

processes of change – to transform skills, business processes, and institutional relationships. They need to build partnerships across business, the public sector, and civil society organizations – to innovate new ways of doing business, identify knowledge and competencies, and induce sustainable institutional change. Leadership is also critical to integrating cross-sectoral components of a holistic strategy while maintaining focus and exercising selectivity in the face of competing demands from powerful stakeholders.

While the decision to create the ICT Agency came early, recognizing the need to build a new cadre of e-leaders in the government and other stakeholders took time. During program preparation, some progress was made in engaging mainstream policymakers by appointing "chief innovation officers." Not surprisingly, however, most top policymakers did not appreciate how central ICT can become in transforming sectors, industries, and institutions. This remained a challenge, particularly as e-Sri Lanka began to promote ICT investments to transform core processes and services within government.

Securing the synergies among the pillars of e-development also continued to be a challenge for the ICT Agency. Some key actors like the Ministry of Education pursued critical but parallel programs. But without leadership at the Cabinet level, the potential synergies between ICT literacy, ICT use in schools, technical education, and other elements of e-development remained elusive. Tapping such synergies takes time, champions, and perseverance. A pilot e-leadership development program tailored to the Cabinet and agency heads was launched in 2006 to address this challenge. But given the continuing changes in government and the breadth of the target group, such a program needs to be sustained and scaled up.

Integrating Pilots into Strategies

Pilots, strategically selected and managed, proved critical in securing and sustaining political interest in and support for e-Sri Lanka. These pilots also proved vital in establishing the legitimacy and autonomy of the newly created ICT Agency. Some pilots were designed to bring visible benefits to key political constituencies like the Parliament. Still others were designed to test first steps toward working across government agencies in difficult areas of collaboration, such as developing and sharing a national database on citizens. The challenge was to avoid viewing these pilots as ends in themselves – a common practice of political sponsors and donors.

Beyond being politically necessary, pilots enable learning and innovation. They deserve more emphasis as applied research to explore hypotheses, test capacities and social responses, accelerate learning about mainstreaming ICT in priority areas, and provide timely information before scaling up programs. They should be standard features of innovative programs like e-Sri Lanka. Aid agencies like the World Bank are often reluctant to support such experimentation on large scale while other aid agencies pursue pilots separately or as ends in themselves.

Multiple, rapid-results pilots are consistent with a "learning process approach" to program development that emphasizes evolutionary, participatory, and demand-driven methods of design and implementation. Pilots proved critical to shaping the e-Sri Lanka strategy by moderating expectations, identifying institutional constraints, and providing timely and practical experience. For example, pilots to develop new telecenters or expand the services of existing ones helped identify some key factors in their sustainability and the multiple partnerships needed for success.

Pilots also helped speed learning by the ICT Agency. The agency is expected not only to make the independent evaluations of such pilots available to the public, but also to internalize the findings and institutionalize the lessons in its practices and in the program. And with its partners – consultants, service providers, and other implementing agencies – it is expected to discuss what lessons can be learned and how to incorporate them into the evolving program.

The ICT and innovation literature suggests that most innovative ICT pilots "fail" in the narrow sense of fully meeting sponsors' expectations about costs, benefits, and delivery time. Yet over time, ICT can transform large organizations and perhaps entire governments. The apparent disconnect can be bridged by viewing ICT projects as embedded in an organizational learning process. Even failed pilots and projects leave a legacy in a learning organization. The sequence of pilots can have a cumulative effect in learning and transformation.

This learning process also occurs at the societal level. Some of the e-Sri Lanka pilots helped advance that learning process, such as the early telecenters. Others proved to be a poor fit in the emerging e-Sri Lanka strategy, such as the distance learning centers.[34] But even in this case, "failures" and subsequent adaptations may have provided important lessons for the emerging national e-learning strategy.

Learning from Regional Examples

Successful regional models exerted a powerful influence on Sri Lanka. The experience of Andhra Pradesh inspired the e-government program. India's visible achievements motivated the original proposal by the software industry. The integrated e-strategies and commitment of top leadership in Andhra Pradesh, the Republic of Korea, Malaysia, and Singapore also provided inspiring models and best practices. Such role models and South–South peer pressures are likely to be more motivational and effective than abstract arguments, conceptual frameworks, or even empirical research on the contributions of ICT and the merits of integrated e-development.

---

[34] Distance learning centers appeared to be attractive pilots at the start. But they did not develop within a national e-learning vision or strategy. Moreover, they demanded substantial attention from the ICT Agency at a time that it was fighting for credibility and survival. They also attempted to solve too many problems at once: lack of local content, partnership with universities and other content providers, and a need to build the capacity of the implementing agency.

But using regional models as blueprints can also be limiting or misguided. Adaptation is critical, and expectations must be managed. Singapore invested over more than two decades to transform government services with ICT, and its success was made possible by a relatively stable and activist government and a strong public–private coalition. Similarly, India's success in the software industry is due in part to an advantage that Sri Lanka lacks – a huge cadre of highly trained engineers. Sri Lanka must seek its own niches and build on its own strengths. Even so, a deeper understanding of the regional models proved critical in assessing the options for Sri Lanka's software and IT-enabled services.

By building on its own strengths, Sri Lanka too can become a regional or even an international model in using ICT for social development, especially for other low-income countries. Sri Lanka has relatively high literacy rates and human development indicators and strong grassroots development movements. It can leverage these strengths to innovate ICT applications appropriate for poor and rural areas, such as applications for local NGOs, microcredit, and rural education. This vision of serving as a regional laboratory inspired the development of the e-society fund.[35]

Integrating Innovation and ICT into Development Assistance

Integrating a new dimension like ICT into development practice calls for both process and product innovation. The business and innovation literature shows that innovation often comes out of engaging with demanding situations and clients.[36] It also comes out of the edge, from staff with passion and in touch with clients, not the center of the organization. And business-driven organizations have learned that clients often are the source of much innovation and learning. But the conventional wisdom that dominates the logic of development assistance – focusing on top-down mandates, knowledge transfer, blueprint design, and universal standards – misses these opportunities for learning and cocreating with clients.

In the case of e-Sri Lanka, creating the ICT Agency and organizing the focus groups unleashed a great deal of creative energy and local experimentation. Simple concepts relating to pilots, proposals for human resources, and grants for communities were transformed into rich sets of content and programs. This energy was particularly evident when the ICT Agency and the Bank team engaged small enterprises, associations, and NGOs in cocreating key parts of the program.

[35] Since its implementation some of the pilot subprojects supported by the e-society fund have won international awards and recognition at international forums, such as the Global Knowledge Partnership.

[36] The business and innovation literature is rich with lessons and techniques that are also relevant for international development assistance, to promote innovation and manage the associated risks in developing countries. See, for example, Prahalad (2005), Kotter (1996), Tushman and O'Reilly (1997), Peters and Waterman (1982), and Porter (1990).

Yet innovations involve high risks and learning costs for both institutions and individuals. They require substantial research and development to create new models that can be tested then scaled up. These investments are seldom anticipated or acknowledged by aid agencies. In the World Bank, for example, budgets for project preparation do not allow for such critical yet practical R&D. Budgets for project supervision (implementation assistance) are even tighter – precluding investment in learning with clients during implementation – because the Bank typically deals with blueprint designs and recipes rather than innovations that require intensive process-oriented implementation support and learning.[37]

The challenges of dealing with new, cross-sectoral dimensions of development are magnified when there is no clear home to protect the proposed venture. Both developing countries and their counterpart aid agencies often lack a home or locus for e-development. As noted, the Bank had to launch the e-Sri Lanka program outside its regional structure, in a unit that lacked the authorizing environment, reporting structure, and operational routines available to the regional units. As a result, the project team had to devote substantial time and resources to nurturing legitimacy, learning internal routines, building bridges and alliances with the South Asia regional unit, and managing bureaucratic politics. That was time taken away from clients and from attending to a complex and challenging innovation. Similarly, the ICT Agency had to struggle for access, influence, and credibility to get its programs initiated. At times, this struggle may have diverted its attention away from helping established ministries mainstream ICT into their business strategies.

Aid agencies need to create an intellectual and operational home for mainstreaming ICT and deepening e-development.[38] At times, groups focusing on technology dominate. That poses barriers to mainstreaming ICT into development assistance. It can also lead to serious distortions, such as when ICT specialists lead assistance for e-education with engagement from education specialists, or e-government with no engagement from experts in governance or public sector management. Aid agencies need to develop new ways for ICT experts to work with substantive sector experts in such key fields as education, governance, and private sector development.

Implementation Experience So Far

As of August 2010, the e-Sri Lanka program has been under implementation for 5 years. During these years, the program has evolved, as anticipated from the initial design, both in response to a fluid political environment (including a continuing

[37] To overcome some of these constraints to learning, the Bank team has been experimenting with a new learning model of connecting the Sri Lankan team with peers in other countries through a series of videoconferences.

[38] In 2003 the World Bank founded an e-development thematic group, with membership extending to many aid agencies and developing countries. But this informal network can only complement, not substitute for, formal organizational strategies and structures.

civil war), and in view of lessons learned during implementation. Despite major political turmoil, and changes in the World Bank's capacity and resources dedicated to implementation support, program performance remained satisfactory, and in some areas, even exceeded targets. Early attention to building the capacity of the national ICT Agency proved critical to continued adaptation of the program, respond to political priorities, and to draw on home grown innovations. The deliberate strategy design remained a constant and robust game plan, but was complemented and improved over time by an emergent strategy borne out of constant testing and learning on the ground.

Although many activities of e-Sri Lanka have been focused on creating the enabling policy environment and building blocks, and on changes in institutional processes and capabilities, some notable results can be measured. Internet usage has increased from 2% in 2005 to over 8% in 2010. ICT literacy improved from 9% in 2004 to an estimated 25% in 2009. Sri Lanka has also improved its rankings on a number of indices under the Network Readiness Index: it moved its overall ranking from 83 out of 115 countries in year 2005, to 72 out of 134 in 2009.[39] Progress in component ranking was highest in government prioritization of ICT and its vision of the future (from 84 to 36), ICT use and government efficiency (from 93 to 51), government success in ICT promotion (from 75 to 31), laws relating to ICT (from 87 to 53), and extent of business Internet use (from 84 to 40). Moderate progress was made in the rankings in several other areas like the availability of online services (from 104 out of 115 countries in 2005 to 89 out of 134 in 2009).[40]

It is interesting to note that the progress made since the launch of e-Sri Lanka has been mainly in the areas under the influence or direct control of the e-Sri Lanka program or the ICT Agency, as reflected in the relative rankings of the three major NRI components: environment, readiness, and usage. While Sri Lanka has advanced in overall NRI ranking to 72, its strength is now primarily reflected in the readiness component (at 44) and particularly in government readiness (at 36). Sri Lanka's overall ranking on the market, regulatory and infrastructure environments is 84, significantly behind its overall NRI ranking of 72, as most of the underlying indicators of these environments are beyond the influence of the e-Sri Lanka program alone. Usage also lags behind, at 82, particularly for individuals who still lack connectivity and affordability, but government usage appears to have advanced significantly and now ranks 59. It is anticipated that as readiness has been now advanced or established, and as the overall environment improves with the end of civil strife, Sri Lanka may be positioned to advance on usage and reap the benefits of increased ICT-enabled transformation.

Information on any government process, service, or application is now just a phone call away – using Government Information Center (GIC). Civil registration

---

[39] Sources: ICT Agency, Sri Lanka and the World Economic Forum.

[40] It should be noted that this progress was made under very severe country implementation conditions due to civil war that peaked in 2009, the last point in this ranking. Progress on Internet use may also have been hampered by legal challenges to investment in broadband.

(Birth, Marriage, Death certificates, etc.) documents are in hand within a matter of minutes, thanks to digitization. Government institutions (Ministries, Departments, District and Divisional Secretariats, etc.) are now connected online in secure and reliable ways through Lanka Government Network (LGN). Over 300 Government organizations are on the Web. A single-window, multichannel access to all e-services has been created – Lanka Gate. Several e-services are underway or already functioning, such as Vehicle Revenue License Renewal, which was the first, end-to-end, e-transaction. Consistent with the notion that e-government is also about leadership and change management, an ICT Capacity Building program has completed awareness raising and training sessions for over 10,000 government officers.

Another area of significant achievements is ICT industry and human resources. Over 40,000 new jobs have been created in the IT/BPO sector since 2005. The IT/BPO sector has become the 5th largest foreign exchange earner for the country – US$ 250 million in 2008 (Export Value Survey 2008). Sri Lanka has ranked 16th in the A.T. Kearney Out-Sourcing Location Index of 2009; its 2007/2008 position was 29th. Over 3,000 schools have been equipped with computer labs under the e-Sri Lanka program. Over 40 Distance Education Learning Centers have been set up, offering 35 online graduate level courses. Sri Lanka has been the host of some notable regional events, such as the e-Asia 2009 Conference.

E-Sri Lanka also made significant advances on the broad front of digital and social inclusion. It has increased access to ICT for citizens across the country – 600 Telecenters and 250 Science and Technology centers across the island. These centers now provide market prices and agriculture information to farmers. One e-society application now provides educational material both at primary and secondary educational level to students in the rural areas. Another is providing e-health/telemedicine facilities to rural patients. Other pilots have developed digital talking books for the visually impaired and visual hearing aids for the hearing impaired. Finally, the program helped set up rural BPOs to create job opportunities for youth in rural communities.

E-Sri Lanka has been recognized internationally and has since influenced several flagship projects of the World Bank. For example, the country became one of the few developing countries in Asia (and the only one in 2009) to win two World Summit Awards. The awards were for GIC (a project under e-government program) and impaired aid (a project under e-society) and the e-Learning tool, which won the Stockholm challenge awards.

A brief update on each of the key components of e-Sri Lanka and pertinent lessons follows.

ICT policy, leadership, and institutional development. This component proved to be at the heart of program success and sustainability. Establishing the ICT Agency, and particularly the legal basis through extensive parliamentary debate and stakeholders mobilization, was a cornerstone to building the authorizing environment for the new agency and the e-Sri Lanka program. It made all the difference between its predecessor, CINTEC, which did a lot of policy analysis and technical work for e-laws, but could not enact or help implement any, and the new agency's ability to link to top policy makers and parliament, set a road map for policy reforms, and to pass the necessary acts and legislations. Outreach, strategic communication, and awareness training of public CIOs also proved to have high payoffs, even though such payoffs were diffused and intangible, such as building and maintaining a supportive authorizing environment.

Many key policies and legislations were developed, such as the Electronic Transactions Act (legal recognition of electronic documents), electronic evidence regime, the Computer Crimes Act (dealing with cyber security), the proposed data protection (privacy) legislation, and the recent adoption of an e-Government Policy (policies and procedures for ICT usage in government and the use of electronic payments for government services).[41] E-laws were subject to extensive parliamentary debates. These legislative achievements were not easy in the context of Sri Lanka, where such adoption has been historically slow and subjected to much legislative debate. These policy and legislative improvements were pushed in part by the need to meet international standards and local pressures from strong constituencies that are interested in securing transactions in a global market – financial services and business-process outsourcing. They were driven by the vision of transforming Sri Lanka into a service and financial hub.[42] As a result, Sri Lanka has been first in signing on several international standards and treaties among South Asian countries.[43]

Legislative and policy actions do not stop with formal adoption, and much of the effort and innovation must come through implementation and institutionalization. For example, the Electronic Transaction Act required the creation or designation of certification authorities and establishment of certification service providers. So far, Sri Lanka has established one for the banking and one for the government sector. The one for government is under ICTA to provide public key infrastructure capabilities and secure transactions under the LGN. Similarly, dealing with computer crime requires parties (investigators, prosecutors, and judges) to agree to an enforcement process and coordinate their work – creating the need for an independent group of experts to assist law enforcement agencies in their investigation. A continuing challenge is to ensure effective enforcement and implementation of these laws and to create the new institutional models and make them work. For a poor country like Sri Lanka, the cost of regulation (for personal data protection against abuse by the public sector) is also a critical factor, and options must be sought to share such costs with the private sector, and to phase coverage, perhaps starting with relatively mature sectors, such as finance and BPO. A learning process to create and enforce a legally secure environment for the digital world has become a key element of e-transformation in Sri Lanka.

[41] For an excellent review of these developments, see Fernando (2010).

[42] They intended to facilitate domestic and international electronic commerce by eliminating legal barriers and establishing legal certainties, encourage the use of reliable forms of electronic commerce, promote public confidence in the authenticity and reliability of electronic communications, and deal with technology and data abuses.

[43] Fernando (2010).

The ICT Agency is also a significant institutional innovation for Sri Lanka and elsewhere. By relying on extensive partnership and outsourcing for a large number of innovative and diverse activities, the Agency was burned by a large number of small contracts that did not disburse money fast. This appeared as a problem for the funding agency, the World Bank, which is used to large and/or standard and repetitive contracts for large investments. But this kept ICTA lean, innovative, and seeking diverse partnerships with business, NGOs, and academic experts, both local and international. ICTA has been nimble enough to adapt to changes and implement an evolving e-Sri Lanka. Being regularly in the public eye meant that ICTA had to get its processes right and transparent. Early criticisms helped ICTA take a partnership role and to outsource or create spinoff institutions for specialized activities. For example, ICTA helped to create two important institutions, namely, SLASSCOM (unified body representing the IT BPO industry and Software exporters) and Sri Lanka CERT (to address cyber threats and incidents). Both are operating on private sector models.

Monitoring and evaluation frameworks and indices were established for each component of the program, but measuring outcomes and impact remained a challenge, particularly in a politically charged environment. A key issue is to use M&E as a tool to redesign and implement new programs for e-Sri Lanka. Perhaps most difficult and lagging aspect of this component is the development of an inter-ministerial steering committee and other governing structures to enhance ownership and accountability for the whole program. Continuous organizational development and renewal of governance structures are critical for new agencies, a fast changing technology, fluid political environment, shifting coalitions, and emergent strategies.

ICT human resource development and industry promotion. The limited and selective support of this program component covered learning seminars for ICT professionals, career fairs, business linkages events, ITES awareness and training, quality certification, and innovation grants, among others. Growth of this sector proved to be robust, despite limited program support, uncertain business environment, and lower priority given by the current government for promoting the private sector. Job creation in the sector exceeded program targets, and foreign investment increased substantially. This component also benefited from the dynamism of IT services and IT-enabled services of Sri Lanka's neighbor, India, and of the ongoing global services revolution. It has signaled the country's commitment to the sector and helped maintain the support of a key constituency for e-Sri Lanka.

Telecommunications network development. This component was expected to be the easiest to disburse foreign funding for, as a single large contract with a private telecom operator. Yet, it proved the most intractable to implement. It was reconfigured to take advantage of changing conditions in the telecommunications industry, and thus facilitate the deployment of affordable broadband services throughout Sri Lanka by establishing a national communications backbone network. Several factors led to implementation delays: changes in leadership in the Telecom Regulatory Commission (outside the control of ICTA), complicated procurement requirements of the funding agency (the World Bank), and unfamiliarity of implementing agencies with such procurement practices. Many of these challenges could not have been anticipated. These delays had negative impact on the connectivity and profitability of telecenters. Overcoming these delays is critical since Internet penetration remains very low at 8%, but forecast to reach 25% and broadband at 13% in 5 years, as a result of current broadband rollout plans and end of the civil war.[44]

Telecenter development program. This component was subjected to analysis and much debate at the design stage, as it involved a large-scale program to create small enterprises in a new field for Sri Lanka and the Bank. But such analyses could not eliminate the uncertainties surrounding the program: the untested grassroots capabilities of telecenter operators, connectivity solutions and coordination with the telecommunication component, demand and affordability for Internet-based services, coordination with e-government applications, development of local content, hardware support and maintenance, and institutional innovations for decentralized monitoring and support program, among others. The ICT Agency has since continued to experiment with the program, in part to respond to political push to spread the program in the rural areas, and in part to ensure long-term ownership and sustainability of the program beyond the period when external subsidies are available from the Bank.

As of December 2009, a total of 620 centers were established (as compared to 200 in the original design), of which 600 were in operation. The program proved very popular with the current government, as it provided visible and quick wins for delivering information and IT-enabled services to the rural population. Problems of connectivity and risks to sustainability were deemphasized so as to achieve ambitious targets for broad coverage relatively quickly.

A telecenter ecosystem is emerging; it had to be nurtured and its elements coevolved. ICTA was consolidating the program's achievements and learning in various ways: continuing entrepreneurial education for telecenter operators, broadening the technological options for connectivity (taking advantage of the spread of wireless solutions), building regional impact teams to assess progress and usage, creating a telecenter academy in partnership with India's National Open University and Sri Lanka's University of Colombo, and organizing national awareness seminars for telecenter operators to share experience and best practices, among others. Monitoring and evaluation also proved to be most critical to managing and adapting this program, synthesizing inputs from multiple stakeholders and actors. Learning to learn has become an indispensable aspect of program design and management.

Reengineering government. This is the largest component program and perhaps the most technically complex of the e-Sri Lanka program – establishing the key building blocks for a coherent e-government program, and starting almost from scratch. Not many quick wins were anticipated here, as much more ground work in terms of enabling policy framework, interoperability, process reengineering, and

[44] http://www.companiesandmarkets.com Summary-Market-Report/Sri Lanka Information technology report Q3 2010

shared infrastructures (e.g., LGN, Lanka Gate) had to be put in place before e-services could be delivered. The LGN provides the underlying information infrastructure that connects all organizations of the government with a highly available, reliable and secure manner. The Lanka Gate was envisioned to deliver practically all e-Services (including online payments) via an open-standard integration platform for both government and private sector entities and for a collection of portals and applications. A long consultative process of about 5 years has contributed to bringing in the expertise academia, industry, civil society, and government to finalize the e-government policy and to get the approval of the Cabinet of Ministers.

Apart from these foundational projects, the reengineering government program also has reengineered processes and began to roll out final transfer of priority e-services to participating government institutions: e-population registry, e-pension, e-district services, e-foreign employment, e-motoring. The key challenge remaining is the change management process that must proceed in line with this roll out of new businesses and practices.

While building key foundations for improving government services, the e-government program took a longer lead time than anticipated. It covered many and major contractual arrangements, involving partners with little experience in managing such contracts or establishing public–private partnerships. World Bank procurement practices provided some rigor, but also led to delays. Fortunately, some pilots and initiatives were encouraged, even though they were not fully envisaged at the design stage. These microinitiatives and quick-wins helped provide much needed popular support for this program.

One of the most visible and unanticipated initiatives has been the development of a government information call center and Website to enable citizens to obtain government information and services. The Website is highly interactive and customizable, based on Web 2.0 technology. The call center is now in high demand and with high user satisfaction. The overall e-government program might have benefited from more quick wins of this nature.

E-society Program. This is perhaps the most visible component in terms of international recognition for grassroots innovation and digital inclusion. It intended to promote innovative use of ICT to meet the needs of the rural areas and most vulnerable groups through community grants and partnership grants. Visible successes of pilots included: reaching the disabled, improving incomes of fisherman, making learning materials available to rural students using e-curriculum via telecenters, supporting e-village applications, and developing relevant local content to be accessible via telecenters, among others.

This component program was initiated on a pilot basis, with a small sum from the e-Sri Lanka program. The deliberate strategy of e-Sri Lanka anticipated that successes of pilots induce new partners to cofund the program, sustain specific pilots, and/or scale them to a national level and help contribute to emergent strategies. The e-society fund was thus envisaged as a grassroots innovation or venture capital fund for learning about ICT for social and rural development, and for building awareness more widely about the relevance of ICT for poverty reduction and bottom-up development. The key challenge at this stage of program evolution is to harvest the grassroots learning and innovations involved for wider dissemination and scaling up. This requires widening distribution channels for e-society solutions by further collaborating with NGOs, private sector, and relevant government agencies, build capacity of grassroots organizations to host content, and engaging the donor community and ICT multinationals in replication of successful pilots. In sum, this component was a major institutional innovation that is likely to spawn many innovations for an emergent e-Sri Lanka strategy that would support community-driven and broad-based development.

Conclusion

ICT-enabled development is not easy, and success is far from assured.[45] The case study of e-Sri Lanka presents neither a perfect design nor a final solution to the challenges of integrating ICT into development at the national level. It is the start of a journey toward profound change and transformation – and true transformation always involves creative destruction, risks, and uncertainties. Much of the final outcome of this pioneering e-development program in Sri Lanka depends on political developments beyond the control of the ICT agency. It also depends on effective, consistent, and long-term support from aid agencies like the Bank.

What has fundamentally changed is that in a country where ICT was simply at the margins of the development agenda in government and the business agenda in the private sector, e-Sri Lanka brought in an irreversible momentum in developing policies and programs for e-transformation and in placing ICT center stage in the country's development strategy. In addition, e-Sri Lanka gained international recognition as it has garnered many awards in many regional and international forums. In the latest Asia regional event, at the Future Gov Asia, hosted by Malaysia with 17 countries participating, ICTA was recognized as the "public sector organization of the year," and the Lanka Gate (government portal) and the telecenter (Nanasala) program were given excellence in innovation and digital inclusion, respectively. These and many leading indicators (such as Sri Lanka's rise in the international ranking of Network Readiness Index) suggest that the final outcome is likely to be highly satisfactory.

The case study suggests many rich lessons for Sri Lanka and other developing countries. It is important to examine and evaluate e-Sri Lanka as a process and not

[45] Firm-level data show much variation in the returns on investments in ICT: some firms do well, but many do not (Dedrick et al. 2002). There is also a substantial body of evidence documenting government failures in ICT investments. The more important increases in productivity arising from ICT investments come about because of parallel investments in organizational and process changes. These parallel investments usually require substantial changes in work flows and take a long time to bear fruit (Brynjolfsson and Hitt 2000).

only as a final blueprint plan or in terms of final outcomes. An innovative program that is built on experimentation and adaptation typically requires intensive learning by both the aid agency and recipient country. While there is a growing (but grudging) acknowledgment of the importance of experimentation and innovation in development programs, there is less willingness to provide the necessary resources to learn from this experimentation. As of this writing, it is not clear that the World Bank will be devoting the necessary resources to learn from this innovation.[46] This reinforces the key role that monitoring and evaluation by local stakeholders must play to match implementation challenges, capture and share the lessons to be learned, and further scale up and sustain such programs.

An integrated approach to e-development appears promising to enhance the impact and sustainability of ICT for development. But it adds to complexity and coordination challenges. In Sri Lanka, the risks are magnified by implementation constraints. We opted for a comprehensive and ambitious program, and put upfront effort to build local capacity, build partnership, and outsourcing practices, and internalize the necessary coordination and integration requirements of holistic approaches to e-transformation. Our hope was that World Bank implementation assistance and skills would match the challenges and address such synergies and complementarities, rather than be content with fragmented pilots and isolated e-development interventions – leaving local agencies to do their own integration.

The e-Sri Lanka program demanded a quantum leap in performance. It needed champions and visionaries as well as effective program managers, knowledgeable local consultants, and competent partners. Achieving success will also require sustained commitment to a comprehensive vision – a vision that underscores the promises, which are plentiful, but also acknowledges the critical choices that need to be made, the potential pitfalls to be overcome, and the coalitions to be nurtured and sustained along the way.

References

Adelman, Irma. 2000. "Fifty Years of Economic Development: What Have We Learned?" Paper presented at the Annual World Bank Conference on Development Economics–Europe 2000, Paris, June 26–28.

Brynjolfsson, Erik, and Lorin M. Hitt. 2000. "Beyond Computation: Informational Technology, Organizational Transformation and Business Performance." *Journal of Economic Perspectives* 14 (4): 23–48.

Broadbent, Marianne, and Ellen S. Kitzis. 2005. *The New CIO Leader: Setting the Agenda and Delivering Results.* Boston: Harvard Business School Press.

Dawson, Ross. 2005. Developing Knowledge-Based Client Relationships. Boston: Elsevier.

[46] Annual budgets devoted by the Bank to support project implementation and provide expert advice to local counterparts have been declining over the duration of implementation, and attention has been increasingly devoted to speedy disbursement rather than learning and impact. This is the norm for Bank leading, and this project was not given an exception during implementation.

Dedrick, Jason, Vijay Gurbaxani, and Kenneth L. Kraemer. 2002. "Information Technology and Economic Performance: Firm and Country Evidence." University of California, Center for Research on Information Technology and Organizations, Irvine. http://repositories.cdlib.org/crito/business/296/.

Denning, Stephen. 2005. The Leader's Guide to Storytelling. San Francisco: Jossey-Bass.

Ellerman, David, Stephen Denning, and Nagy K. Hanna. 2001. "Active Learning and Development Assistance." In "Tacit Knowledge Exchange and Active Learning," special issue, *Journal of Knowledge Management* 5 (2): 171–79.

Fernando, Jayantha. 2010. *"e-Enabling Legislation" A catalyst for ICT Based Banking and Financial Sector Growth in Sri Lanka.* Sri Lanka ICT Agency. Colombo, Sri Lanka.

Fukuyama, Francis. 1995. *Trust: The Social Virtues and the Creation of Prosperity.* New York: Free Press.

——. 2004. State-Building: Governance and World Order in the 21st Century. Ithaca, NY: Cornell University Press.

Hanna, Nagy K. 1991. *The Information Technology Revolution and Economic Development.* World Bank Discussion Paper 120. Washington, DC: World Bank.

——. 1994. *Exploiting Information Technology for Development: A Case Study of India.* World Bank Discussion Paper 246. Washington, DC: World Bank.

——. 2004. *Why National Strategies Are Needed for ICT-Enabled Development.* Information Solutions Group Paper. Washington, DC: World Bank.

——. 2007a. *From Envisioning to Designing e-Development: The Experience of Sri Lanka.* Directions in Development Series. Washington, DC: World Bank.

——. 2007b. *e-Leadership Institutions for the Knowledge Economy.* Washington, DC: World Bank.

Hanna, Nagy, Ken Guy, and Erik Arnold. 1995. The Diffusion of Information Technology: Experience of Industrial Countries and Lessons for Developing Countries. World Bank Discussion Paper 281. Washington, D.C.

Hanna, Nagy K., and Robert Picciotto, eds. 2002. *Making Development Work: Developmental Learning in a World of Poverty and Wealth.* New Brunswick, NJ: Transaction Publishers.

ILO (International Labor Organization). 2001. *World Employment Report 2001.* Geneva.

Jomo K. S. and Ben Fine, eds. 2006. *The New Development Economics.* London: Zed Books

Knight, Peter Titcomb, Ciro Campos Christo Fernandes and Maria Alexandra Cunha, eds. 2007. *e-Desenvolvimento no Brasil e no mundo: subsídios e Programa e-Brasil.* São Caetano do Sul, São Paulo: Yendis.

Kotter, John P. 1996. *Leading Change.* Boston: Harvard Business School Press.

Lall, Sanjaya. 1999. "Competing with Labor: Skills and Competitiveness in Developing Countries." Issues in Development Discussion Paper 31. International Labor Organization, Geneva.

——. 2001. *Competitiveness, Technology and Skills.* Cheltenham, England: Edward Elgar.

Moore, Mark. 1997. *Creating Public Value: Strategic Management in Government.* Cambridge, MA: Harvard University Press.

Moragoda, Milinda. 2002. Parliamentary speech, Appropriation Bill 2002. Committee Stage Debate on the Ministry of Economic Reform, Science and Technology. *Daily News* (Colombo), April 12.

Perez, Carlota. 2001. "Technological Change and Opportunities for Development as a Moving Target." United Nations University, Maastricht.

Peters, Thomas J., and Robert H. Waterman Jr. 1982. *In Search of Excellence: Lessons from America's Best-Run Companies.* New York: Harper & Row.

Porter, Michael. 1990. *The Competitive Advantage of Nations.* New York: Free Press.

Prahalad, C. K. 2005. *The Fortune at the Bottom of the Pyramid: Eradicating Poverty through Profits.* Upper Saddle River, NJ: Wharton School Publishing.

Rodrik, Dani. 2000. "Development Strategies for the Next Century." Paper presented at the Annual World Bank Conference on Development Economics, Washington, DC, April 8.

Rodrik, Dani. 2004. "Getting Institutions Right." *CESifo DICE Report* (University of Munich), no. 2: 10–15.

Scott, J. C. 1998. Seeing Like a State: How Certain Schemes to Improve the Human Condition Have Failed. New Haven, CT: Yale University Press.

Stiglitz, Joseph E. 1998. "Towards a New Paradigm for Development: Strategies, Policies, and Processes." 1998 Prebisch Lecture, United Nations Conference on Trade and Development, Geneva, October 19.

Stiglitz, Joseph E., Peter R. Orszag, and Jonathan M. Orszag. 2000. "The Role of Government in a Digital Age." Study commissioned by the Computer and Communications Industry Association. http://www.ccianet.org/govt_comp.php3.

Sri Lanka, Ministry of Science and Technology. 2002. ICT Road Map. Government Print, Colombo, Sri Lanka.

Tushman, Michael L., and Charles A. O'Reilly III. 1997. *Winning through Innovation: A Practical Guide to Leading Organizational Change and Renewal.* Boston: Harvard Business School Press.

UNDP (United Nations Development Program). 2001. *Human Development Report 2001: Making New Technologies Work for Human Development.* New York: Oxford University Press.

Wade, Robert. 1990. *Governing the Market: Economic Theory and the Role of Government in East Asian Industrialization.* Princeton, NJ: Princeton University Press.

Wilson, Ernest J., III. 2004. *The Information Revolution and Developing Countries.* Cambridge, MA: MIT Press.

——. III. 2005. "Engaged Scholars and Thoughtful Practitioners: Enhancing Their Dialogue in the Knowledge Society." *Information Technologies and International Development* 2 (4): 89–92.

World Bank. 2002. Information and Communications Technologies: A World Bank Group Strategy. Washington, D.C.

Yusuf, Shahid 2003. *Innovative East Asia: The Future of Growth.* New York: Oxford University Press.

Chapter 6
Comparative Experience and Lessons in E-Transformation

Nagy K. Hanna and Peter T. Knight

The four country case studies presented in this book cover different periods of time and are not part of an experimental design, but rather attempts by their authors to explore national experiences with some guidance from a common e-development model. A companion book covers four additional countries of diverse size, conditions, and levels of development: Singapore, Finland, South Africa, and the Philippines. Taken together, the two books cover a broad sample of countries at different levels of development and take an international comparative approach to the study of e-transformation.

Country experiences are rich and diverse. Yet, the case studies are selective abstractions of the messy realties of e-transformation. These country cases inevitably capture one phase or another of a country's long journey toward e-transformation. They are often a composite of espoused policies and formal plans of a national ICT strategy, combined with implementation practices and results of such plans. Any attempt to make comparisons among these cases along any set of criteria or common dimensions is, therefore, fraught with many difficulties and limitations. Yet, a common set of core criteria for comparing the design and implementation can be most helpful in capturing the diversity of country approaches and experiences and in generating some important conclusions or hypotheses to be tested by further research in the sample countries and across more countries.

This chapter starts with a summary of country economic levels and characteristics as well as country rankings on Network Readiness Index (NRI) and its key components.[1] Table 6.1 shows the diversity of countries covered in terms of size of population, level of economic development, mobile and Internet penetration, overall NRI country rankings (of 2009/2010), and key components of environment, readiness, and usage. These indicators provide a summary of some hard data on the context within which e-development strategies have been pursued and both hard and soft

[1] For details, see Dutta and Mia 2010. As of this writing, this is the latest issue of the World Economic Forum's annual publication: *The Global Information Technology Report.*

N.K. Hanna and P.T. Knight (eds.), *Seeking Transformation Through Information Technology*, Innovation, Technology, and Knowledge Management,
DOI 10.1007/978-1-4614-0353-1_6,

Table 6.1 Selected key indicators and Network Readiness Index (NRI) and selected component rankings by country

Country/Criterion	Brazil	China	Canada	Sri Lanka
Population (millions), 2008	192.0	1,325.6	33.3	20.2
GDP per capita ($PPP), 2008	10,466	5,970	39,098	4,589
Mobile phone subscriptions per 100 pop., 2008	78.5	47.9	66.4	55.2
Internet users per 100 pop., 2008	37.5	22.3	75.4	5.8
NRI 2009/2010 (rank of 133)	61	37	7	72
Environment	74	57	6	84
Market	87	72	7	60
Political and regulatory	73	47	13	90
Infrastructure	63	70	6	89
Readiness	62	19	13	44
Individual	99	9	16	47
Business	38	34	11	77
Government	68	14	27	36
Usage	47	36	8	82
Individual	61	71	12	101
Business	37	16	8	61
Government	45	30	6	59

Source: Dutta and Mia (2010)

data on progress or actual usage of ICT by individuals, business, and government. While these readiness indicators suffer from several shortcomings, they can be useful in relating country e-strategy practices to some of the most common indicators being measured and shared internationally. Other contextual factors not captured in the table, such as the political and institutional development of the country, can be gleaned from the country cases themselves. Such factors should be taken into account in generating hypotheses or conclusions about how key parameters of e-strategies are contingent on a country's sociopolitical and economic development.

The next part of this chapter is about setting the main criteria or dimensions along which cross-country comparisons are made. These dimensions are key e-strategy design and implementation issues. They include the degree of centrality, linkage, or integration of e-transformation into the country's development strategy; search for comprehensiveness, synergy, and coherence of the strategy; and attention to e-leadership, stakeholder engagement, and institutional mechanisms for implementation. They also cover the balance taken between top-down direction and bottom-up initiative, between pursuing long-term and short-term objectives, and between ICT as a cross-sector enabler and as an industry or sector on its own. The final set of issues or criteria for comparing e-strategies includes degree of reliance on innovation and adaptation during implementation, emphasis on monitoring and evaluation or measuring outcomes, and attention to the digital divide and social inclusion. These criteria or dimensions of e-transformation strategies correspond to the uses or value added expected from adopting the e-transformation framework, as set out in the first chapter.

We give a tentative grade (overall characterization of e-strategy) for the countries covered along these dimensions, based on both country policy and implementation for the period covered by the case study (Table 6.2).

Table 6.2 Assessing e-transformation strategies across countries

Country/Criterion	Brazil	China	Canada	Sri Lanka
Integrating into development strategy	L	H	M	H
Coverage, coherence, synergy	L	M	M	H
Leading, institutionalizing, and engaging	M	M	M	M
Balancing central direction with local	M	M	H	M
Balancing long-term and short-term objectives	M	H	M	M
Innovating, adapting, and learning	L	M	H	M
Balancing ICT as enabler and sector	M	M	M	M
Emphasizing digital inclusion	M	M	M	M

Key: *H* high; *M* medium; *L* low rating for each criterion

It should be noted that there may not be a high correlation between the scores on the characteristics of the e-transformation strategy process (in Table 6.2) and e-readiness indicators or NRI (Table 6.1), since process criteria are expected to influence e-readiness outcomes only over a long time horizon, and the countries included in this book have started their e-transformation journey at different times and from different initial conditions and levels of economic development. Over time, however, a country's high scores on the e-transformation process should lead to higher e-readiness, and in turn, higher e-readiness should lead to increases in per capita GDP growth.[2]

We can conjecture that those countries pursuing e-transformation more effectively will move faster in terms of their development goals and competitive position than other countries with similar initial conditions. Moreover, we suggest that countries successfully pursuing e-transformation over the long term will be able to leverage ICT to catch up in terms of their overall development and perhaps even surpass slow adopters of the new technologies that started at a higher level of development. Korea, Singapore, Finland, and to some extent, China and India, among others, support these hypotheses.

In this sample of countries, China, starting from low levels of development and NRI rankings, has persisted with a relatively effective e-transformation process over a long period, and over this long term, it has risen significantly in its NRI rankings and in comparison to other countries at its level of economic development.[3] Sri Lanka is given relatively high scores on its e-transformation process,

[2] More research is needed to understand the relationships between such process indicators, NRI (and its component indicators), and impact on GDP growth using much larger number of sample countries. Using cross-country growth analysis, some researchers argue that connectivity and Internet penetration contribute to higher growth rates. By one estimate, for a high-income economy a 10% increase in broadband penetration would enjoy 1.21% increase in per capita GDP growth, and for developing countries, a corresponding 1.38% increase (Qiang and Rossotto 2009, pp 35–50). Given the lag effects and the importance of complementary inputs to ICT investments, we are cautious to make the case for mechanical payoffs or high correlation. It is critical to understand how broadband and other elements of e-development affect specific contexts and key variables that are good for economic growth, including innovation, education, finance, public expenditure management, FDI, etc.

[3] NRI methodology has changed over time, and NRI rankings have exhibited significant volatility from year to year, so it is best to look for changes in rankings over a long period to get a more reliable reading of comparative progress.

but since it started its journey quite late and from low per capita GDP, its NRI is relatively low. Despite its initial conditions and the short time of pursuing e-transformation, Sri Lanka has risen in its NRI ranking since 2006/2007, perhaps reflecting high scores on its e-transformation process. Canada, in the 1990s, pursued a highly effective e-transformation process, which led to high score on its e-readiness or NRI in 2002/2003 and plausibly contributed to higher per capita GDP growth rate. But with the changes in government, Canada has been flagging in its e-transformation process, although that was not fully reflected in its volatile NRI ranking and since the e-transformation process scores assigned to the Canada case were averaged for this period. Brazil remained relatively low in its process scores, and its NRI rankings correspondingly declined consistently since 2002/2003.[4]

The remaining and main part of this chapter draws on the above two tables to generate lessons and hypotheses and is organized along these key design issues and options.

Integrating ICT into Development Strategy

This is perhaps the most important criteria for assessing e-strategy as an enabler and transformative tool for economic development. There is a vast literature on the importance of aligning or integrating ICT strategy with business strategy, and the evidence of the impact of ICT–business alignment on business performance and competitiveness has its parallel at the national level (Chan and Reich 2007). As a general purpose technology, ICT is both pervasive and context-dependent, and thus must be strategically integrated into national and sectoral strategies to leverage its transformative potential (Hanna 2009a).

Openness, export orientation, and competition from local and international sources can help build pressure to leverage ICT more strategically across the economy (as increasingly evidenced by efforts of China). Some advanced countries may take ICT for granted and opt for a less-proactive role for ICT in their competition and innovation policies once they achieve a high level of connectivity and e-literacy, as Canada may have done. Yet, even in the most advanced countries facing increasing global competition, there is a growing recognition of the role of innovation in general and ICT-enabled transformation in particular in securing sustainable economic growth and competitiveness (Ezell and Atkinson 2010).

Integrating e-strategy into overall development policy and programs is difficult for larger countries with regions at very different levels of development, such as Brazil and China. Brazil's three-level federal system, where different coalitions or individual parties with relatively weak programmatic content can control different federal units, further complicates policy making and implementation. In such

[4] For NRI rankings over the period 2002/03–2008/09, see http://www.networkedreadiness.com/gitr/main/previous/.

contexts, it is often likely that e-development is better integrated with the development strategies of the most advanced regions and municipalities, with the poor regions left disconnected. Poor regions have a difficult time establishing unambiguous linkages between ICT and their local development or setting ICT as a clear priority. China may be an exception, as it moves beyond leveraging ICT for export and competitiveness in the coastal cities and puts an increasing emphasis on rural informatization as a tool for social inclusion and harmony.

Most interesting are the challenges of integrating ICT in development in poor countries. For poor countries, it is difficult to conceive and communicate the linkages of ICT to growth and poverty reduction. These countries face many daunting development challenges and ICT may be perceived as lower among a long list of priorities, particularly when ICT is advocated as a sector rather than enabler of all other development priorities. Moreover, ICT's role in poverty reduction is less understood and more uncertain than in improving productivity or promoting exports and competitiveness. But the leadership of some poor countries has taken a visible and proactive posture in adopting e-development as central to their overall development and transformation strategy, as the case of Sri Lanka. In this case, special measures had to be taken to make ICT central to development strategy: aligning several e-Sri Lanka initiatives to the coalition government's core strategy of rural development and inclusion and initiating visible pilots and quick wins to demonstrate such linkages, particularly for poverty reduction.

Coverage, Coherence, Synergy

Most countries have progressively moved toward broader and more comprehensive coverage of e-development, along the proposed e-development framework (as outlined in Chap. 1). But a strong telecom monopoly or protective ICT industry can narrow the perspective of policy makers and undermine the interests of other stakeholders in pursuing a comprehensive, coherent, and synergistic approach to e-transformation, as has been the case to some extent in Canada. Protective computer policy in Brazil played a similar narrowing role of the ICT for development agenda prior to liberalization in the 1990s.

Pursuing a comprehensive and coherent approach is a dynamic process that often involves balancing the interests of diverse stakeholders, both ICT providers and users. In the case of Sri Lanka, early dominance of the ICT industry (software export) and telecommunications was counterbalanced by creating an ICT agency with a broad and inclusive mandate and adopting a comprehensive e-development framework to guide engagement of all stakeholders, ensure broad ownership, and seek synergies across all elements. To generate support for a comprehensive strategy that would cover less-served areas or weak stakeholders, e-Sri Lanka strategy relied on pilots for testing and demonstration during program design and on innovation funds to stimulate grassroots innovation in e-society.

Even when coverage was comprehensive, this did not guarantee coherence or synergies in most countries. China pursued many parallel, but narrowly defined, programs by various ministries. These programs shared common goals for rural informatization, for example, but they often competed, overlapped, and left out critical gaps, with modest synergy and coherence. The lack of synergy and coherence is most felt in the poor, less-developed provinces, where local competencies for coordination and integration are most lacking.

Brazil has pursued separate and parallel programs for various elements of e-development, but with little coherence, coordination, or synergy. The Brazil case suggests that a comprehensive approach may be easier to do at the vision and policy formulation stages, but most challenging to maintain during implementation through coherence and synergies. The closest Brazil's federal government has come to a comprehensive e-development strategy was during the second administration of President Cardoso with the preparation of an Information Society Program under the leadership of the Ministry of Science and Technology from 1999 to 2000. This effort produced the so-called Green Book on the Information Society in Brazil (Takahashi 2000) with a wide-ranging analysis and proposed goals and actions elaborated with the participation of over 300 specialists from different parts of government, the private sector, academia, and civil society organizations. Some 150 of these participated in 12 thematic groups. The Green Book covered all the key elements in the e-development framework. Legislative, programmatic, and other actions were proposed, though in rather general terms, without budgets. Unfortunately, this integrated and comprehensive strategy was never executed in a coordinated fashion with strong guidance from the President's office, though various elements of it were pursued by separate ministries. E-government got the most attention during the period 2000–2002. In the second Lula administration, the themes of digital inclusion (and a National Broadband Program) began to receive strong coordination from the President and his Chief of Staff, but not other elements of e-development. Yet, despite emphasis on digital inclusion, federal, state, and municipal authorities responsible for finance have been extremely reluctant to reduce the high taxation of telecommunication services, including broadband Internet provision.

Leading, Institutionalizing, and Engaging

Securing linkages to overall development and inclusive coverage of e-development depends to a great extent on e-leadership, e-institutions, and stakeholders' engagement (Wilson 2004; Hanna 2007b). Investing in leadership education, institutional development, and stakeholder participation can strengthen both the integration of ICT across the economy and the synergies among elements of a broader coverage of e-transformation. The countries covered in this book are ranked at medium level on the issues of leadership and institutionalization. Leadership was never given or simply static. In the case of Canada, after a successful decade, federal government institutions with a wider mandate to develop policy or learn from national experience were later marginalized. In the case of Sri Lanka, they had to be developed and nurtured through an energizing vision and active recruitment. In the companion book, case studies show that Finland and Singapore created and nurtured such institutions over decades, and are therefore ranked high on leading and institutionalizing.

Experience indicates that it is easier to engage stakeholders and create effective leaders and e-leadership institutions when countries are endowed with a civil service that is effective and ready to lead and partner with the private sector and civil society. It is also easier, where populations are more educated and urbanized and where national consensus on development is well-established. Canada comes closest to meeting these conditions, hence early achievements in connectivity and e-government programs. Yet, leadership and institutions could and should be nurtured and developed on a continuous basis. In Canada's case, later change in political ideology undermined government leadership after early achievements. In Sri Lanka's case, such leadership and institutional development and stakeholder engagement had to be initiated at the outset of developing a first e-strategy.

Countries characterized by economic inequalities, polarized societies, and underdeveloped civil service systems face significant challenges in establishing the leadership and institutions necessary for e-transformation. In these contexts, e-transformation strategies must give special attention and resources to develop appropriate leadership and institutions for e-transformation and to establish the incentives and authorizing environment for these institutions to function and become self-sustaining. Innovations in institutions and in participatory processes are often necessary under these conditions, as was the case for e-Sri Lanka. For large and unevenly developed countries like China and Brazil, decentralized approaches are likely to be necessary to establish the necessary leadership, institutions, and stakeholder engagement for e-transformation.

A common theme among the case studies is the balance of power of stakeholders from government, the private sector, and civil society and their representation in the leadership, institutional mechanisms, and participatory processes involved in designing and implementing e-strategies. The pioneers and advanced economies have consistently engaged political and business leadership in managing e-transformation. Countries with long traditions of democracy and decentralized government have also given NGOs, academia, and media a stronger voice in these e-leadership institutions. Countries with substantial inequalities have also sought to engage their NGOs, academia, and the media, as in Brazil and China, albeit with mixed success. Political instability, civil strife, and inequalities have often constrained the degree of balanced representation and inclusive engagement of stakeholders, as in Sri Lanka.

A common lesson in all cases is the importance of proactive government polices and incentives in overcoming weaknesses in the investment climate for the ICT industry and barriers to ICT diffusion. For example, China ranks poorly on the World Bank's investment climate indicators, yet it has been able to nurture a globally competitive ICT industry, particularly in hardware manufacturing. China continued to work on first-best solutions for improving the overall investment climate – which is a long-term process. But it sought to create "microclimates" in the short term through second-best, ICT-specific interventions, like the special economic zones and ICT parks and incubators, and benefitted from returns to scale in a huge domestic market supplemented by an aggressive proexport policy. Similarly, none of the successful ICT diffusion cases (in this volume and the companion one) were the result of laissez-faire government.[5]

Balancing Central with Local

It is not easy to generalize about the optimal balance between top-down direction and bottom-up initiative that should be pursued in e-development. This balance is conditioned by the political and social culture of the country. Canada's case suggests that central policy and program leadership were influential and perhaps optimal in the early phases of e-development, but with a political shift, e-development at the federal level moved off center stage, and had to rely primarily on community-level initiatives. Given the early achievements of connectivity, e-government, and e-literacy and political culture of openness and participation, bottom-up initiatives and community-led e-development may now provide a better fit for the political and social culture of the country.

Observing e-strategies over time indicates that countries at early stages of e-transformation tend to rely on top-down push for reforms and central coordination in investing in shared infrastructures and capabilities. In such phases, they also often relied on the highest political authority of the country and a powerful central ICT agency to provide central direction and an enabling environment. Sri Lanka has sought to start its e-transformation journey along these lines. Canada made a more abrupt shift toward a decentralized mode relying more on market forces, perhaps reflecting a vacuum in central leadership or a takeover of national policy making by private interests, mainly by the telecom and IT industry lobby.

China started with central directions provided by the central ministries, but has progressively recognized the limits to this approach and has recently encouraged the provinces to take more of the lead for investing, coordinating, adapting, and experimenting at the local level. The optimal balance between central and local initiatives is, thus, likely to change over time even within the same country. Striking the right balance is particularly hard for large countries with high inequality and/or regional diversity, such as China and Brazil.

In Brazil, many state and municipal initiatives have to a moderate extent influenced the development of various federal policies as well as complemented them and provided a wide range of different experiences that can and have been adopted and/or adapted for use in other subnational governments – good examples are São Paulo's and Bahia's integrated citizen service centers that have inspired

[5] The strategic leadership role of government in ICT diffusion extends to most OECD countries, including the most advanced economies. This role is evident in the long-standing national programs for the diffusion of new technologies, particularly targeted at small and medium enterprises.

similar initiatives in many other states and municipalities. As countries move further into empowering local governments with authority and resources, the central–local balance in e-transformation strategies is also likely to shift in the same direction.

Balancing Long- and Short-Term Objectives

These country cases indicate that political and economic stabilities have both been essential to set and sustain commitment for long-term objectives. China exemplifies this. Canada shifted its emphasis from long- to short-term objectives as the government changed to one with a conservative economic philosophy, leaving much of goal and target setting to market forces and local initiatives.

From 1999 to 2000, Brazil articulated early on a long-term vision of its information society, led from the Ministry of Science and Technology, a relatively weak ministry with a rather small budget. This vision and most corresponding programs were neither articulated for the medium term nor executed in a coordinated fashion by the different ministries in the federal bureaucracy. Such coordination over the medium term would have required strong support from the President's office and Ministry of Finance. Short on resources and also subject to changing political leadership, many state and municipal initiatives have focused on the short term. In e-government, for example, the temptation was to pursue window-dressing Web sites and front-end e-service delivery as quick and visible wins, but to lag far behind in attempts to secure interoperability, information sharing, back-end process transformation, and fully integrated transactions. Despite grandiose visions, many developing countries share with Brazil many of the limits on addressing the long-term objectives.

The Sri Lanka case illustrates in some depth some of the tensions involved in pursuing and balancing the short- and long-term objectives toward e-transformation. Political turmoil and instabilities demanded special efforts to continually balance the investment portfolio and programs to seek quick wins and visible payoffs while developing the enabling environment, governance mechanisms, and building block for e-government, for example. Pilots, demonstrations, and quick payoffs proved critical to sustain political commitment to a long-term program and build a coalition for sustainable policies and institutions. At times, the pressures for the short-term and political objectives have tended to compromise long-term goals, such as building, evaluating, and adapting sustainable telecenters throughout the country.

Innovating, Adapting, and Learning

Canada has an advanced innovation, monitoring, evaluation, open, and learning culture. With a federal structure and decentralized public sector and programs, much of the learning, adaptation, and innovation occur at the provincial and local levels. Regional diversity in a large country also sets limits to centrally designed and rigid programs. Now that communities have become e-literate and electronically connected, such learning and adaptation are expected to occur much more at the local levels. Developed statistical systems and online feedback also allow for advanced and timely feedback at higher levels of governance. But political factors and industry lobbies (like the telecom industry) can still hijack the policy-making process and stifle policy and program learning at the federal level, and consequently for supporting learning at the local level and the sharing of innovation and learning across communities.

In contrast, large and diversified countries, like Brazil and China, have not adopted a systematic innovation, adaptation, and learning strategy to identify and draw on the rich and varied innovation and experimentation that may be occurring at the local level and to scale up the most promising programs. Brazil gave relatively little attention to learning, adaptation, and evaluation at the federal level. Obviously, there were exceptions, such as the programs like Softech, to incubate ICT entrepreneurs, and the Observatory of Practices of Information and Communication Technology in Public Management, to share innovative applications at the state levels. There appear to be many examples of innovation and learning at the state and municipal levels in both countries, for example, in promoting telecenters, IT parks, and digital inclusion. But there have been few efforts at evaluation or systematic processes for identifying innovative ICT applications and programs and learning across regions and state governments. One exception in Brazil is the national meetings on e-government that have helped showcase federal, state, and municipal best practices. Nevertheless, e-government applications have proliferated at all levels, in many cases approached as if they were first in Brazil, thus "reinventing the wheel," with little cross-learning or consolidation to benefit from economies of scale. A good example is e-procurement systems. Similarly, many of the innovative applications of ICT among NGOs are not shared or scaled up.

Although China is known for innovation, adaptation, and pragmatism in its development and technology policies, there is little evidence that such innovation and adaptation are being systematically evaluated and captured for national policy making and scaling up promising programs. The diversity and size of the country set limits to imposing standard solutions beyond common infrastructures and building blocks (e g., the golden projects). However, provincial governments still have limited capacity to adapt standard applications to their own specific conditions or to integrate silo programs that are designed and directed from the center. The search to meet centrally determined targets may have also constrained integration, adaptation, learning, and innovation at the local level. Monitoring and evaluation is not taken seriously at the local level, perhaps for fear of criticizing central ministries. Why would local governments invest in monitoring and evaluation activities if they are not allowed to direct and adapt these centrally driven programs? Why would they learn about programs they do not "own"? The more advanced regions and municipalities may offer rich lessons, innovation, and locally adapted applications for the poorer and lagging regions, but this potential is not tapped.

As in most developing countries, a monitoring and evaluation culture is weak in Sri Lanka and the civil service is particularly averse to risk taking and innovation. Taking this into account, the e-Sri Lanka program and the ICT agency were designed to start with a variety of pilots and competitions to invite innovations before the full-scaled program was designed. Moreover, innovation funds were designed to promote competitive proposals for innovative applications of ICT for societal applications and to learn from these innovations for scaling up the most promising. E-Sri Lanka also tried to build a systematic monitoring and evaluation (M&E) system to secure its independence and reporting to the highest levels of policy making and to invest in its development from the start of the program. Political factors, however, still intervened and may have constrained objective and timely evaluation of innovations, like the telecenter programs.

M&E is perhaps the weakest feature of e-strategies in developing countries. Setting M&E systems for learning and indicators for measuring progress for e-strategies present a dilemma. On one hand, e-transformation is a novel and poorly understood change with profound implications for all economies, and hence needs to be piloted and adapted in diverse local contexts with much attention to innovation and learning. On the other hand, applying quantitative M&E systems and indicators to a new and poorly understood phenomenon runs the risk of measuring inputs rather than outcomes, emphasizing hard data over soft, but more relevant and critical information, and at times using aggregate indicators that tend to ignore poorer regions and constituencies. Weak M&E systems, however, often lead to heavy reliance on rigid and centralized plans for accountability, rather than local learning, as may be the case in China.

Balancing ICT as Enabler and Sector

The ICT sector can play diverse and even contradictory roles, as a lobby for monopolistic and anticompetitive policies for telecom and protectionist policies for ICT producers or as a promoter for ICT application and diffusion, that is, ICT as enabler and transformer of all economic sectors. Policy makers, broadly mandated ICT agencies, producers of content, and intensive ICT users and NGOs can play counter roles and balance the interest of domestic beneficiaries of ICT use vis a vis ICT producers and telecommunication operators. Development strategists may give even more prominence to ICT as enabler, recognizing that it offers broader and higher payoffs by transforming the whole economy. Countries with large and highly competitive IT and telecom sectors can also opt for balancing the priorities set by these leading sectors with those of users throughout the economy. They can create a more virtuous cycle by promoting those segments of the ICT sector that are most critical to broad ICT diffusion in the economy, and at the same time giving most attention and resources to the cross-sectoral and transformative role of ICT. But reforms and liberalization to promote ICT diffusion are never easy under these conditions.

Brazil and China have sizable ICT sectors, including both producers and telecom service operators. Balancing the interests of the sector and of the users has shifted over time. Many developing countries, including Brazil and China, put early emphasis on the ICT industry, particularly manufacturing of computers and telecommunications equipment, over ICT use and adaptation for the local market. The reasons are several: the promise of fast growth in ICT exports and foreign investment (in case of China), the strong and focused power lobby of the national computer industry and telecommunications companies and their supporters inside the military governments (Brazil), the weak and diffused lobby for ICT users, and the low awareness among policy makers and the public at large of the higher benefits arising from e-transformation. However, in both countries, the governments have moved progressively toward policies and programs that give at least equal emphasis to both roles of ICT, as producing sector and as catalyst for productivity and inclusion across all sectors.

One exception may be China's setting of technology standards in areas, such as wireless communications and others, by the government without foreign or public input. Even large countries, like China, take a risk in attempting to manipulate standards to shield domestic firms from international competition, as this may raise the price of the new technologies for domestic users or lead to adopting an inferior standard that would not become a global standard.

Over the last decade, the telecom and computer industries in Brazil have lost some lobbying power in part due to liberalization and the opening of the industry and the whole economy to global competition. These developments have been beneficial for the development of new segments of the industry, like mobile and software services. The telecom industry has also been flexible about converting its obligations for universal access to digital inclusion programs in support of connectivity for government, schools, universities, cities, small towns, etc. when pressed by the federal government, but continues to resist pressures to unbundle services and share key facilities, like fiber-optic backbones. In fact, the case study demonstrates that the telecom industry has been taxed more than other sectors despite continual protests by its lobby. Thus, there is some room for using taxation reductions to achieve national and state objectives through private sector investments in the context of the emerging National Broadband Program, which also embraces the suppliers of relevant equipment. The threat of intervention by the revived Telebrás may also provide incentives to extend Internet service and lower prices. Meantime, most federal programs have tended to have cross-sectoral emphasis, e-government, digital inclusion, computers and Internet for schools and universities, etc.

Canada also has a sizable and dynamic ICT sector, producers, and telecom service providers. But its user market is also sizable and aware of the potential role of ICT for its sectors. In this case, Canada started with comprehensive programs for connected government and connectivity throughout the economy and achieved advanced levels and highest rankings for some time, providing a model for other countries. But, as the case study argues here, this stance has shifted dramatically with a more conservative government letting the telecommunications industry gain an even more powerful role in shaping current policies and perhaps undermining further progress on policies and programs to promote an inclusive information society.

In Sri Lanka case, the intent was to create such synergistic programs between the ICT sector (telecommunications, software services, BPO) and the user sectors (government, business, and local communities). As the case indicates, the e-Sri Lanka vision started mainly in the ICT sector, and particularly the software subsector that had export potential. By engaging other stakeholders over time, the program was broadened to become more comprehensive and to give most attention for enabling the whole economy. But with changes to a more populist and rural-oriented government and oligopolistic fights set by dominant operators in the telecom services, the program turned its sights toward ICT as enabler for government and society at large. The synergistic potential received little attention from political leadership, but was sustained to some extent by the holistic mandate of the ICT agency.

Emphasizing Digital Inclusion

Almost all countries in this review have emphasized digital inclusion, at least in terms of espoused policy, if not in practice. Canada focused on building an inclusive information society early on in its e-strategy. It could be argued that for small and urbanized countries with high income and relatively homogenous populations, it is easier to adopt and implement digital inclusion programs. Canada's population is not that small (33 million), but is relatively concentrated close to the border with the USA and just over 80% urban. The Community Access Program (CAP) was only one of several national digital inclusion programs, including specialized programs for isolated and indigenous communities, though federal support for such programs has flagged under recent, more conservative governments. As there are two national languages, all Canadian Federal Government Web content is bilingual in English and French.

In countries with high levels of inequality and urban–rural divides, the rhetoric for digital inclusion and the information society was loud. In Brazil, the gap between formal digital inclusion policies and implementation has been significant, and coordination of multiple federal digital inclusion programs has been weak and their funding limited until very recently. Virtually no use has been made of the Fund for Universalization of Telecommunications Services (Fust) for this or any other purpose – despite the substantial revenue it has accumulated, which has been diverted to service the national public debt. In part, this is due to deficiencies in the underlying legislation, in part to resistance from the Ministry of Finance, and in part to lack of consensus on how these financial resources should be applied. Some of the gap has been taken up by NGOs, with innovative programs to benefit the poorer communities and youth with training and income-generating activities that benefit such target groups. But problems of partnership with government or business and of scaling up have limited their reach and impact in overcoming the digital divide. The development of private fee-for-use Internet access points, called lan houses in Brazil, has exploded in recent years, and government is now moving to harness this dynamism in the context of the National Broadband Program.

China has also adopted rural informatization programs in various ways to redress the rising inequality between the urban and coastal regions on the one hand, and the rural and poorer central and western regions. But these programs are relatively recent and often driven by central ministries in terms of ICT access and digital content, with little adaptation from the local governments in the rural and poorer regions. Practicing holistic and inclusive e-development remains a formidable challenge in China. Building capacity at the provinces and local levels to lead and practice inclusive e-transformation is an urgent and long-term effort, particularly for the poor and highly rural areas.

The e-Sri Lanka strategy has been deliberately inclusive of the rural and poor areas of the country. But the telecenter program, e-society, and key elements of the e-government and e-education programs were focused on inclusive or shared access to ICT, telecom infrastructure, Internet, relevant content, and e-government services. This was driven by the political mandate and commitment of the government to use ICT for broad-based growth and social development. During implementation, the intent to include the poor regions of the North and East was frustrated by the civil war in these regions and, thus, the lack of security to achieve much progress. Progress was slowed by resources devoted to crush the rebels, and at times by trying to achieve visible targets and political priorities without due attention to impact, evaluation, and sustainability.

Changing Technology, Constant Fundamentals

The ICT revolution promises changes in economies and societies at least as profound as the industrial revolution and the invention of the press (Hanna 2010; Tapscott and Williams 2010). Each revolution induces a techno-economic paradigm shift as it demands new organizational models and practices to take advantage of the new potential – reaching beyond the organization of production to involve the socio-institutional sphere (Hanna 2010; Perez 2002). But as in earlier technological revolutions, we expect too much in the short term, but vastly underestimate or miss the long-term implications (Perez 2002; David 1990). The macroimpacts of technological revolutions are typically long delayed and involve profound and often painful changes in institutions, culture, and business practices. Old ways of work die hard. Vested interests fight the transformations and disruptive changes unleashed by revolutionary forces. Thus, anticipated changes take decades to unfold.

The Internet and particularly recent advances, such as the participative Web (Web 2.0), cloud computing, social networking, mobile devices, open source, and business intelligence, are challenging old, hierarchical (industrial) models of organization and innovation. They provide a new engine for innovation, and in particular open and collaborative innovation. They promise new options to cocreate and coinnovate solutions to local, national, and global challenges and to rebuild many industries and sectors of economy on a profoundly new, open, agile, networked model. They offer a new set of bottom-up institutions that are being built up on principles, such as openness, collaboration, and the sharing of information (Tapscott and Williams 2010). Other complementary technologies, like Global positioning system (GPS), radiofrequency identification (RFID), sensing devices, the Internet of Things, and business intelligence (analytics) further promise data-driven, in-real-time decision making and accelerated innovation.

Given the fast pace and seemingly endless changes in ICT, should countries continuously revise their e-transformation strategies or even give up strategizing and just respond incrementally in all directions to continuous waves of disruptions? Or should countries find ways to persist with desired transformations that will require long-term strategic commitments, transformational leadership, and smart change management? How can aid agencies catch up and develop up-to-date competencies in this new and fast-paced area of development assistance?

Country case studies presented in this volume suggest some fundamentals that should guide countries through this technological upheaval. E-transformation is not about constant chasing of the "next new thing" or the adoption of the latest technology. It is about securing some fundamentals to guide and enhance desirable and sustainable change. Some countries, like Finland and Singapore, have patiently built institutions and governance mechanisms to guide change agents and technology adopters. Successful countries (and organizations) did not rush into investments in new technologies without strategy, governance model, prioritization, experimentation, and continuous evaluation and learning. They attended first and foremost to building blocks or pillars of e-transformation, such as shared vision, e-leadership, capacity building, and information infrastructure. To ensure that transformation is sustainable and equitable, they addressed the digital divide in all its forms, starting with access and e-literacy. They induced appropriate changes in the culture to support openness, collaboration across sectors, and tolerance of the risks associated with transformation and the adoption of new organizations and practices. They created zones or ecosystems for experimentation and innovation. They managed expectations to match resources and patient capital and, at times, set stretch goals and then mobilized local and global resources to meet them. They coinvested in both technology and organizational reforms. They focused first on culture and human resources, not technology per se. Governments and businesses constantly sought to understand the needs of their clients and to engage them in the design and innovation of services.

The recent trends in ICT, such as social networks and the participative Web, suggest increasing reliance on collaborative, networked, and grassroots innovation as the driver for transformation. Even countries like Singapore, that traditionally had a more top-down driven strategy, have recently reoriented their strategies to rely on collaborative government and collaborative innovation. Government still steers the fundamentals, such as developing an enabling policy environment, coinvesting in broadband, securing and harnessing public information resources, and promoting partnerships for innovation and technological capabilities. But it is learning to listen to clients, to seek partners, and to collaborate with all segments of society. This means relearning skills and changing attitudes. The new collaborative technologies make the process easier, but changing attitudes, habits, and practices take time, persistence, and leadership.

Aid agencies have to collaborate with many partners and intermediaries to keep up with this fast-changing field. In particular, they need to develop platforms for knowledge sharing and collaboration that engage developing countries with ICT multinationals, consulting firms, research centers and universities, and advanced governments. The World Bank and other aid agencies can act as facilitators, connectors, and honest brokers in sustaining these platforms and in addressing information asymmetries between global ICT vendors and local users. Aid agencies cannot maintain the latest expertise in all technological fields on their staff, neither should they do so. While they need to keep up-to-date knowledge of technological trends and the policy and institutional implications of technological shifts, they should not focus on chasing the "next new thing" as the basis for their advice and support to client countries in their journey for e-transformation. Rather, aid agencies should focus on the fundamentals, that is, the policies, institutions, and capabilities, that would position countries to negotiate their path into global connectivity, technology diffusion and adaptation, and broad transformation. They need to assess the soundness of the national e-transformation strategy design and implementation, perhaps along the criteria discussed above. To the extent possible, aid agencies should remain technology-neutral and strive to broaden the options for their clients and safeguard them from technological or vendor lock-ins.

Conclusions

The relevance and effect of the eight criteria and other factors, such as those mentioned below, need to be tested through more systematic research and learning on a larger number of countries using more measurements of outcome. We hope that this initial effort at cross-country comparisons of strategy design, implementation, and outcomes will encourage much future research and learning.

Implicit in the eight criteria on which we have sought to compare the e-development strategies analyzed in the case studies of this volume is the hypothesis that the higher the rank on each of these criteria, the more likely the national strategy is to be successful in promoting comprehensive e-development as set forth in the model presented in Chap. 1, and to some extent reflected in the country rankings on the

NRI. For example, we expect that a country following a strategy is supportive of and integral to overall development goals and programs. One with a high focus on digital inclusion and a high degree of balance between top-down and bottom-up initiatives, other things being equal, do better at achieving e-transformation than one with low ratings on these criteria. The same goes for high rankings on the other criteria.

In our criterion-by-criterion analysis and the in-depth treatment of each country case, many other suggestions and hypotheses have been put forward or emerge as factors that can facilitate comprehensive e-transformation. Some of the more salient are:

- Commitment of top political leaders and continuity in such commitment over long periods of time
- A widely shared vision of ICT's strategic role in national development (especially among the business community, public policy makers, labor leaders, academia, and NGOs)
- High and broad-based education levels
- Highly professionalized civil service
- Low economic and social inequality
- High incomes
- High population density and urbanization
- High degree of homogeneity of the population (ethnic, linguistic, cultural, etc.)
- Real competition in the IT and telecommunications sectors
- High availability of attractive content in the national language(s)

Causality is generally not only one-way. In fact, ICT offers powerful tools for improving income distribution and increasing education, health, incomes, competitiveness, and many other desirable economic, social, and political outcomes. So the fact that a country ranks low on these and other factors should not be taken to imply that e-transformation should not be undertaken, only that strategies, policies, programs, and projects need to be carefully designed to use ICT effectively to achieve development objectives.

Put differently, some of the factors, like low income or low urbanization or high heterogeneity of population and regions, do not condemn a country to low or slow e-transformation. In fact, some diversity in population and regions can be a source of innovation, learning, and strength at the national level. But these and other factors should be taken into account in strategy design, program content, monitoring and learning processes, and implementation mechanisms of e-transformation. Most of these factors can be addressed in a systematic way, such as building awareness at the leadership level, generating a shared vision, improving the legal and regulatory environment for the competitive telecom and ICT industries, and building the necessary skills for adopting ICT in policy and the private sectors. In the end, we believe that all countries must undergo e-transformation, and the sooner they start on their learning and transformation journey taking account of their strengths and vulnerabilities, opportunities and risks, the faster they can become knowledge- and innovation-driven economies and inclusive information societies.

References

Chan, Yolande E and Reich, Blaize Horner (2007). "IT alignment: what have we learned?" *Journal of Information Technology* 22, 297–315.

David, Paul. 1990. " The Dynamo and the Computer: A Historical Perspective on the Modern Productivity Paradox". *American Economic Review*, 80 (2), pp. 355–361.

Dutta, Soumitra and Mia, Irene. 2010. *Global Information Technology Report 2009–2010: ICT for Sustainability*. INSEAD and World Economic Forum, available online at http://www.networkedreadiness.com/gitr/.

Ezell, Stephen, and Atkinson, Robert. 2010. *The Good, the Bad, and the Ugly of Innovation Policy*. Washington, DC: The Information Technology and Innovation Foundation.

Hanna, Nagy K., and Picciotto, Robert (editors). 2002. *Making Development Work: Development Learning in a World of Poverty and Wealth.* New Brunswick, USA: Transaction Publishers.

Hanna, Nagy K.. 2009a. *e-Transformation: Enabling New Development Strategies*. New York: Springer.

—–. 2009b. *Enabling Enterprise Transformation: Business and Grassroots Innovation for the Knowledge Economy.* New York: Springer.

—–. 2010. *Transforming Government and Building the Information Society: Challenges and Opportunities for the Developing World.* New York: Springer.

—–. 2007a. *From Envisioning to Designing e-Development: The Experience of Sri Lanka.* Directions in Development Series. Washington, DC: World Bank.

—–. 2007b. *e-Leadership Institutions for the Knowledge Economy.* Washington, DC: World Bank.

Perez, Carlota. 2002. *Technological Revolutions and Financial Capital.* Cheltenham, UK: Eduard Elgar.

Qiang, Christine Zhen-Wei, and Rossotto, Carlos M. 2009. "Economic Impacts of Broadband", in World Bank. 2009. *Information and Communications for Development 2009*: Extending Reach and Increasing Impact. Washington, DC: World Bank. pp 35–50.

Takahashi. Tadao (ed.). 2000. *Sociedade da Informação no Brasil: Livro Verde*. Brasília. Ministério da Ciência e Tecnologia. September. Available in pdf format at www.mct.gov.br/index.php/content/view/18878.html.

Tapscott, Don, and Williams, Anthony. 2010 *Macro Wikinomics: Rebooting Business and the World.* New York: Portfolio/Penguin.

Wilson, Ernest. J., III. 2004. *The Information Revolution and Developing Countries*. Cambridge: MIT.

World Bank. 2006. *Information and Communications for Development 2006: Global Trends and Policies*. Washington, DC: World Bank.

Index

N.K. Hanna and P.T. Knight (eds.), *Seeking Transformation Through Information Technology*, Innovation, Technology, and Knowledge Management, DOI 10.1007/978-1-4614-0353-1,

GPSR Compliance

The European Union's (EU) General Product Safety Regulation (GPSR) is a set of rules that requires consumer products to be safe and our obligations to ensure this.

If you have any concerns about our products, you can contact us on ProductSafety@springernature.com

In case Publisher is established outside the EU, the EU authorized representative is:

Springer Nature Customer Service Center GmbH
Europaplatz 3
69115 Heidelberg, Germany

Batch number: 10704039

Printed by Printforce, the Netherlands